LIVE PROJECTS
LIVE PRACTICE

DS3.2+DS20 2017-2025
MARIA KRAMER

STUDIO AS BOOK
NO. 11

SCHOOL OF ARCHITECTURE + CITIES
UNIVERSITY OF WESTMINSTER

SERIES INTRODUCTION

Studio as Book is a series of publications that tender the extraordinary creative work undertaken in the School of Architecture + Cities design studios – in detail. Each book in the series covers the work of a single design studio, either undergraduate or graduate, and sometimes both, over the course of at least two years. Its objectives are:

- To record, archive, and present the pedagogical programme and creative student outputs of a design studio.
- To position the work of a design studio within a broader intellectual, scientific or aesthetic field.
- To advance the design driven research being undertaken in the School's design studios.
- To provide a reference for future iterations and variations of a design studio.

Compressing the creative output of a multi-year design studio into a single volume, using a pre-designed book template is no easy undertaking, and it is necessarily selective. At the same time, it provides a consistent, sure platform for the wide range of approaches to the discipline of teaching architectural design which characterise the school.

Each Studio as Book has been peer-reviewed on the basis of a proposal submitted by the studio's tutors to an editorial committee. In addition to studio briefs and student work, each book includes content that draws out the studio's research and pedagogical agenda. The format that this takes varies from book to book – reflective essays by tutors or past students, interviews, theoretical essays from parallel fields, and so forth.

I wish to acknowledge the contribution of the following in bringing this project to fruition: Lindsay Bremner, Director of Research and Knowledge Exchange, who was the driving force behind the series when it was launched in 2016; Mark Boyce, author of Sizes May Vary, A workbook for graphic design (Lawrence King, 2008) – and the designer of Studio as Book; Filip Visnjic and Mirna Pedalo, who have given the books a presence on OpenStudioWestminster: http://www.openstudiowestminster.org/studio-as-book/; and the design tutors and students who have given of their time and energy to collate and edit the books into this unique series.

Professor Harry Charrington
Former Head of the School of Architecture + Cities
University of Westminster

LIVE PROJECTS
LIVE PRACTICE

DS3.2 + DS20 2017–2025
EDITED BY MARIA KRAMER

STUDIO AS BOOK
NO. 11

SCHOOL OF ARCHITECTURE + CITIES
UNIVERSITY OF WESTMINSTER

CONTENTS

INTRODUCTION — 007

Live Projects Overview — 008
Acknowledgements/Support — 011
Preface — 013

DIALOGUES BEYOND — 021

Second Nature, *Harry Charrington* — 022
Educating the Architect-Arbitrator, *Dr Jan Kattein* — 024
Live projects' Journey through the Archipelago of Pedagogies... *Julian Williams* — 028
Live Projects from Social Science Perspectives, *Arlene Oak* — 032
Reclaiming the Architect's Role Through Live Projects, *Interview with Steve Webb* — 034
What Future for Architects in the Age of Capitalist Realism? *Student Perspective Kitty Emery Rainbird* — 036
Socially-Engaged Education+ Practice - Why It Matters, *Alicia Pivaro* — 040
Objects Of Repair, *Yara Sharif, Nasser Golzari* — 042
The Ramadan Pavilion, *Shahed Saleem* — 044
The Portal at Ekawa, *Elle McIntyre and Sergio Pineda* — 046
Dressing Space, *Conor Clarke* — 048
From Agency To Structure, *Interview with Sandra Denicke-Polcher* — 050
Practical Academia, *James Soane* — 052

COLLECTIVE AGENCY — 055

Engaging People+Place, *Maria Kramer* — 056
In Common, Reimagine, Voices, *Krystallia Kamvasinou* — 067
Co-Creating Just Streets, *Enrica Papa, Sabina Ciobata, Maria Kramer* — 070
Student Reflections — 075

CIVIC PERMEABILITY - BRENT CROSS — 077

An Architect's Dilemma in The Age of Capitalist Realism, *Kitty Emery Rainbird* — 084
Our Canopy at Clitterhouse Farm, *Live Project* — 088
Brent Cross Textile Commons, *Anna Long* — 098
The Adhoc Agora, *Hardeepak Singh Panesar* — 102
Industrial Domesticity, *Alex Marton* — 106
The Hearth, *Kitty Emery Rainbird* — 110
Feathered Connections, *Yuelin Zhou* — 114
Civic of many Voices, *Joseph Kuforiji* — 118
— 128

APPLIED MAKING THROUGH COMMUNITY+ ECOLOGY AT THE RIVER LEA — 125

The River Lea, *Maria Kramer*	126
THE Floating Forum, *Live Project* Mussel Meadow, *Steven Op*	142
Weaving Gender, *Maria Saraguro*	148
River Repair, *Jenny Foster*	154
Kinship and Stakeholders at the Lower River Lea, *Corinna Dean*	160

ECOLOGICALLY LED COMMUNITY REGENERATION AT CODY DOCK — 163

The Growing Space, *Maria Kramer*	166
Eco-Expansionism, *Blessing Sulaiman*	184
Tidal Walk, *Hamza Khan*	188
Ruderal Autopoesis, *William Lambert*	194

UNIVER**CITY** — 199

Mini Meadow, *Maria Kramer*	204
Northwick Craft Collective, *Rebecca Weller*	216
Connecting the Campus, *George Sorapure*	220
CollaBuild, *Alex Marton*	224
Pavilion Prototype, *Live Project*	228

CAMPUS LIVE PROJECTS — 237

Tatlin Tower, *Maria Kramer*	238
Tension Pavilion, *Maria Kramer*	242
The Oculus Pavilion, *Maria Kramer*	244
Woven Pavilion, *Maria Kramer*	254
Sensory Bench, *Maria Kramer*	262

MATERIAL EXPLORATION — 267

Applied Making, *Maria Kramer*	269
Repairing The River, *Jenny Foster*	276
Reeds Making, *Maria Saraguro*	278
Slowing Fast Fashion Down, *Anna Long and Tugce Yigit*	282
Waste+Native Materials Making, *Hardeepak Singh Panesar*	286
I Made It Myself, *Kitty Emery Rainbird*	290

LIVE PROJECTS AS EMBEDDED PRACTICE — 293

Afterword	297
Bibliography	298

INTRODUCTION

LIVE PROJECTS OVERVIEW

Tea Pavilion by Finnish Institute,
S.Rintala + FabLab

Mobile Sauna by Finnish Institute,
S.Rintala + FabLab

Oculus Pavilion DS3.2

Pavilion Prototype DS3.2

2017/18   2018/19   2021/22

Woven Pavilion DS3.2

Mini Meadow DS3.2

Shelter at Finnish Museum of Forestry by Finnish Institute, S.Rintala

Environmental conservation of the River Lea, Corinna Dean, DS2.1

Architects for Gaza: mobile clinic by Nasser Golzari, Yara Sharif, François Girardin

The Growing Space DS20

Our Canopy at Clitterhouse Farm DS20

2023/24

2022/23

2024/25

Sensory Bench DS3.2

Floating Forum DS20

Ramadan Pavilion at the V&A Shahed Saleem, DS2.3

Radical Speculations Natalie Newel, DS2.2

Image: The Growing Space Live Project at Cody Dock

ACKNOWLEDGE-MENTS/SUPPORT

"Live Projects in Architecture represent everything that is best about learning at the University of Westminster. Giving students the opportunity to work with external partners and seeing their designs translated into real structures offers so many benefits in relation to preparation for their future careers. But more fundamentally, we would say this is the archetype of 'authentic learning' - students have significant intrinsic motivation because they can see purpose in their endeavours, they have agency and the freedom to work creatively and collaboratively. This environment facilitates high levels of engagement, enjoyment and satisfaction. Students love Live Projects and it is easy to see why. Long may they continue at Westminster." Andy Pitchford, Head of the Centre for Education and Teaching Innovation (CETI)

"To truly unlock the transformative potential of our 'Live Projects,' fundraising is essential. Funding for raw materials our students need enables the physical build of innovative designs to happen, allowing students to gain invaluable hands-on experience from concept to completion, whilst contributing to local communities with accessible spaces. Funding also supports bursaries to enable talented students to fully immerse themselves in these demanding, real-world builds, rather than being pulled away by their part-time jobs due to financial pressures. This support helps develop the next generation of socially conscious and skilled design professionals who are ready to make a tangible difference in our communities." Jordan Scammell MinstF(Dip), Head of Development and Fundraising

"The Capital Development team at UoW delivers multi-million-pound projects in collaboration with external architects and consultants, so our involvement in small-scale Live Projects might seem unexpected. However, working alongside academic colleagues and students from the School of Architecture and Cities has been genuinely inspiring. These Live Projects are rooted in research and innovation, particularly in exploring the nature of a brief and infusing meaning and vision into proposed schemes. Their creative, boundary-pushing approach is refreshing and challenges us in the Estates team to rethink how we define value and purpose in every project. Adopting this approach in large-scale capital projects would be a bold and innovative step - embedding academic research and teaching into real-world delivery and unlocking new potential for transformative design. Maybe something to consider in the coming years?" Alessandra Foderaro, Deputy Director of Estates- Capital Development | Estates Planning and Services

This publication would not have been possible without the support of the studios I have taught over the years. First of all, thank you to all the students - from whom I continue to learn - for making this a truly mutual process. In particular, I would like to acknowledge the BA DS3.2 and MArch DS20 studio partners: in BA, Eric Guibert, Bruce Irwin, and Roberto Bottazzi; and in MArch, Corinna Dean and Shahed Saleem.

Thank you to all the students who participated in this publication, with special mention to Kitty Emery Rainbird, without whom this would not have been possible. I am also grateful to Joseph Kuforiji for offering his help. Special thanks to: Francois Girardin, for always assisting us with generous advice, most recently in helping erect the prototype canopy in our studio for the end-of-year exhibition. Ed Lancaster, for his continuous practical advice in the FabLab and unfailing helpfulness.

Harry Charrington, for his support over the years, along with his wide-reaching advice and motivation.

Thanks to: Kate Cheyne, William McLean, Ro Spankie, Julian Williams, Alastair Blyth, Maja Jovic, Paul Dwyer, Marius Brodeala, Alexander Fleming, Enrica Papa, Andy Pitchford, Paul Dwyer, Anke Boehme, Guy Sinclair, Bill Erickson, Daniel Scroggins, David Scott, Nancy Guest, Ken Kinsella, Victoria Watson, Justine Kenyon, Jules Attanayake, Wilfred Achille, Mervyn Rodrigues, Peter Barber, Chris Meloy, Linsey Cole, Simon Myers, Nic Henninger, Nick Runeckles, Ben Stringer, Tobias Schaffrin, Steve Webb. We also thank our collaborators, visiting critics, and external partners who generously contributed their time and expertise. Thank you to all the participating communities, the estate team both at Harrow and Marylebone campuses. Many thanks to the 'University Records and Archives' at Titchfield Campus who made available the images and articles of the Tatlin Tower at the Marylebone Campus and thanks to Richard Watson for making me aware of this.

The Quintin Hogg Trust is delighted to support the Live Projects that are included in this Studio Book. The sole purpose of the Trust is to support the advancement of education at the University of Westminster, when we consider the projects to fund, we prioritise those that have the greatest impact on students. The Trust is delighted to see the student work that we have supported, included in this book; it is very impressive to see what students have achieved. We are delighted to have been able to support them in their accomplishments. Liz Duff, Chair of the Grants Committee, Quintin Hogg Trust

Image: Floating Forum Live Project at Cody Dock by Kitty Emery Rainbird

PREFACE

"Learning is better than teaching because it is more intense: the more we teach, the less students learn." Joseph Albers

Live Projects sit at the intersection of practice, research, and pedagogy

This book offers an opportunity to record, analyse and reflect on the processes and methods employed in Live Projects, as well as engagement strategies developed within the Live Studios BA DS3.2 and MArch DS20 programmes since 2017. In addition, a selection of individual student projects is included, developed alongside and adjacent to the Live Projects, offering visionary conceptual ideas that contribute to the overall themes. It also features contributions from collaborators including Jan Kattein and structural engineer Steve Webb, as well as voices from others who have provided inspiration over the years.

We often either practice, teach or research - rarely do we combine all three. Live Projects provide a unique opportunity where these three strands intersect, mutually enriching one another and creating outcomes greater than the sum of their parts. There is significant value in being able to cross-fertilise ideas between these areas.

Built Live Projects extend beyond the conventional academic focus of RIBA Developed Design work stage 3 and Technical Design Work Stage 4, see diagram below. They offer learning opportunities across the full spectrum of project phases- including construction and inhabitation, while involving a wide range of stakeholders, including consultants, makers, and local communities.

"A Live Project comprises the negotiation of a brief, timescale, budget and product between a client and an educational institution." liveprojectsnetwork.org

The freedom and privilege of the academic environment allows for experimentation, testing, and an investigative, research-led approach, including innovative project set ups, engagement processes, and hands-on making. This aligns with the idea of "the reinterpretation of Live Projects as research tools, whilst, at the same time, requiring architect-makers to adopt a broader role."[1] While Maurice Mitchell presents this in the context of working with those in greatest need, we believe this approach can-and should-be extended to the wider, mainstream architectural discourse.

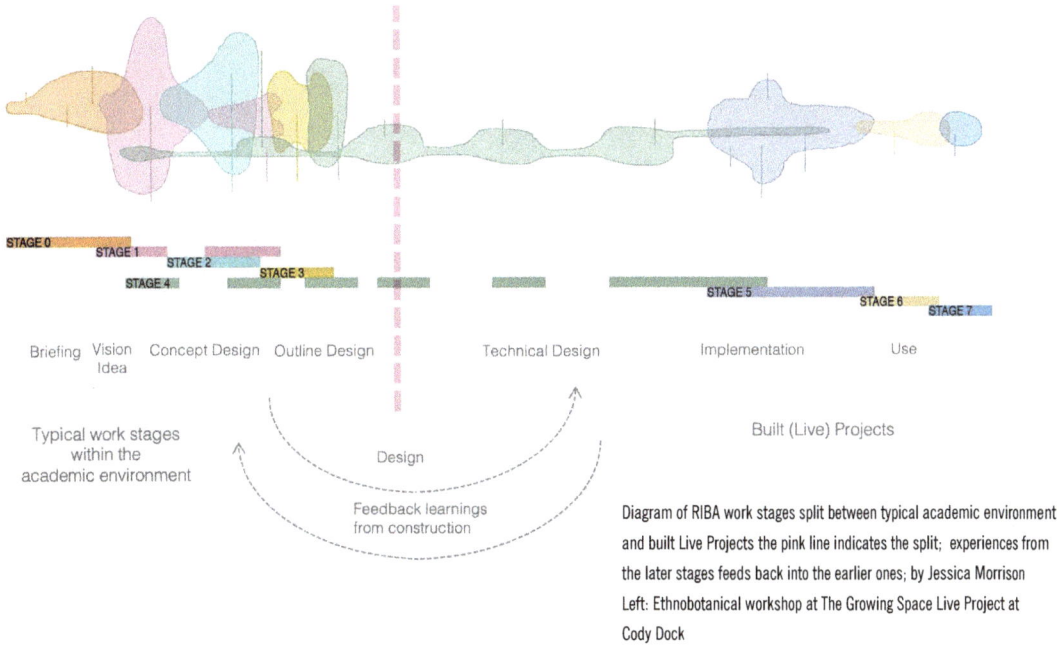

Diagram of RIBA work stages split between typical academic environment and built Live Projects the pink line indicates the split; experiences from the later stages feeds back into the earlier ones; by Jessica Morrison
Left: Ethnobotanical workshop at The Growing Space Live Project at Cody Dock

Image: The Oculus Pavilion Live Project

Live Project briefs are rooted in society, addressing its social, economic, political, and ecological dimensions as they relate to lived experience. By immersing students in real-world scenarios, Live Projects enable first-hand engagement with the often-invisible and complex decision-making processes that shape the built environment. These projects also empower local communities, demonstrating the potential of slow, bottom-up developments driven by regenerative values. Through collaboration, students encounter alternative models of practice and new ways of doing, that challenge normative processes.

Pedagogically, Live Projects are embedded within experiential learning and the theories of tacit and embodied knowledge, drawing on frameworks such as constructivism, David A. Kolb's Experiential Learning Cycle, and John Dewey's theory of experience in education[2]. Live Projects are inherently challenging, fraught with risk, unpredictability, and unknowns. As Amy-Jane Beer aptly states:

"Risk is something we can be taught to manage, but there's no better instructor than experience."[3]

The building industry is notoriously risk-averse, constrained by contractual, regulatory, financial, political, and insurance-related factors, as well as widespread skills gaps. This environment often suppresses innovation. By contrast, the academic live-research context offers a space to test, promote, and apply novel ideas-including those around regenerative design and knowledge exchange.

Live Projects serve as a platform for questioning existing systems, fostering experimentation and encouraging creative engagement and transformative action. Insights and research developed through these projects can be scaled up to contribute to civic culture and perhaps to even help inform policy and: "Bottom-up learning through making can create a more vibrant and democratic city than the more flattened, top-down, centrally planned, factory-made version."[4]

Reflecting on Live Projects and Live Practice involves critically analysing experimental processes and outcomes, from which we distil applied research and generate new knowledge. This knowledge can then inform innovative design methods and practices. By understanding Live Projects as manifestations of method and process, we shift the framing of architecture beyond formal expression, toward a connected, systems-based mode of thinking - a shift that is increasingly urgent in our time of climate crisis.

Our goal is to build a cross-disciplinary platform that fosters collaborative, place-based projects. Through Live Projects, we aim to contribute to social cohesion, civic engagement and the green transition of neighbourhoods.

The university can - and should - act as a civic catalyst and anchor.

Bottom Diagram: Live Projects provide the unique opportunity to combine theory and practice. They provide a micro cosmos where we can reflect and learn from processes and practice. Being a project initiator provides agency which is empowering.
Left: The Oculus Pavilion at Marylebone Campus

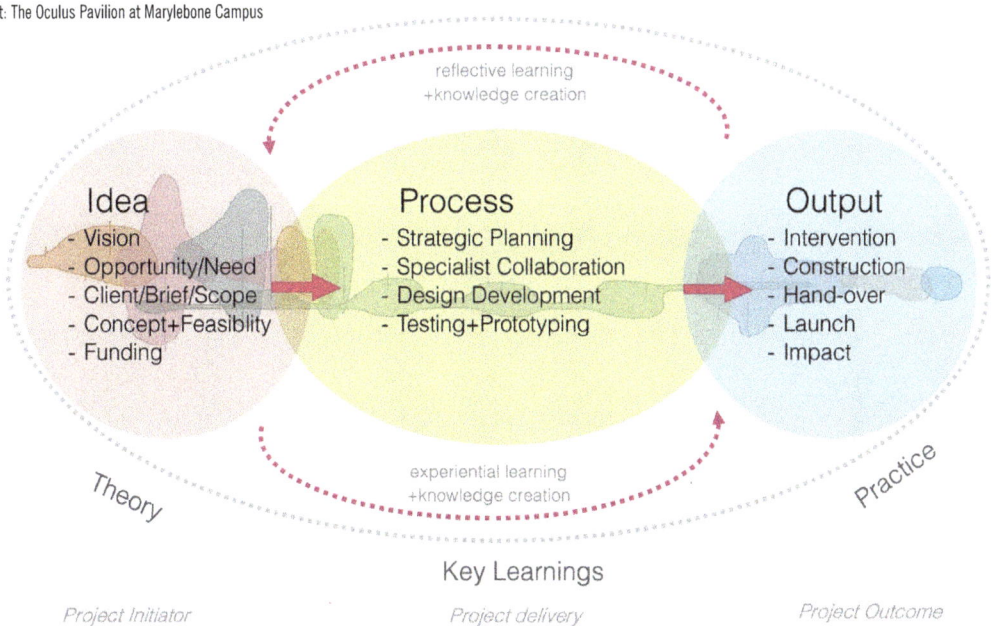

Image: Testing Plywood under tension as part of the Woven Pavilion development

LEARNING AS A SOCIAL PROCESS

Lev Vygotsky's social learning theory emphasises that learning is a social process, where interaction with peers, mentors, and the environment plays a central role. His concept of the Zone of Proximal Development (ZPD) highlights the importance of collaboration, where learners advance through guided support (scaffolding) from more knowledgeable individuals. In the architectural education, the studio environment is often collaborative, with students working together on design projects, such as Live Projects, learning from peers and industry collaborators whilst receiving guidance from tutors. Students often learn more effectively through group critiques, peer feedback, and collaborative design charrettes which are at the heart of Live Projects and Live Practices.

As previously mentioned, Live Projects offer the opportunity to extend beyond RIBA Work Stages 3/4, allowing students to engage in the entire process. There's a compelling argument for integrating more making and construction knowledge into design phases by involving makers early in the process, fostering innovation. Instead of a rigid separation between planning + design and making + construction, there is potential for these stages to overlap, influencing each other holistically.

RECLAIMING THE ARCHITECT'S ROLE

The traditional split between design and construction, and even earlier between concept design and detailed/technical design, often leads to non-architects taking the lead in these design stages and onwards, particularly in larger-scale projects, such as with a contractual Design & Build setup. Introducing students to the design and construction cycle early in their career aims to demystify this process and cultivate a wider understanding of the different roles architects can play throughout various work stages.

Experiential Learning and Embodied Knowledge provide a theoretical frameworks for integrating the 'applying' and 'doing' stages more meaningfully, tying these back into the 'reflecting' and 'thinking' phases. Connecting learning to real world situations: John Dewey, recognised that experience alone does not produce learning, it involves the "reconstruction or reorganisation of experience that adds to the meaning of that experience; increases ability to direct the course of subsequent experience", see Kolb's ELT diagram below.

Right: David A. Kolb's Experience Learning Cycle applied to Live Projects
Left: Experimenting with plywood under tension

Image: The Woven Pavilion Live Project

FOR WHOM?

Live Projects resist reducing architecture to mere physical form or a commodified shell. Instead, they highlight the tensions between inhabitation and design, lived experience and constructed envelope. This approach demands bridging divides - between business and values, commercial imperatives and ecological responsibility. Where business often feels exploitative, Live Projects invite us to reimagine it as a system of mutual benefit, recognising that we are all part of an interconnected habitat. Architecture transforms from mere buildings to an ecology of relationships, resources and responsibilities.

It is based on ecological humanism, acknowledging the complex web of life that both sustains and is sustained by the environments we create. The political philosopher Hannah Arendt's concept of natality provides profound insight. Natality is the uniquely human capacity to begin anew - to act in ways that introduce something unprecedented into the world. Arendt writes in The Human Condition that this ability to initiate newness through action is at the heart of what it means to be human. Arendt urges us to remember that humanity is defined not only by survival or production but by acting together in a shared world. Architecture, especially when rooted in public engagement and Live Projects, is an embodiment of this capacity to begin anew. It is a practice that does not simply produce buildings but facilitates collective action and renewal in communities. Each project becomes a space where people come together to shape their environment - a new beginning in the ongoing journey of community.

Central to this process is the idea of collective intelligence: the shared knowledge, creativity, and problem-solving capacity that emerges when diverse individuals collaborate. Live Projects harness collective intelligence by inviting multiple voices and perspectives into the design process, creating solutions that reflect the complex realities of lived experience. This collective wisdom strengthens the social fabric and enriches the built environment, making it more adaptive, inclusive and resilient.

BEYOND THE DISCIPLINE

The principles underpinning Live Projects in architecture-experiential learning, community engagement, iterative problem-solving, and the integration of theory with practice-are increasingly relevant to disciplines beyond the built environment.

In legal education, for example, clinic-based models offer students opportunities to work with real clients, mirroring the real-time negotiation and ethical responsibility seen in architectural Live Projects. Similarly, in business and management education, Live Practice equivalents emerge in consultancy projects, social enterprise initiatives, or start-up incubators, where students engage with real stakeholders, market constraints, and evolving briefs.

What these pedagogical approaches share is a

shift away from abstract (case) studies toward lived, situated learning experiences that develop professional judgement, adaptability and critical thinking.

Crucially, they allow students to engage with uncertainty and complexity - skills essential to contemporary practice in any field. By foregrounding collaborative knowledge production and socially embedded practice, Live Projects challenge linear, siloed modes of education and propose a more integrated, relational model of learning. As architecture claims a broader, civic role through these methods, there is a parallel opportunity for other disciplines to do the same - expanding their social relevance, addressing systemic challenges and fostering ethical, responsive forms of practice.

1 Maurice Mitchell, Bo Tang: Loose fit city: the contribution of bottom-up architecture to urban design and planning (Taylor & Francis, NY : Routledge, 2018)
2 Dewey, J., 1938. Experience and Education. New York: Macmillan
3 Amy-Kane Beer: The Flow (Bloomsbury Publishing, 2022)
4 Maurice Mitchell, Bo Tang: Loose fit city: the contribution of bottom-up architecture to urban design and planning (Taylor & Francis, NY : Routledge, 2018) p.209

Left: Woven Pavilion at the rear podium at Marylebone Campus

DIALOGUES BEYOND

Top: 'Lastu' Shelter at the Finnish Museum of Forestry, Punkaharju. DS3.6, Tom Raymont with Sami Rintala for 2017 Finland 100 Centenary, Finnish Institute with Harry Charrington; Bottom: Construction of 'Lastu' Shelter at the Finnish Museum of Forestry.

SECOND NATURE

HARRY CHARRINGTON

Live Projects and students working on building sites have been around for as long as architects have been trained. What is relatively new is how complex it has become to do them. A growing awareness of risk, health and safety, and safeguarding has made working outside controlled workshop conditions far more involved (I ran a second-year elective project at the University of Newcastle in 1993 with a primary school in Meadow Well in which the students worked alongside the school children redesigning and painting their playground. We pretty much just turned up and got on with it). At the same time there has been an increasing theorisation of live projects as distinct elements within university-based courses. While critique and feedback is always helpful, attempts to define live projects as a pedagogical method can seem paradoxical, apparently contradicting the serendipity of learning-by-doing (what Donald Schön calls 'knowing-in-action'). When we did the Meadow Well school we weren't aware we were doing a Live Project' but I'm not sure that reduced its impact.

ENGAGEMENT AND EMBODIMENT

As a student in the late 1980s, I encountered a series of collaborative building projects that Peter Hübner and Peter Sulzer undertook at Stuttgart University; projects in which harnessing the tacit knowledge and ability (what we now call 'agency') of students and end-users seemed second nature. At the same time, I read Paolo Friere's Pedagogy of the Oppressed while studying J.F.C. Turner's work in South America. It's advocacy for a praxis of action and reflection in opposition to the inevitable class action of asserting a priori knowledge or expertise, has been a personal touchstone ever since.

Friere, Hübner, and Sulzer imply that a vital and engaged architecture lies in a willingness to lose control. This view could not have contrasted more than with those promoting an architecture of 'essence' and 'embodiment' at the same time, an approach tied to the Martin Heidegger's phenomenological philosophy. The inherent passivity of which Hannah Arendt had already identified in 1946 as a dangerously irresponsible "naturalistic superstition", in which the moral and political value of human spontaneity is dangerously downgraded.

SPONTANEITY

Eighty years later, nevertheless, the baleful influence of Heidegger on architectural education is still seen in studio projects that promote 'rising above' contingencies and projecting a singular 'pure' intention. In contrast, DS20 and DS3.2s live projects possess a vitality that reflects Arendt's advocacy of spontaneity – no small achievement given ever more prescriptive conditions, not least those of the ARB. Three particular qualities stand out:

Making The Studio's commitment to making and testing is the most evident commonality of the diverse projects shown here. Intention gives way to action as fabrication demands that, instead of trying to predict things from afar, students attend to the matter in hand. The dedication to making also reflects a wider School belief that if making is not mere production but also a way of thinking, as with the shelter students designed and built on location at the Finnish Forestry Museum in 2017 (see images to the left), and in a very different environment, PARTs Gaza Mobile Clinic conceived and manufactured from its site.

Evolving Just as the students develop their practice as they carry out the Live Projects, so the Studio's approach has evolved with each year's iteration. The self-contained sequence of earlier campus-based small-scale pavilions has led to more ambitious and complex projects. These reach beyond their immediate manufacture to address fluid and contested situations which can only be addressed through collaborative working and cross-disciplinary cooperation. The entanglements and action of the live project also help shape students' subsequent individual projects.

Funding and Clients Mutual interest, partnership and funding are the basis of live projects, as I know from instigating the three pavilions that we built with the Finnish Institute. But that was one partner which pales in comparison to Maria Kramer's remarkable record of finding and building relationships with a range of clients and her astonishing ability to garner support and funding from myriad sources and partners within and without the university. Without her persistence these projects wouldn't have happened.

Left image : Pavilion Prototype at the rear podium of the University of Westminster, developed in collaboration with Jan Kattein Architects and DS3.2

EDUCATING THE ARCHITECT-ARBITRATOR

DR JAN KATTEIN

"We had the fortune to collaborate with Jan Kattein Architects on the Prototype Pavilion Live Project, particularly from the Detail Design stage onwards, see image to the left - it was fantastic to have Jan's support and experience at the beginning of the three-year initiative, which ultimately became The Growing Space at Cody Dock."

The Skip Garden - Jan Kattein Architects

ARCHITECTURAL EDUCATION AT UNIVERSITY REWARDS INDIVIDUAL EXCELLENCE, YET THE SUCCESS OF THE ARCHITECT IN PRACTICE HINGES ON THEIR ABILITY TO COLLABORATE AND CO-ORDINATE. COLLABORATION AND CO-ORDINATION TAKE ON EVER GREATER SIGNIFICANCE IN OUR RESPONSE TO CLIMATE CHANGE. LIVE-BUILDING PROGRAMS PRESENT A UNIQUE OPPORTUNITY FOR ARCHITECTURE STUDENTS TO LEARN SKILLS THAT TRADITIONAL EDUCATIONAL PATHWAYS DO NOT TEACH.

My book, the Architecture Chronicle, Diary of an Architectural Practice (Ashgate 2014) define the persona of the architect as three distinct characters, each of which has a unique skillset that is needed to practice. The architect-inventor brings ideas and employs their creativity to solve problems. The architect-arbitrator has the ability to communicate spatial concepts and to collaborate with others to realise the project. The architect-activist innovates by transgressing disciplinary boundaries. In his book Architecture Depends, Jeremy Till characterises architecture as a 'dependent' profession. This ingrained dependency, the Architecture Chronicle argues can only be overcome by the three architect characters acting in concert.

Formal architectural education can be traced back to the Academie Royale d'Architecture established in Paris during the 17th Century. The Academie established an atelier-based system where students' design education was directed by a studio master who set design briefs and

Top image: Will McLean, Mervyn Rodrigues, Bruce Irwin, Jan Kattein and Maria Kramer discussing the student Prototype Pavilion models
Bottom image: Skip Garden at Kings Cross - Jan Kattein Architects

critiqued the students' work. Despite attempts to renew the way design is taught, most university-based design education today continues to gravitate around the design studio. A studio group of 15 to 30 students is supervised by a team of design tutors who set a design brief and each student proceeds with the development of speculative designs expressed in sketches, drawings, computer visualisations and architectural maquettes. Design progress is reviewed in individual tutorials and during communal design critiques. In order to progress from year to year, students submit a design portfolio which is assessed by academic staff and graded individually.

The design studio excels in teaching the skills of the architect-inventor. The regular challenge of the students' work by their design tutors hones their visual and practical design skills. Design studios at architecture schools around the world deliver hugely ambitious and visually stunning student work. Yet, the skills of the architect-activist and the architect-arbitrator are under-represented in the traditional curriculum.

Despite attempts to introduce group work, collaboration and co-ordination are largely absent in an environment where students are compelled to compete for the highest marks and end of year design prizes. And disciplinary boundaries are ill-defined on speculative projects where the design parameters are largely set by the students and their design tutors.

When Dr Julia King and I took over degree studio 3 at the Bartlett School of Architecture in 2014, we were intimately aware of these deficiencies. Julia had been working on sanitation projects in informal settlements in India and I had been working on grass-roots regeneration projects in London. We had both experienced that tackling real world challenges and the collaboration with people outside of our profession were essential to meet the objectives of the projects that we had been tasked to deliver.

In pursuit of a new, more integrated form of design education, we struck up a partnership with environmental charity Global Generation. Global Generation had been building community gardens in London for several years and they had recently been given a site for a new, temporary garden in King's Cross, in Central London. That, year, our design studio brief would prompt students to develop designs for a real site. The parameters of their design project would be defined by real world challenges and their design critiqued by the needs of a community outside our profession.

In the guise of the architect-activist, who strays beyond traditional disciplinary boundaries, the students were initially based at the university workshop, progressing their design proposals by building 1:1 prototypes under the guidance of specialist technicians. Projects advanced in

The Skip Garden - Jan Kattein Architects 'Projects advanced in response to the properties of the materials they used and the technical challenges inherent to making in a workshop setting.'

response to the properties of the materials they used and the technical challenges inherent to making in a workshop setting. When student projects finally moved onto the building site, collaboration and co-ordination took centre stage. Realising a project that's larger than life required the students support each other to procure materials, transport and to lift and assemble large construction elements.

'Realising a project that's larger than life required the students supported each other to procure materials...... and assemble large construction elements.'

Sharing skills and knowledge allowed students to tackle technical and logistical challenges through combined and complementary effort. And all along, liaison with stakeholders including the resident charity, future garden users, statutory authorities such as Camden Council, structural engineers and the site owner advanced the students' ability to communicate their ideas, to compromise and invest others. On completion, the site, which became known as The Skip Garden was visited by 10k people each year. It received internationally recognised design awards and was publicised in the professional press worldwide. That year, the students from degree unit 3 graduated with a design portfolio, their first built project, a network of collaborators who had supported the project and an understanding that

architecture is an integrated process of activism, innovation and collaboration.

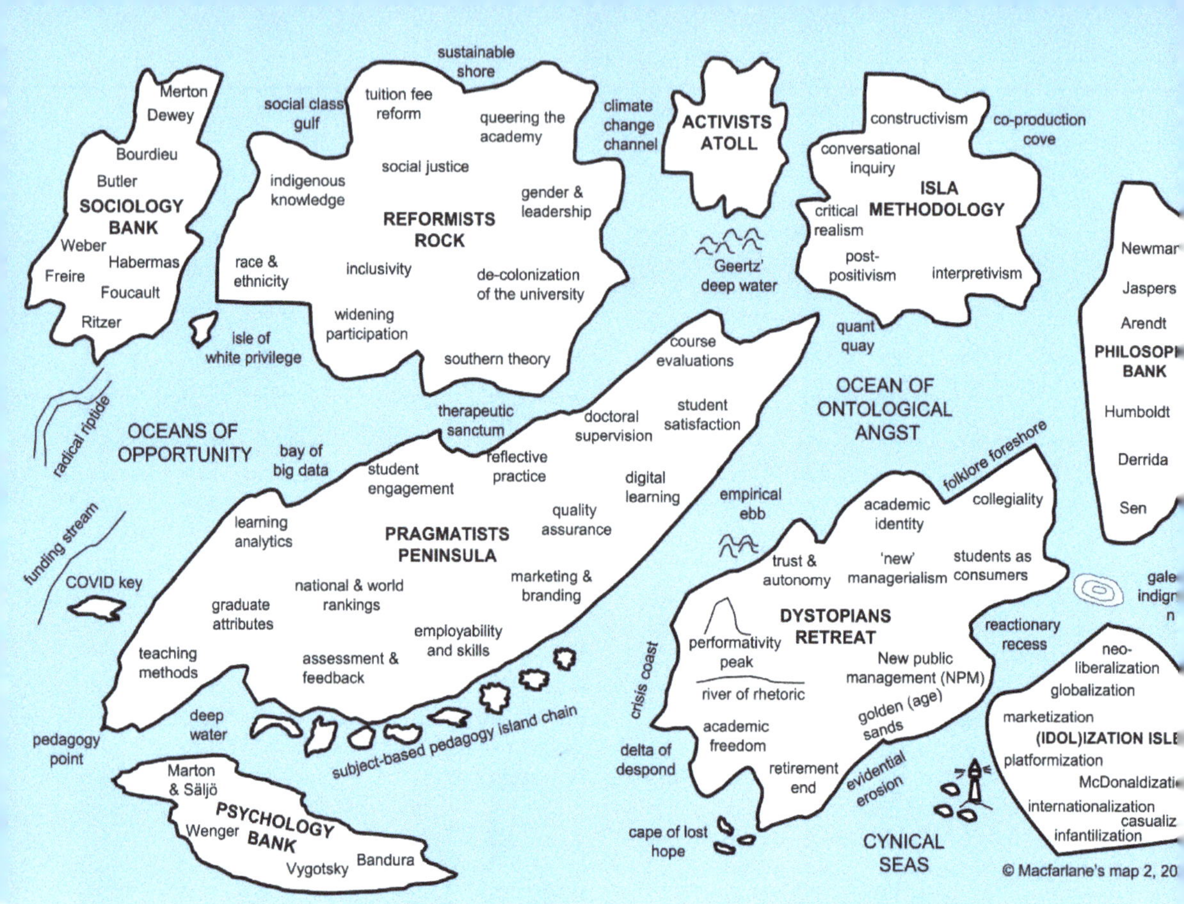

The Ideological Seascape of Higher Education Research by Bruce Macfarlane; reproduced with the kind permission of Bruce Macfarlane

Public Engagement structure and content about Greening the Campus developed by Julian Williams, Catherine Phillips, Alex Fox and Foundation Year students; we have since been awarded funding from Westminster City Council to develop the project in collaboration with the author of this book.

LIVE PROJECTS' JOURNEY THROUGH THE ARCHIPELAGO OF PEDAGOGIES...

JULIAN WILLIAMS

Back in 2019, Maria Kramer and I were awarded funds from the University's Quentin Hogg trust to support a live project collaboration with community partners. Maria's work involved large live-build projects, whilst the funds supported more modest work on my part on a series of collaborations with the umbrella title ClimateDemonstrator, involving primary school partners in the London Boroughs of Lambeth, Camden and Westminster. In Maria's project work and mine, external collaboration with partners was a key feature, and one that, perhaps more than anything, distinguishes the live project as a vehicle for learning the practice of architecture.

Possibly because of the spatial dimension of our field, the question of where we learn the practice of architecture comes up a lot.

Where do we best learn our craft?

Is it in the lecture theatre or studio of an architecture school, in the so-called real world of the building site, or perhaps its inverse, through blogs and online content?

To respond to the question, and hopefully lead to some useful and practical conclusions, we need explore two terrains not one. The first one is as discussed- the location in which learning takes place: is this at the side of an experienced practitioner, surrounded by 'old timers', with other students in an academic environment of self-exploration and imaginative freedom, or at the site of physical change and with parties drawn from beyond the academic fold.

In each of these places, the question arises as to what the mechanism of learning is.

Do we learn by emulating model actions, by a process of transmission, through trial and error, or by learning through practice? And is one way of learning more effective than another- for example, is practising the difficult bits repeatedly better than experiencing the whole thing over and over? Is learning with other learners in a social environment better than being a lone learner watching those with expertise? And what about the real world- is this more complex and more uncertain space more effective again?

Every teaching method is underpinned by a guiding concept, even if it is the outcome of practical evolution. Architectural education is, in the field of teaching and learning scholarship, considered a 'signature pedagogy', and like medicine or law, shaped by long-standing traditions of learning outside of the orthodoxy that shapes university education. These different ways of doing excite academic curiosity. Are they better, less egalitarian, more egalitarian, more expensive, less academic… and so on. And most importantly, how can they be conceptualised?

This brings me to the second terrain. In 2021, Bruce Macfarlane published a map of pedagogical entitled 'The ideological seascape of higher education research' (see diagram on following page). It presents educational concepts and ideologies together with prevailing policies and social and technological changes as a series of islands and seas through which any research journey on pedagogy would need to navigate. Where does architectural education and indeed live projects lie? Understanding our work in the context of educational theory can help us shape and refine our approach.

Perhaps to be found off the Psychology bank in the subject-based pedagogy island chain of Macfarlane's map in the field of Donald Schön. Supporting architecture's signature pedagogy tutorial tradition, he argued for the student tutorial as an emulation of the master-apprentice relationship. Schön's controversial research set an agenda for educational research focusing on the particular qualities of studio-based teaching, perhaps at the expense of the wider picture.

Nearby would be Lave and Wenger, whose work on communities of practice has been argued as a good reflection of studio learning. Within a community of practice, those with less experience learn through a process of observing more skilled members and through peripheral participation. As tutors, we like to think of ourselves as central to the studio space, but my own research suggests otherwise- students' experience is that we are in the space for very little of the time, do not demonstrate in such a way that students might peripherally participate, and do not work with groups of learners made up of students of significantly different levels such that there is meaningful mentoring.

In a live project, something much more like a community of practice might be happening- project parameters are more closely set by a tutor or external partner, and the creation of these is carried out with the students so they might observe, peripherally, the

Crumbles Castle Live Project, built from the granite paving blocks of the demolished 'Crumbles' tenements, Author's own image. Taken 24/07/2025

events unfold. Students are not at the centre of things- stakeholders occupy real rather than conceptual space and wield greater capital.

Much of live practice resonates with the ideas of the social nature of learning beyond the university, reflecting many aspects of the long-standing North American traditions of service learning supported by John Dewey's work, located by Macfarlane on the Sociology Bank.

Dewey argued that education and learning are social and interactive practices and that institutions of learning should be drivers of social change, with students engaging with the curriculum and structuring their own learning experience. In Experience and Education, he argued for experiential learning (provided that it was part of a positive and connected curriculum) and against isolationist learning environments (we could include the design studio in this category). In live projects, the 'rules', if you like, are set by the tutors, students and external stakeholders, so students feel less that the parameters have been arbitrarily drawn by the tutor. Dewey characterised the learning activity in this scenario as having 'genuine purpose'.

Mobilising the agency of students and educators has been a marginal but consistent strand in architectural education- from the work in Birmingham, to the teaching of Brian Anson and Cedric Price. Recognising that the call 'to build' is not the only route to what is now called 'authentic learning'. Back in 1971, three architecture students from the University of Westminster's predecessor, the Polytechnic of Central London, got involved with an adventure playground organisation in Islington and local tenants, and together built a castle- the outcome of asking the local children what they wanted their new place to be like. Crumbles Castle, built from the granite paving blocks of the demolished 'Crumbles' tenements, continues to thrive as one of Islington's Adventure Playgrounds (see image to the left).

The emphasis of Dewey's approach is on the impact of social learning on the individual, and of the learner as a social being. The focus is on the construction of social contexts that can support the learner and their journey. But how is this experienced by that individual, above and beyond the social learning experience and the getting to grips with the know-how and the know-what in a live setting?

For Hannah Arendt, located on the far side of Macfarlane's archipelago alongside Humboldt, the transformational process of learning served not only to transform the shape of society itself, but to prepare the individual to lead on this. In her essay, The Crisis of Education, she wrote:

"Education is the point at which we decide whether we love the world enough to assume responsibility for it and by the same token save it from that ruin which, except for renewal, except for the coming of the new and young, would be inevitable. And education, too, is where we decide whether we love our children enough not to expel them from our world and leave them to their own devices, nor to strike from their hands their chance of undertaking something new, something unforeseen by us, but to prepare them in advance for the task of renewing a common world."

This perspective allows us to consider the experience of learning as more than that of self-enlightenment, but as connecting an enlightened self-realisation with action in the world. Elsewhere, Arendt, in her essay on Walter Benjamin, alludes to the practice of the pearl diver, seeking 'thought fragments' from the depths, and bringing them into the present as a 'rich and strange' lens through which to challenge our present-day world.

In the live project, the unpredictability of both the process and the outcome is, I would argue, an integral part of experiencing the complexity of achieving anything in the world. And because the process positions the tutor at the side, the student is confronted directly by external agencies and their vicissitudes rather than a carefully foreseen and construed version of reality. For this reason,

Live Projects are loved in theory but feared in practice.

Live project educators should remember Arendt's emphasis on the process of learning being a reflective experience for the learner in getting to know themselves and their relationship with the public sphere.

In this voyage through McFarlane's archipelago of learning theory, I believe it is this final realm that offers the most value for the pedagogy of the live project, as it asks us to consider education as a journey of becoming in the world, not just as a social learning process, or as a vehicle for creating beguiling artefacts.

"ClimateDemonstrator.org.uk" accessed Aug 27, 2025

Bruce Macfarlane, "A Voyage Around the Ideological Islands of Higher Education Research," Higher Education Research & Development 41, no. 1 (January 2, 2022), 107–115. doi:10.1080/07294360.2021.2002275.

Donald A. Schon, The Reflective Practitioner: How Professionals Think in Action (Basic Books, 1984).

Helena Webster, "Architectural Education After Schön: Cracks, Blurs, Boundaries and Beyond," Journal for Education in the Built Environment 3, no. 2 (2008), 63–74.

Jean Lave and Etienne Wenger, Situated Learning: Legitimate Peripheral Participation (Cambridge University Press, 1991).

Julian Williams, "Design Studio: A Community of Practitioners?" Charrette 4, no. 1 (-04-01, 2017), 88–100.

John Dewey, Experience and Education (Free Press, 1997).

James Benedict Brown, "A Critique of the Live Project" (Queen's University Belfast, 2012).

The Crumbles Castle Ekistics 43, no. 255 (1977), 87–91. https://www.jstor.org/stable/43618792.

Hannah Arendt and Jerome Kohn, Between Past and Future (Penguin, 2006), 196.

Hannah Arendt, Men in Dark Times (Houghton Mifflin Harcourt, 1968), 205.

LIVE PROJECTS FROM SOCIAL SCIENCE PERSPECTIVES

ARLENE OAK

The following outlines some aspects of Live Projects that are of interest to social scientists, particularly those who work in the area of qualitative, interpretive social science (e.g., social psychology, ethnographic anthropology), where the aim is not to measure human behaviour but to better understand its nuanced complexities. Live Projects (and the related area of Design-Build (Brown & Russell 2022)) education offer to social scientists a rich variety of individual, social, material, pedagogic, and community-oriented experiences to consider. Such phenomena may be explored and analysed through observing (and, ideally, video and/or audio recording) some of the activities of Live Projects participants, and/or otherwise acquiring information through e.g., interviews, questionnaires, and other forms of data collection (Woodward 2020). I'll briefly outline a couple of areas that I, as a social psychologist, find particularly interesting about Live Projects: these include aspects of communication, and some forms of contemporary social theory in anthropology and related areas that offer interesting perspectives through which the practices of Live Projects could be considered.

As a social psychologist who studies design-related activities, I'm interested in how groups influence individuals, and how individuals influence groups, particularly through the social interaction (mainly conversational talk) that occurs during design and architecture practice (Oak 2009, 2011). To study talk in design-related settings, it is useful to have access to the naturally-occurring conversations that happens in everyday situations: that is, conversations between participants that would happen whether or not the researcher was present. This kind of talk can be distinguished from that which occurs when, for instance, a researcher asks questions in an interview. Conversation is a particularly interesting aspect of human behaviour to study because, if the talk can be recorded and transcribed, it is possible to explore topics such as misunderstandings, explanations, and accounts or justifications for beliefs and actions (Oak 2011). During Live Projects (where students work with community clients, their teachers, and others to design and create plans, drawings, digital or analogue models, and at times full-scale, useable structures), the talk that takes place contains a great deal of fascinating information about how decisions are made concerning what should be created (Nicholas & Oak 2020; Oak 2019).

There are many situations that social scientists who study interaction explore, for instance, conversations in medical situations (Maynard & Heritage 2005), office-based settings (Mondada & Miranda da Cruz 2024) or business contexts (Niemi & Hirvonen 2019) which, like Live Projects, involve cooperation, negotiation, and complex decisions (Anderson 2017; Harriss & Widder 2014). However, what makes Live Projects a particularly interesting area to study is how participant talk involves more than decisions about relationships and processes, it also involves decisions about materials, structures, tool-use, sites, etc. That is, while Live Projects requires participants to communicate in face-to-face and/or online contexts that are similar to the situations mentioned above, Live Projects also involves its participants in making decisions about the worlds of material culture (i.e., materials and tools – from paper and computers to wood and concrete, and from X-Acto knives and laptops to hammers and circular saws), and the worlds of the environment (i.e., the land and climate of the proposed site). Further, Live Projects is an interesting location to study because its participants have to navigate between the 'real' situations of designing and/or making for 'real' people (e.g., community-based clients), and also between the pedagogic situations of academic schedules, grading and assessment, and other institutional demands. Participants in Live Projects are continuously shifting between managing the experiences and expectations of students, teachers, and/or clients, while also considering the pragmatic logistics of budgets, materials, tools, and sites (Anderson 2017). The resulting conversations are, unsurprisingly, complex and therefore offer rich areas of consideration for those interested in communication and culture (Nicholas & Oak 2020; Oak 2019).

The ways that Live Projects requires participants to engage, simultaneously, in social, material, and environmental contexts means that the activities of Live Projects can be considered through a range of social theory, some of which is associated with the area of 'new materialism'. A new materialist approach to investigating and/or interpreting the world explores human connections with 'nonhumans, 'i.e., with 'matter', including materials, equipment, technologies, land/earth/sites, and other species and organisms. Humans are understood to live with and through such non-human matter in ways that see both humans and non-humans as being active or having agency (Bennett 2010). While some critique new materialism for inconsistencies and an at times disinclination to acknowledge the power of human action (Boysen 2018), nevertheless, these approaches have opened space to consider, e.g., ethical issues as these link to areas of materiality alongside social issues. For instance, in architecture, the familiar ethical concerns of relationships between clients and architects or, in education, between teachers and students, might, through a new materialist perspective, also consider the ethics of land use and materials acquisition and deployment (Krasny 2019; Puig de la Bellacasa 2017).

Some aspects of new materialism overlap with aspects of Actor Network Theory (ANT), a philosophical and social science field of interpretive scholarship that has for some time been associated with the practice of architecture, and that some consider to be a precursor to new materialism. The work of ethnographer/anthropologist Albena Yaneva (2017) and anthropologist/sociologist/philosopher Bruno Latour (Latour & Yaneva 2008; Yaneva 2022) are especially associated with ANT-based approaches to architecture. ANT's awareness of how designed objects emerge through networks of humans distributed in and through, e.g., governmental policies, technologies, materials, and forms of representation (drawings, models, etc. (Latour 2017) mean that it is an effective way to describe the complexity of architectural projects without resorting to limited discussions of individual 'genius' creators. An ANT-oriented approach has been taken to some research concerning Live Projects and other experiential education projects (e.g., Doucet 2016; Fenwick et al. 2011; Schwarz et al. 2025; Sharif 2020).

Other social scientists whose work might be considered as (loosely) associated with aspects of a new materialist perspective–because they consider human activities as always occurring with and through material contexts–include the anthropologist Tim Ingold, who explores 'making' in terms of the way it brings humans and materials into "correspondence" with each other (Ingold 2013, 2021); and, anthropologist Trevor Marchand (2007, 2009, 2010) who considers the processes of making in architecture, with building knowledge enacted by and across bodies, skilled gestural movements, talk, and materials. In terms of Live Projects, Ingold has influenced the scholarship of some Live Projects educators such as Piers Taylor (2021) who explores the relatively unplanned aspects of collaborative making, while Marchand's interest in 'situated learning' (Lave & Wenger 1991) and 'experiential education' (Schenck & Cruickshank 2015) link to elements of teaching and research in Live Projects (e.g.,

Note taking for social science data collection at Live Projects field site by Arlene Oak (right); photo by Claire Nicholas

the work of Jane Anderson (2019)).

In settings of experiential education, students engage in direct action, and reflection on those actions. Taking an interpretive, social science approach to Live Projects through perspectives associated with experiential education, means recognizing that each Live Project is a unique set of experiences and so both students and their professors need to puzzle through situations to solve problems of design and making (Nicholas & Oak 2020). This aspect of Live Projects–that students and instructors are often designing and making together and so equally learning together–raises interesting issues of the potential of Live Projects (and research into Live Projects), to disrupt or challenge some of the traditional assumptions of pedagogic structures and social hierarchies that are often associated with education-based situations.

This brief outline indicates a few reasons why Live Projects education is, or could be, of interest to interpretive social scientists who are concerned with human behaviour, social contexts, communication, materials, and wider environments; and, particularly to those social scientists who are interested in the interrelations between these. Architecture as professional practice has been considered through social science perspectives including, e.g., psychology (Donald 2022), social psychology (Oak 2011, 2013), sociology (Jones 2011), and anthropology (Cuff 1991; Ingold 2013; Yaneva 2017); and, traditional modes of architecture education have themselves on occasion been the subject of social science inquiry (Mazalán, Vinárčiková, & Hronsky 2022). As this discussion suggests, Live Projects open up rich, situated opportunities for the social sciences to engage with real-world dynamics-where research, design and social practice intersect through ongoing collaboration and critical reflection.

For references, please see the end of the book.

RECLAIMING THE ARCHITECT'S ROLE THROUGH LIVE PROJECTS

INTERVIEW WITH STEVE WEBB FROM WEBB YATES ENGINEERS

Steve Webb, co-founder of the multi award-winning Webb Yates Engineers, is celebrated for pushing the boundaries of structural engineering by integrating craft, sustainability and design intelligence. Whilst leading the MArch DS20 Live Studio, I had the opportunity to work with Steve on several Live Projects, where his input significantly elevated both our designs and structural thinking. I often remind students that the quality of a project is shaped by the people you collaborate with—and Steve is a prime example of that.

THE ROLE OF LIVE PROJECTS

In this conversation, we reflect on Live Projects and their broader implications for architectural education and the built environment. Webb highlights how such projects bring relevance and practicality to academic settings. He also contrasts the roles of engineers and architects-engineers almost always work on projects destined for construction, architecture often remains theoretical.

SW: "Doing Live Projects with a university is a kind of combination... they're quite experimental because they're in an academic situation... but also grounded in some kind of reality...Designing speculatively on paper, can lack rigour because you don't deal with the constraints or realities. For me, I'm more interested in the destination, the actual building."

MK: "The beauty of a Live Project is that one can focus on the process, where a lot of learning takes place, but then you have an output as well."

Live Projects offer students a unique opportunity to engage with real constraints—like budget and materials-while retaining the freedom to innovate.

SW:

"Constraints shouldn't necessarily mean that their response has to be basic but rather an opportunity for true innovation."

ARCHITECTURE VS ENGINEERING

Webb reflects on the differing expectations between disciplines: SW: "Nobody calls an engineer unless they're actually going to build something...The joy of teaching in different academic institutions is that you work on things that are never going to be built... It can be much more dreamy...

Frequently I sit there thinking, 'What a stupid idea, you could never build that,' and then suddenly... 'Oh, maybe in a certain way you could what an amazing idea"

A central theme was the evolving definition and scope of architecture, particularly its tension between physical form and abstract ideas.

SW: "In the real world, architecture is about designing buildings that get built...Architecture as a broad profession can sometimes define itself in cloudy, self-aggrandising ways, social engineering art philosophy... but most outsiders would define architects as the people who do the drawings that make the building."

MK: "Sometimes we don't even know where architecture starts and ends... Some architects [especially in academia] are not interested in the built environment at all."

Webb expresses frustration with uninspired responses to current architectural challenges:

SW: "Today's [architecture], despite some really interesting constraints, like climate and carbon and reuse... the responses can sometimes incredibly boring...and many reasons are given for the failure to innovate or move the dial on carbon but ultimately it is a failure to steer the project in the right direction."

MK: "That's the skill of the innovative architect—convincing clients to go beyond what they've imagined... Live Projects question the role of the architect - we can make design decisions beyond the brief."

MK: "In some ways we are creating new projects with Live Builds, which probably wouldn't exist otherwise."

Live Projects bridge conceptual thinking and physical reality. They empower students, question professional norms, and produce meaningful, imaginative and buildable architectural outcomes. Live Projects, while still grounded in the real world, offer a middle ground-a co-created brief with clients, yet more realistic than purely academic studio work. However, even these face challenges when briefs are unclear or too loose.

SW: "You can stretch the constraints of the real

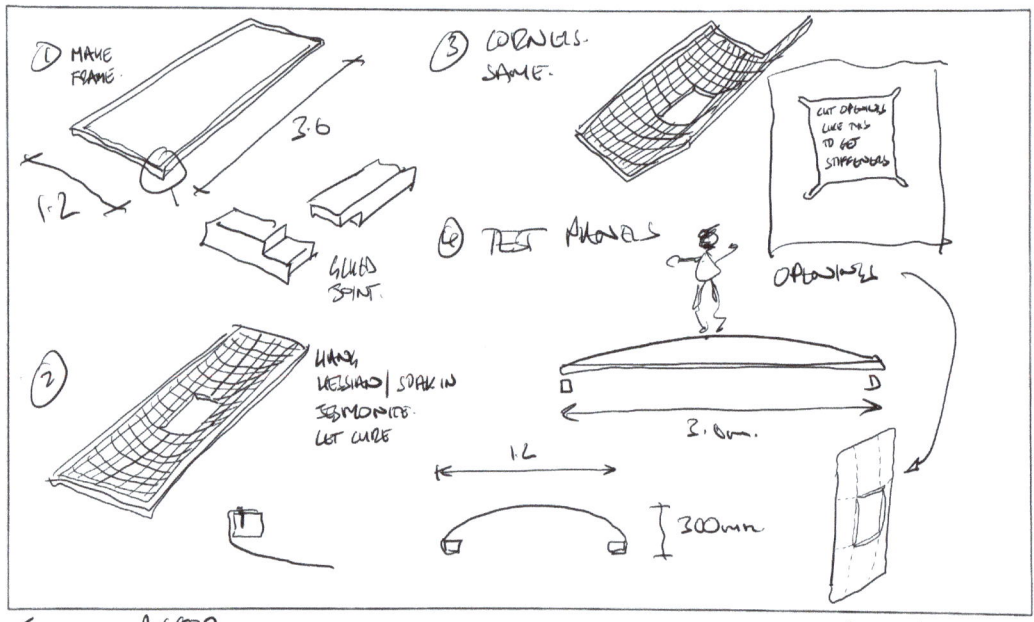

Top Image: Photo of discussion with Steve Webb developing the Floating Forum Live Project at the University of Westminster architecture studios; Sketch above by Steve Webb world... but you're still dealing with restraints...That is intelligence... to still be able to bend all of those things into something beautiful, ecological, buildable and affordable. Having a blank chequebook and a blue sky... and producing something pretty is not so intelligent."

> *"This idea that there's a dichotomy between being artistic and being technical is not true...You can absolutely be coexisting on both ends of that spectrum at the same time."*

THE IDENTITY CRISIS IN ARCHITECTURE

We touch on the unclear role of architects today: Are they designers, builders, thinkers, or something else?

MK: "Architecture is not only the built environment."

SW: "I would say architecture is only the built environment." This exchange reveals a deeper philosophical tension about what architecture is and who it serves. Webb argues that the UK currently lacks a culture of architectural innovation, constrained by limited technical education and mindset. He urges a return to materially and structurally grounded design and embracing the technical as well as the artistic.

SW: "If you don't have the education and technical freedom to innovate, then you're always at the mercy of those who do."

EDUCATION, PRACTICE AND THE TECHNICAL GAP

We reflect on the disconnect between architectural education and professional practice. In studios, students are encouraged to devise imaginative programmes. In practice, briefs are mostly fixed. I criticise over-reliance on representation, which can distance students from the act of building: MK: "Everything is a representation... and we become quite removed from the real thing ....We take students [to site]; they help build the projects... we build 1:1 prototypes to test ideas."

Webb critiques the myth of the architect as lone genius: SW: "95% of architectural work is really bloody boring... specifications, drawings, dimensions... only 5% is creativity." We both note that design-build contracts often stifle experimentation. I praise firms like Herzog & de Meuron for embedding prototyping into contracts to allow innovation.

SW: "There's a poetry in the pragmatism... something clever and pure in just clipping timber together."

CRAFT, COLLABORATION, AND THE MYTH OF THE DESIGN HERO

We agree that successful architecture relies on collective effort and shared vision. We advocate for deeper collaboration with fabricators, arguing that innovation often comes from on-the-ground knowledge. The best outcomes emerge when there is mutual "pull" rather than imposition, particularly when the craftsperson has deep material knowledge. Webb critiques the "design hero" narrative: SW: "The kind of icon at the head of the pile of designers is probably not very helpful for a collaborative multi-disciplinary industry because it fails to reward or recognise everyone else who contributed ideas and expertise and inspiration."

URGENCY, RESPONSIBILITY, AND THE FUTURE OF ARCHITECTURE

Finally, we express a shared frustration at the lack of urgency in the industry around climate and housing challenges. Webb calls for a return to material and structural innovation, rooted in risk-taking and technological integrity. He praises early modernism for its bold use of new materials:

> SW: *"The most interesting architecture... is vernacular... true to the technological roots of the construction itself..."*

The beginning of modernism was really the birth of a new vernacular embracing new materials of the time like concrete, steel, and glass... new materials made new architecture possible."

This conversation with Steve Webb invites us to rethink architectural education, re-evaluate the architect's role, and reimagine innovation as something grounded in collaboration, craft and constraint. Though not without limitations, Live Projects offer a compelling vision of what architecture can become when it re-engages with reality—while still embracing the power of imagination. They create new interventions that might not otherwise exist, placing the architect at the heart of the process-as initiator, collaborator and an active partner with stakeholders, consultants and makers throughout.

WHAT FUTURE FOR ARCHITECTS IN THE AGE OF CAPITALIST REALISM?

STUDENT PERSPECTIVE: KITTY EMERY RAINBIRD

Acknowledgements: Special thanks to Lindsay Bremner for your help and support, and to Alessandro Toti for introducing me to the key theories of this dissertation.

ARCHITECTURE IS A PROFESSION OF CONTRADICTIONS

The task of an architect, if boiled down to the simplest terms seems easily definable: design buildings. Yet to achieve this goal, they are faced with complex and conflicting hurdles of which the correct course to navigate is not always clear. In the UK, contemporary architectural practice is profoundly shaped by the capitalist system, within which neoliberal ideologies have flourished since the 1980s. To contextualise the discussion, it is essential to understand the framework within which architects operate: architects now find themselves a product of an education which equips them to design high quality structures, driven by social, environmental, and contextual considerations – yet they find themselves employed in an industry which is dictated chiefly by profitability and efficiency. This poses profound moral and professional challenges for architects.

The role of the architect is made clear to us throughout our education. We must be more than simply a designer of buildings; we must be an environmental advocate and community enricher; we must strive to benefit society and the planet through the built environment. Although on the surface, the stated goals of private development companies appear to align with the values taught within architectural education, when the actions of these companies are examined in depth, a different reality is exposed.

THE FRICTION BETWEEN UNIVERSITY EDUCATION AND WORK IN PRACTICE

In the UK, architectural education typically consists of a Bachelors (RIBA Part 1), a masters (RIBA Part 2) and a post graduate diploma (RIBA Part 3) in addition to industry practice in various forms [NB this is currently being reviewed by the ARB with some integrated courses being offered]. Usually the structure of courses are focused on studio projects, with smaller modules in areas such as architectural technology, history and theory, and architectural practice. Whilst the structure of architectural education has remained relatively unchanged for decades, there has been a noticeable change in recent years from the practice of "the master tutor and willing servant students, the privileging of the visual, the inculcation of absurd modes of behaviour (sleep deprivation, aggressive defensiveness, internal competition)"[1] to a much more collaborative process. Tutors support students as they navigate the sociopolitical context and environmental factors, while also exploring a range of cross-disciplinary influences. This system places high value on students implementing this critical thinking in their work[2], with factors such as feasibility and planning regulations being considered later on in the process. Whilst this rounded education provides the knowledge to evaluate the built environment and the skills to better it, the student can feel that their technical skills, and knowledge of real-world design are lacking once they enter the workforce;

Students can be faced with a sense of frustration at their inability to practically implement their theoretical knowledge.

Architects start out instinctually optimistic, and even if this hope is tempered and frustrated over time by the barriers that have to be overcome, the initial motivation of betterment still remains.[3]

The reality of working in practice is a vastly different world from the one we are exposed to in architecture school. When starting out in practice, it can feel like most of what we've been taught is completely irrelevant, and the basic day to day tasks are completely new. When lamenting on what the point of architecture school was, I was told by a colleague, that architecture school was invaluable to the architect because it teaches us how to think. At the time it seemed far more important to know how to design a building that won't fall down, or how to navigate the complex planning system; it didn't seem to require much socioeconomic analysis to plan the layout of a two bedroom flat, but some basic knowledge of Part M would have been useful. I couldn't understand how students could graduate after three years of university with only a basic technical and regulatory knowledge of architecture, when this seemed to make up the majority of work in practice.

Image: A Space of Expression by Kitty Emery Rainbird

Yet the longer I spent in the industry, the more I recognised the validity of his words, and those of educators who have been defending the current system, such as Sean Griffiths, who argues:

> *It is emphatically not the job of architecture education to mimic practice and generate workers for the profession in its present mode. The task of architecture education is to carry out experimental research, to critique practice and provide the tools, skills and attitudes needed to reinvent it* [4].

Whilst it has proven relatively straightforward to learn the technical aspects of architecture on the job, the foundations I developed in Architecture school meant I could question, if only inwardly, the implications of our designs. As an architectural assistant, I had an even more limited influence over the work I was producing, but I could perceive the implications of the decisions being made around me. I adjusted to working in practice swiftly, picking up the practical skills I felt I lacked at the start, yet I was however, left with a gnawing feeling that I was somehow forgoing what I'd learnt in architecture school.

There are those however, who believe at the disparity between architectural education and practice is too great, and that closer ties between education and practice would lead to architects becoming a more productive workforce. Some suggested changes to architectural education place skills which benefit the market and streamline productivity in the workplace above those which allow the architect to critically assess designs from a socially and environmentally ethical standpoint.

Standard architectural education places high value on the role of the architect in society, championing that good design must consider the relationship between people and places, and the impact of buildings on communities and the environment. Whilst this might not be the most efficient way to produce a building as a consumer product, it aims to ensure that the public have access to a built environment which addresses multiple socio-environmental considerations. Although it is true that vocational routes offer a greater development of the practical skills required for work in practice, there is little opportunity for future architects to study the subject more broadly and develop a more rounded view which would allow them to challenge designs more robustly. Whilst vocational training is an excellent supplement to a traditional architectural education, it is vital that it remains alongside a foundation of architectural, environmental, and social theory.

1 Nishat. Awan, Tatjana. Schneider, and Jeremy. Till, Spatial Agency: Other Ways of Doing Architecture (Abingdon: Routledge, 2011). P.46
2 The Architects Registration Board, 'Prescription of Qualifications: ARB Criteria' (The Architects Registration Board, 2011).
3 Awan et al., Spatial Agency: Other Ways of Doing Architecture. P. 37
4 Sean Griffiths, 'It Is Emphatically Not the Job of Architectural Education to Mimic Practice', Dezeen, 2019, https://www.dezeen.com/2019/08/02/architecture-education-opinion/

SOCIALLY-ENGAGED EDUCATION + PRACTICE - WHY IT MATTERS

ALICIA PIVARO

In our age of multiple crises, we must embrace the opportunities and unexpected outcomes that come from involving citizens in shaping cities and communities. Live Projects and genuine community collaboration are essential in developing the ethics, politics, and skills to create positive change.

It has always struck me as bizzare that you can go through 5 years of architectural education and never speak to a 'real' person. As you learn the skills, knowledge and processes of designing you are tested within a very particular environment – that of the educational institution filled with a variety of architectural academics and practitioners. There are rules here - ways of talking, thinking, communicating and presenting and rules about what is important to be studying, how to design, criteria to operate within, briefs to be responded to – all within a hierarchical, top-down structure.

I studied in the 1980s when architectural education was predominately male, modernist, myopic and introverted – none of which resonated with me as a student that sought out the alternative or radical people and ideas that could be found of the edges of what was considered important for my education.

The good news is things have changed radically- academia and the profession are more open, diverse and socially-minded. My belief in live projects or socially- engaged architectural education is multi-faceted mixing ethics, politics and practicality. Some basic advantages for students include;
- Getting out of the studio with action/site-specific research
- Talking to people outside of architectural academia about ideas – their families, users, clients, stakeholders
- Working with others learning skills of collaboration, negotiation and communication
- Hearing multiple viewpoints, lived experiences and opinions, which enrich briefs and more critically robust design responses

My own ethics, values and politics have been shaped by various ideas and thinkers:

1 Gentle and practical anarchism
We can advocate new forms of participation in spatial practice to reconnect knowledge, power, and civic life - aiming for a co-produced, just and sustainable city, rooted in anarchism. My anarchist hero, Colin Ward, championed 'pragmatist anarchism' - replacing top-down authority with bottom-up, self-organised systems built on mutual aid, collective action, and respect for people and nature. A prolific writer and teacher, he celebrated people over profit, documenting community growers, self-builders, council estate kids, and rural squatters.

In Anarchy in Action (1973) he wrote: "An anarchist society… is always in existence, like a seed beneath the snow." I see this in wikis, open-source projects, co-operatives, mutual aid, co-housing, Community Land Trusts, and Libraries of Things.

2 Marxist urban thinking
Marxist Urban Theory and Radical Geography, shaped by Henri Lefebvre, contrasts the dominant "representations of space" created by planners and engineers with the lived, dynamic spaces of users. Central to his ideas of the Right to the City and the Right to Difference is the diversity of urban life and the public's role in shaping social space. Lefebvre embraced the messy, ever-changing nature of urban culture as a source of new practices and needs.

Proposed in his 1968 book Le Droit à la Ville, the Right to the City has since been adopted by social movements and progressive authorities as a

call for co-created, collectively managed cities

a response to rising social and spatial inequalities. David Harvey expanded this, describing it as a common right to transform ourselves by transforming the city through collective power. Much pioneering work comes from the Global South, documented in Design Like You Give a Damn! by Architecture for Humanity, and seen in practitioners such as Rural Studio (US), muf architecture/art, Civic Square, Resolve, Poor Collective (UK), Raumlabor (Germany), and R-Urban (France).

3 Participatory and collaborative creative practices
The idea of social or socially-engaged art and architecture practice has a rich and varied lineage from the 1921 Paris Dada Season which involved the citizens on the streets to the radical experiments of the 1960s/70s to the 1990s&2000s as documented in the book Living as Form edited by Nato Thompson. One of the first texts to address the political status of participation was by German theorist Walter Benjamin using the plays of Bertolt Brecht to explain the shift from mere spectators to collaborators.

Peoples' Map: "The Plan will start from our needs, rather than the developers' profits" In 2023 DS 2.7 based the student brief on the The People's Plan for the Royal Docks. Developed in 1983 by local residents and community members the Plan proposed an alternative, bottom-up scheme - contesting the financialised and extractive model of development in the form of the City Airport; Tutors: Alicia Pivaro and David McEwen

Peoples' Plan 2030; Based upon the ideas and concerns of the local community and incorporating the new challenges of the 21st century, students emphasised the role of the commons, shared resources and amenities for all, furthering the role of communities in the developments that shape their neighbourhoods, local activism and the importance of collective ownership; Tutors: Alicia Pivaro and David McEwen

So maybe we need to rethink our relationships to our communities and users – reframe them not as abstract actors or consultees but as genuine collaborators, with unique knowledge and equal levels of expertise that the sociologist Antony Giddens would see as "the sharing of mutual knowledge so the instinct of the amateur is accepted as having equal potential as the established methods of the supposed expert."

In the book Participation, edited by Claire Bishop, she asks "So what are the connections between the earliest days of participatory art and practitioners today?
• desire to create an active subject, one who will be empowered by participation
• authorship ceded to others fosters egalitarian, democratic collaboration, embracing risk, unpredictability and non-hierarchical creativity
• community cohesion and collective experience

These three concerns – activation, authorship and community – are central to artists and other creatives including architects – that have sought to encourage participation. These concerns also appear in the writings of Guy Debord including The Society of the Spectacle. In his analysis of spectacle he states that the separation, passivity and non-communication of spectacle is the opposite of dialogue. For Debord the idea of the audience or user should disappear altogether into a new idea of the viveur (one who lives) with the construction of 'situations' aimed at producing new social relationships and social realities.

4 Critical pedagogy and radical education ideas
Paolo Freire, Brazilian educational theorist and philosopher saw education the learning of how to think critically and creatively. The book 'Pedagogy of the Oppressed' attempts to help students question and challenge the beliefs and practices that dominate.

Building on Freire's thinking the Canadian-American educator Henry Giroux sees "teaching as an inherently political act," insisting "that issues of social justice and democracy itself are not distinct from acts of teaching and learning."

"Education, is about the production of agency...

What kind of narratives are we going to produce that students can understand, that enlarge their perspective not only on the world but on their relationship to others and themselves? What is the basis for knowledge? In what way does it speak to a particular kind of future? Because all education is an introduction in some way to the future. It's a struggle over what kind of future you want for young people".

Today, citizens have more opportunities to shape their world through activism, social justice work, and urban movements - from citizens' assemblies and neighbourhood plans to Transition Towns, community-owned enterprises, and local hubs. All aim to deliver spatial, economic and social justice while offering alternative visions for developing and maintaining our towns and cities. For architect-activists, this means reframing communities not as abstract actors but as genuine collaborators with unique knowledge equal to that of experts. As sociologist Antony Giddens suggests, the instinct of the amateur can be as valuable as professional methods, provided relationships are non-extractive and citizens benefit from their involvement.

The Ladder of Participation, developed by Sherry Arnstein in 1969, maps levels of citizen involvement in decision-making from tokenism to citizen control. Valuable resources on this include Collaborate by Just Space, Towards Spatial Justice by DSDHA, and the Practising Ethics Project by David Roberts, curated by Jane Rendell.

Colin Ward, Anarchy in Action (George Allen and Unwin Ltd., 1973)
Henri Lefebvre, The Right to the City, (Anthropos, 1968)
Ed. Architecture for Humanity, Design Like You Give a Damn! Vol. 1 + 2 (Metropolis Books, 2006)
Ed. Nato Thomspon, Living as Form (MIT Press, 2017)
Ed. Claire Bishop, Participation (Whitechapel Gallery with MIT Press, 2006)
Guy Debord, The Society of the Spectacle (Editions Buchet-Chastel, 1967)
Paulo Freire, Pedagogy of the Oppressed (Bloomsbury Publishing, 1968)
Just Space, Collaborate: London Universities and Community Groups working Together (justspace.org, 2019)
DSDHA, Towards Spatial Justice (DSDHA.co.uk, 2022))
D. Roberts, Practising Ethics Bartlett School of Architecture, practisingethics.org, 2022

OBJECTS OF REPAIR

VENICE BIENNALE AS LIVE PROJECT
YARA SHARIF, NASSER GOLZARI

The Travelling Lab

The Travelling Lab brings together building materials salvaged from Gaza's rubble which, in collaboration with Gazan families, have been used here to reconstruct fragments of their homes and neighbourhoods. These fragments illustrate alternative uses and spatial possibilities of recycled crushed concrete, sandbags, repurposed reinforcement bars, fired and unfired clay bricks, recycled metal, timber, cardboard, and fabric. Rather than a prototype for reconstruction, The Travelling Lab stands as an evolving framework - continuously assembled and reimagined to cultivate hope.

Objects of Repair

Palestine lies near the northern-most point of the Great Rift Valley. In 1920, in the aftermath of the First World War, it became a British Mandate and was governed under de facto British colonial rule until 1948. These years set the course for subsequent widespread geographical misappropriation and geological extraction, which continues today, tearing apart the terrain and reducing Gaza's coastal edge to rubble.

Objects of Repair explores fracture and repair in the architectures and geologies of Palestine, drawing from the Palestine Regeneration Team's ongoing work to test and transform available resources for (re)building in the West Bank and Gaza. Echoes in time across 1935, 2005 and 2025 reveal how the current abuse of land, topography and ecosystem are deeply rooted in colonial agendas that continue to leave people and their homes scarred. Confronting these colonial strategies of erasure, Objects of Repair takes inspiration from Gazans' reappropriation of rubble to propose new design tactics in which ruins become active participants in creating new architectural "skins". These fragmentary interventions envision another potential reality - a world of impermanence, resilience and expression, born from architectures of accumulated small changes, healing and repair.

The Everyday Tools of Repair

Gazans have become particularly adept at reusing steel bars from damaged reinforced concrete. Here, experimental fabrication techniques are used to explore the potential of recycled steel bars, alongside other salvaged materials from destroyed buildings, such as timber and bricks. The underlying aim of this work is to develop a repository of techniques - or "library of repair" - that can help foster resilience through material innovation.

Live Build Journey

The Live Build project for the Venice Architecture Biennale was a collaborative process that started with the building of the 'Off the Grid' Mobile Clinic, a University of Westminster QHT funded project that was built in June 2024, part of the London Festival of Architecture, and now displayed at the Venice International Architecture Biennale's British Pavilion.

We worked with a team of six students from different courses MArch, MAA, PhD, Bsc, to test and make the installation with Francios Girardin and build manager Sarah Daoudi. The project was an opportunity for students to engage with the complexity of the making and build process, as well as a chance to apply learned design and problem solving skills in a setting with the real implications of time line, management and budget. The testing and build process began in November 2024, with students each taking ownership of a segment of the installation.

We explored a range of methods, including prototyping components at a smaller scale, utilising card and timber to create moulds and guides, carefully translating the construction drawings into realised structure. This primary stage involved mocking up at full scale, slices of the installation structure, provisionally securing timber columns, beams, and metal frames using clamps. The process was not linear, with students getting a sense of the complexity of the building process and the nature of testing, designing and redesigning- fluctuating constantly between making and drawing. Different parts of the structure progressed at different paces, allowing the students to gauge and form a system of effective communication and feeding back between team members.

Resolving design problems and experimenting meant students were able to observe at first hand the relative difficulty or ease of working with different materials and methods. Bending, manipulating, and drilling metal for the clay screen and curved wall for example, was a challenge, proving to be especially more labour intensive and slower than working with timber.

This experience also allowed students to engage with compromise and navigating the multiple competing needs of a project, in this case metal was a truer representation of materials available in Gaza.

Working on an installation that would be exhibited internationally also brought about critical design and quality output considerations. Ease of assembly and disassembly factored into each part's design, material choice, and method of securing, reflecting the fact that the installation needed to be packed into crates, shipped, and re-constructed by an entirely new team in Venice.

Overall, working with students on a live build is challenging due to its demand for time management, skill awareness and financial management, for the students and staff alike.

The reality of how structure and materials work in real life brings a much needed groundedness to how students approach their work in a very theory-heavy education.

Equally, for practitioners, working on an installation that is not built by professional builders, with a small, extremely tight budget and affixed timetable - requires different project management, design awareness and exchange of skills and knowledge to students.

THE RAMADAN PAVILION

AS A LIVE PROJECT

SHAHED SALEEM

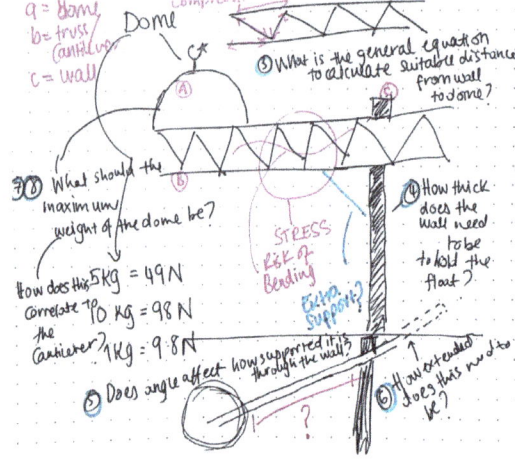

Left: Students working on the fabrication and installation
Top: Sketch with structural engineer exploring initial truss configuration
Right: Event at the Ramadan Pavilion
Bottom: External view of the Ramadan Pavilion at the Victoria and Albert Museum

The Ramadan Pavilion was a large-scale installation erected in the Exhibition Road Courtyard of the Victoria and Albert Museum in spring 2023. It was a playful composition of abstracted architectural elements which are found in the traditional architecture of the mosque, and each element was derived from prints, drawings and photographs of Islamic architecture held in the collection of the museum.

The pavilion served as a space for visitors to the museum to use for rest, play, conversation during their visit. It also provided a space for a series of organised public events, from music workshops, to dance performances, to prayer gatherings. It was thus a multi-functional space which brought people together in group activities as well as providing a setting for people to use in their own way.

Although the pavilion was realised in 2023, the idea for it started some years earlier in 2018 and had been developing since then. Over this period of time I was exploring the design of the pavilion as well as working with the museum to find potential funding sources which would enable these ideas to become a reality.

In 2019 through conversation with Will McClean we thought that we could use the pavilion design as a live project, where 3rd year Architecture BA students could develop the design as part of their Technical Studies module (TS3). This would give the students a real project to work on and served as a rich source of research and development for the design and construction of the pavilion.

A group of TS3 students chose the pavilion for their module project and formed themselves into small teams of 2 or 3, each of them choosing an element of the pavilion to develop further. The result was a rich series of design explorations where each element was explored in terms of its design and fabrication.

Structural design was provided by Hanif Kara and AKTII engineers, and the TS3 student group attended a design meeting with the engineers where ideas and possibilities were explored.

The work that the students produced was useful in informing subsequent design development and decisions, and as the pavilion design evolved over the following years their work was an integral part of this evolutionary process.

Eventually, after delays due to Covid and once funding was eventually secured from a range of donors, the Ramadan Pavilion was launched as the inaugural pavilion for the Ramadan Tent Project, a community organisation organising public and open iftars (fast breaking gatherings) during Ramadan, the month of Muslim fasting.

The final iteration of the pavilion was structurally designed by Corbett and Tasker to be built from plywood and painted in high gloss exterior paint. It was fabricated by Simon Davenport in his Folkestone workshop. This provided a further opportunity for student involvement, this time 2nd year Architecture BA students were invited to assist with the fabrication in the workshop. Students were also then invited to assist in the installation of the pavilion at the V&A, and a number of BA and MArch students took part in this process. The students undertook this in their own time for which they were paid by the University EDI fund.

This long gestation and then eventual realisation of the Ramadan Pavilion allowed for student involvement at different stages of the process, from design to fabrication to installation. It showed how student engagement can actively inform design development and how a live project can be incorporated into the course structure, so offering valuable teaching material leading to rich learning experiences and outcomes.

THE PORTAL AT EKAWA
INTERNATIONAL LIVE PROJECT

ELLE MCINTYRE AND SERGIO PINEDA

Ekawa is at once a territory and a life-project, which embodies a passion for living in symbiosis with nature.

In July 2024 a bamboo portal was constructed in the Colombian rainforest as part of a workshop with architecture students from the UK, including from the University of Westminster, and other countries. The process was one of learning through doing during which participants experienced a three-week immersion into the world of bamboo, co-creation, organic form and architecture in the tropics. Here we tell the story of how the Portal came to happen.

THE BAMBOO LAB

The Bamboo Lab is a crafts-based laboratory exploring the full life cycle of bamboo, in the creation of sculptural architecture through co-creative design. Ekawa has been and continues to be built through the Lab, where every construction is an exploration into new design and structural possibilities, connecting with the wide potential of the materiality of bamboo.

The Lab is a space for insight to arise through the act of creation. Design is explored through dialogue, observation and model-making before construction begins, but does not end there. Deep collaboration is at the heart of the construction process. We encourage the essence of the design to evolve on site as the structural and aesthetic possibilities of bamboo begin to merge with the contextual opportunities.

The Bamboo Lab comprises:
• a design team, who conceive all sculptural spaces, envision the rhythms of the projects and coordinate the overall dynamics of the Lab;
• a creative local crafts-team, that brings ancestral wisdom as well as a powerful impulse to make things happen;
• like-minded participants, who immerse themselves in hands-on learning and wild lifestyle experiences

Annually, we run an immersive programme within the Lab for a group of like-minded participants to deeply connect with the adventure of creation with bamboo. The central aspect of the workshop is the co-creation of a bamboo structure that has an important purpose at Ekawa and the Bamboo Village. Sculptural architecture happens on-site through insightful revelations about the interplay of curved elements, the composition of splays and the human experience of the form. An intuitive design process is led by the act of making, through creative and constructive hands at play. In this way, the workshop is a living organism, where the most insightful learning happens through the creative processes themselves.

Ekawa is a place where sculptural architecture and bamboo craftsmanship meet the arts of personal and planetary healing, through ecological regeneration, creation of edible forests, expansion of ancestral bamboo groves, and a general tone of opening towards insight and wholeness. The territory of Ekawa spans over 750 acres in four watersheds which all feed water into the larger Valley of San Blas, in the region of Antioquia in Colombia.

As architects, we founded Ekawa in 2018. Elle graduated from Bath University in 2015 and Sergio from the Architectural Association in 2004. When we met in the UK, we discovered that each was on a journey of exploration, asking questions about how the act of living in nature could become a space for personal transformation. We came to the Valley of San Blas in Colombia during an exploration of the land of Sergio's grandfather. Sleeping in a tree-tent, we heard the calling of the land, inviting us to connect with the fullness of living in the wild and with bamboo as an incredible materiality.

This was the start of a 4-year pioneering phase - an immersion in bamboo construction, reforestation techniques, and understanding life in symbiosis with nature. The dream to create a Bamboo Village emerged when friends and guests began asking how they too could live in this way. This has evolved into a vision of sculptural bamboo homes, surrounded by the magic of the rainforest, holding space for an emerging regenerative neighbourhood of like-minded families. The process of creating this architecture has become the Bamboo Lab.

The architecture of Ekawa focuses on the creation of sculptures for inhabitation that soften the threshold between inside and out. The surrounding nature becomes an essential part of how we experience the interior spaces. We build with natural materials, especially bamboo, which grows locally in ancient bamboo groves and is being re-discovered as a gift from the wild. This is an architecture of sculptural form that nourishes the human condition beyond functional needs and brings insight to our deeper inner self. Each project is a space for exploration into the possibilities of bamboo and sculptural building in a rainforest setting. Collaboration with the wisdom and strength of local

craftspeople as well as maintaining a flexible approach are essential to the process.

Having built five homes in the Bamboo Village, along with a collective house for guests and visitors, we felt that it was time to build an entrance Portal to Ekawa.

Building the Portal

We designed the project in early 2024. In July of the same year, we organised a Bamboo Lab workshop to build the primary structure of the Portal, together with 20 participants from many nationalities. The team of participants included 5 architecture students from Westminster University in London. The project was also supported by a team of local craftspeople.

The aim of the portal is to dynamise the entrance to Ekawa, through a gesture where the edge of the road spirals up in a helix form, returning back down to connect again with the road line. Two interlocking spirals create a three-dimensional lemniscate which relates to the archetype of the leaf, a form that is in metamorphosis. The challenge of this project was to create two spiralling arches that span the road to create an open, dynamic gateway. The structural bamboo solution for these arches became a technique that we created, the "Spiral beam". In a process of co-creation with the 25 individuals that were present, the form of the spiral beams was set out in space as lidi bundles (an ancestral bamboo technique to create curved structural elements by inter-connecting many bamboo rods), held in position by scaffolding poles which were marked with heights in order to create the three-dimensional form of the design. Once adjusted, the lidi bundles were wrapped with bamboo splits which became spiral beams with many, many layers of splits swirling around a common curved vector. The spiralling of the bamboo "splits" creates a small-scale "diagrid effect" that holds the structural form of the beam. The ridge beam is a helix form, which takes the

Construction with five University of Westminster students; the final Portal

angle of the road line up in a three-dimensional spiral over the gateway, and then back down to the roadside on the other side. A secondary structure of bamboo split beams connects the spiralling arches and the helix ridge to create a leaf-like surface which was woven with bamboo splits to create a rigid form. With a team of local craftspeople, we finished the project by positioning a layer of "bamboo mats" giving a smooth surface upon which metal tiles could be fixed as the final waterproofing layer. The helical ridge line is highlighted using old reclaimed ceramic tiles.

The stonework at either side continues the spiralling gesture, with twisting forms that undulate, connecting the gate and the edges of the roof. The gate holds it's space with a taller wooden post at either side, and with it's translucency, emanates a sense of presence yet a warmth, a welcoming invitation to enter Ekawa.

Credits: Designed by Sergio Pineda and Elle McIntyre, built in co-creation with:
Local craftspeople: Fredy Zapata, Cesar Londoño, Esteban Bran, Dorance Guzmán, Guillermo Morales, Medardo Correa;
International participants: Alana Carmel, Bryan Cano, Gabriela Egas, Gregory Waksmulski, Imogen Power, Ivonne Valencia, Jade Monrose, Keith Struthers, Kevin Kurang, Kitty Emery Rainbird, Lauris Svarups, Lina Castro, Manuela Hincapie, Marieta Dimitrova, Pablo Jaramillo, Ricardo Ruiz, Mauricio Castro.

DRESSING SPACE
NEGOTIATING PATTERNS & CONTINGENT STRUCTURES

CONOR CLARKE

Detail shot of a stage design for a festival, BEAM 2021. The form of the structure is a direct product of the pattern cut and contingent structural relationship, of fibreglass, boning and rope, across its skin.

The urge to dress - the body, the domestic space, the third space - remains a persistent spatial instinct. Long before architecture existed as a discipline, there was the enfolding, tying and knotting of boundary and shelter using fabric, fibre, and skin. Knowingly or otherwise, we all partake in this tradition: wrapping ourselves, marking territories, creating interiors. In this work discussed here, these modes become continuous surfaces between self and world. In the following projects, BEAM Festival (2021) and Transplantia (2025), I discuss the notion of dressing space with fabric as a means of spatial thinking. The first discusses the transmission of this knowledge through a 4 week summer school to a team of students and the second explores a more liberated pedagogy where I facilitated students' experiments over the course of 1 week.

Of fabric architecture I ask, if we free the skin from the structure, how might the material nature of the fabric and the pattern of its cut characterise the enclosure? What structures would these moves necessitate?

"Textiles function, critically and materially, to connect such chasms as between language and space or words and architecture… with dual reference to an interiority and an exteriority in which concept and substance are … twisted together in the initial formation … of thread." (Mitchell, 2006, pg 342). The Beam project was a summer school initiative with a £600 budget, four-week timeline, and a small team of designers and students from the Bartlett and Royal School of Drawing. Building on prior research, the team created 20 textile-based installations for a forest stage in Kent, inspired by the themes of dancing and collapsing.

The structures explored how fabric could define space without a human body, resisting the conventional use of tensile skins and instead focusing on draping and tension that revealed the fabric's cut. This required developing a structural system embedded within the fabric itself.

By the second week, the project shifted into full-scale production. Lead designers created paper maquettes at night, which were scaled up by the team into full-size structures using calico, rope, corsetry boning, and fibreglass rods. The process was collaborative and hands-on, translating ideas through shared making and embodied knowledge. As misunderstandings were resolved through demonstration and experimentation, the team collectively shaped the textile forms. The final collapsible installations were later exhibited in nightlife settings, highlighting the tactile and architectural potential of fabric.

Theorists Jefferies, Conroy, and Mitchell link the origins of enclosure to textile making, where the seam becomes a site of both boundary and social exchange. This tactile knowledge lives on in how fabric is manipulated in space. Transplantia explored this idea, inviting students to test spatial forms by hand, using seamlines and cuts not as decoration but as structuring elements. Rather than defining enclosure, interiors became provisional and shared-a process of continual negotiation.

Supported by Spradling, I led a week-long workshop involving over 100 students and staff, working with faux leather and green willow under tight constraints. Divided into 10 groups, students created assemblable, living structures through direct material engagement. Each team responded to the materials' feedback-tensions, stretches, and shifts-using intuition and collaborative judgment. Pattern became both a physical and social tool for invention. As Emma Cocker writes, new ways of working arise through unfamiliar situations. Transplantia embodied this through hands-on learning, embracing uncertainty and collective spatial experimentation.

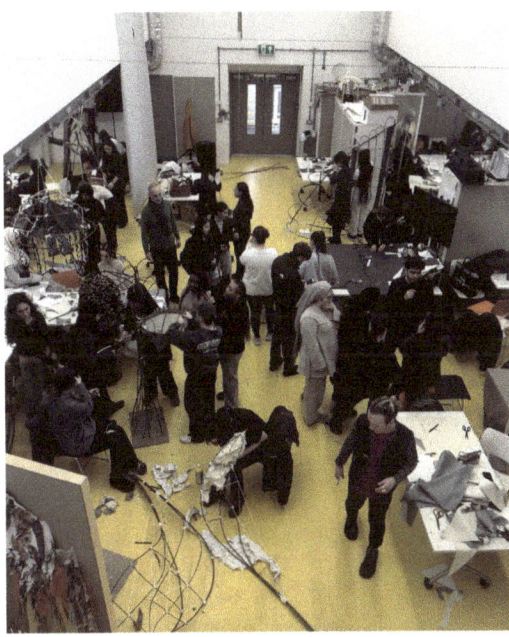

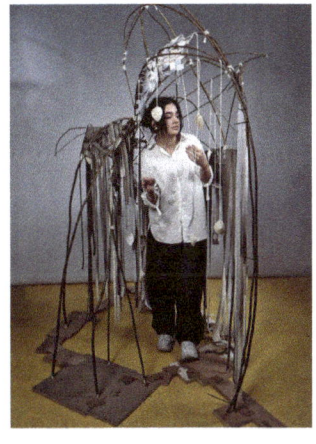

Top right: Installation in Kent forest; middle: 1:50 paper maquettes
Right: Transplantia 2025. A student inhabits her group's willow structure. Designed for an imagined music festival, the installation remains undone allowing inhabitants to continue to weave the construction.
Top: The studios at UoW making the willow structures

FROM AGENCY TO STRUCTURE
LIVE PROJECTS AS CIVIC INFRASTRUCTURE

INTERVIEW WITH SANDRA DENICKE-POLCHER

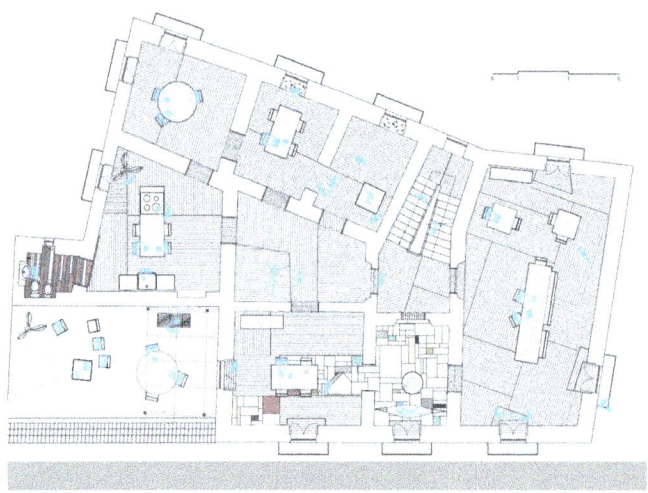

Left: Plan of the Casa di Belmondo, drawn retrospectively, 2021 / credits: LRDS)

Right: The "Golden Gate" was a small but impactful Live Project in which Sandra Denicke-Polcher painted a rusty school gate in a run-down Liverpool neighborhood with glossy gold paint, sparking curiosity, hope, and community engagement around the school's reopening.

As someone whose own path into Live Projects was shaped by Sandra Denicke-Polcher's work, this conversation gave me the opportunity to reflect on the evolution, tensions, and possibilities of Live Projects–both as built interventions and as catalysts for engagement, learning, and systemic change.

We began by discussing the dual nature of Live Projects. We observed that they operate "somewhere between experiment and service." On the one hand, they're open-ended explorations, uncertain in outcome but rich in potential to shift perspectives. On the other, they can be more service-oriented and deliver built outputs within real budget and time constraints. But even then, we're not just delivering, but

"we're also initiators, collaborators and sometimes even the client."

Sandra's work has long reflected this hybrid character and questioned who the client is, who do we owe a "duty of care"? Influenced by her time in Diploma 10 at the AA under Robert Mull and Carlos Villanueva Brandt, and drawing on the Situationist ethos of derive and direct action, she emphasises that Live Projects are not only physical. As she said:

"Live Projects are not necessarily physical. They're also about changing perception, about creating energy between people."

(Image: Sandra's student project Golden Gate in Liverpool, 1996 / credits: Sandra Denicke)

This resonated with my own experience. I recalled spontaneous student interventions on Harrow campus—small actions that generated conversation. "People would stop and ask, 'What are you doing?' And that was engagement in itself." We both agreed that the process is just as important as the product, if not more so, particularly given the pedagogical context. As I put it, "Architecture has these two sides—the output and the process. And it's the process where the learning happens."

Sandra's design approach is also shaped by experimentation. She described a live project by Studio 3, she led with Torange Khonsari at London Metropolitan University. To construct the Mobile Room in London (2009), a mobile live/work prototype to be inhabited by a student and occupying meanwhile spaces throughout London, "everything was found on the street… except the screws." She describes this as a bricolage method, designing not on paper but developing the design hands-on from what's available, which reveals a different kind of design method. "There's an aesthetic of the unfinished," she said, "and there's beauty in that."

Our shared concern is how to sustain and embed this kind of learning. I've long been engaged with the tension between practice-based knowledge and academic theory: "I believe Live Projects generate important knowledge—particularly tacit knowledge… but traditional academia is theory-driven."

Sandra agreed, describing how she found it also impossible to fit live engagement with a live built component beyond the scale of a room into traditional curriculum frameworks.

"You can't fit [Live Projects] easily into the academic calendar," she said. Instead, the later projects Studio 3 engaged with extended beyond university timelines and engaged different student cohorts to work in the same location over up to eight years. We both see Live Projects as fertile ground for innovation:

"Each building is a prototype. Nobody wants to take risks.

But that requires navigating risk, managing community expectations, and help securing funding. That's something I've become clear about in my own practice at Westminster University: "I do Live Projects if there's funding, which bridge academic experimentation and real-world delivery - with engineers, fabricators, and professionals."

Our conversation turned back to pedagogy, Sandra reflected on her earlier focus: understanding how Live Projects benefit students and communities - not just in terms of employability but entrepreneurial learning. "It's not for students to gain conventional skills, but how to raise funds, initiate projects, and develop care for something."

Today, Sandra's focus is increasingly on long-term impact. In collaboration with former student and co-founder of Le Seppie, Rita Adamo, and teaching partner Jane McAllister, a key output of an ongoing village activation strategy in Calabria is Casa di Belmondo. Since 2019, the former nunnery has been transformed through a partnership between the university, the NPO Le Seppie and the architecture collective Orizzontale. The renovation adopts an in situ bricolage design approach, using locally available and discarded materials - a method similar to Mobile Room for London. Rather than beginning with a fixed plan, the design has evolved through the making itself, with drawings produced retrospectively.

This prompted to shift the focus from pedagogy to questions of governance and continuity. "What's the exit strategy for the university?" she asked. "How do you hand over responsibility and don't just leave it?"

This mirrors challenges I've faced. In early community projects, I learned that "the expectation that a building could create a community was false-we would have failed." Instead, as I realised, we had to "find communities already in need of a building," like at Cody Dock or Clitterhouse Farm. The architecture then supports their existing energy.

In our conversation, we returned again to the idea of physical and social structures. Sandra underscored that

sustainability depends on governance and structures-not just physical interventions.

She reflected: "It's actually about systems… subsystem structures that create community." I shared a powerful example from Cody Dock:

"They cleaned up the dock for £65,000 with over 30,000 volunteers – where in comparison a commercial clean-up would have cost over a million." That's the power of community as a resource. I also believe this speaks to a deeper societal need.

"We as humans beings, we need community - loneliness is a significant factor of death."

We must design for connection. We also touched on how design differs from other sectors

"It's about value creation. But we need better ways of measuring that value."

This led to a discussion of Live Project support systems. "There are always gaps that the curriculum doesn't fill," I noted. "Live project leads struggle with extra work and no support network." We both advocated for a more structured "project office" or platform to support this kind of work, both inside and outside the studio.

Finally, we reflected on knowledge sharing. "How do we transfer the tacit knowledge?" I asked. Sandra highlighted how studio pedagogies evolve over time, often without structured reflection, much of it this transitional pedagogy risks being lost. This is part of my motivation to write this book capturing 10 years of studio practice as a form of reflective research. Our conversation reinforced the value of Live Projects-not just for their outputs, but for their power to activate community, shift perceptions and reshape how we teach, learn and build.

PRACTICAL ACADEMIA

RECONNECTING STUDIOS

JAMES SOANE

Front and Rear cover to PO Box 4, showing current projjects submerged in rising seas

What happens when, after five years of academia in the UK, students land in architectural practice? Often the answer is to desperately gain practical experience in order to enrol on the RIBA 'part three' programme, take the exams and become an 'architect'. While this route to qualification is likely to diversify over the next five years, there will always be a schism. This fracture is the cause of a frequent disconnect between academia and practice, between speculation and certainty.

Not only are there different agendas, characterised by

the false binary of 'fantasy' versus 'reality' and 'impractical' versus 'practical'; there is a break in the way architects perceive their education to be in the past.

While the CPD requirements of the profession are important, they focus on the knowledge of regulations, compliance and legals.

Where do the culture, history and theory learnings go in practice?

In my experience they tend to sink to the bottom of a priority list. However, if the practice of architecture is re-framed as a continuity of a collective education, then it is important to keep critical thinking alive. In reverse to many case studies in this collection which look at how insights from industry, brought into the school, offer key skills and knowledge to students; this project looks at

what happens when you bring academia back into practice?

Project Orange Architects was set up in 1997 by Christopher Ash and myself when we were in our early thirties. Over the years we have expanded and contracted, working both in the UK and abroad, as well as being involved in teaching. One of the questions we struggled with was to triangulate our teaching with practice.

The studio in school is necessarily different to the reality of commercial practice, but it felt as though we needed to develop a mechanism to bridge the gap. This evolved into a space for a structured conversation that allowed the practice to reflect on what we were doing with a critical eye, using skills developed at architecture school.

The vehicle for this became a publication or 'zine' that all current members of staff contributed to. We have produced four volumes to date. It was designed to have a light touch, while steering contributors towards academic texts, precedents and alternative ways of representation in order to create some friction. It is all too easy to fall into the banter of banal press releases or PR chatter. We brought in external voices to act as mentors and editors: Dr Matthew Barac, Rae Whittow Williams and Gem Barton. While PO Box 1 had no single theme, PO Box2 looked at questions around representation, PO Box3 was titled, 'Housing House, Home' and PO Box Four, produced during Covid, is simply called 'Help!'.

We have been drawn towards the concept of the 'choral architect', coined by Carlo Ratti, which seems to better reflect the process of working as a team, with many voices contributing to the final production. This approach then informed the History and Theory programme at the LSA (London School of Architecture). Here the traditional dissertation was replaced with the writing of a Manifesto, drawing on an alternative tradition of architectural writing.

The value of such an endeavour is to re-ignite a different sense of creativity and judgement. While the 'zine' was self-published, it was sent to clients, consultants and friends. The subjects covered in HELP! struck a chord with many, and became a gateway into conversations around how a project might become an exemplar of best practice. Our studio was motivated to enter the first regenerative Practice Index (run by Architecture Today and architecture Declares), and were listed as one of the ten frontrunners.

As Rae Whittow Williams wrote in the foreword: "By repositioning the relationship between practice and process, and evaluating processes against outcomes Project Orange have sought to use the latest issue of PO BOX as a vehicle to determine how they can begin to move the debate surrounding the climate emergency forward. It is not intended as a solution but a springboard: to work collaboratively as a team. Craft a renewed set of practice values, challenge the status quo surrounding city making, inspire action and behaviour change in others, and ultimately forge the path ahead."

Collage showing ideas for the future of Thamesmad by Dawa Pratten

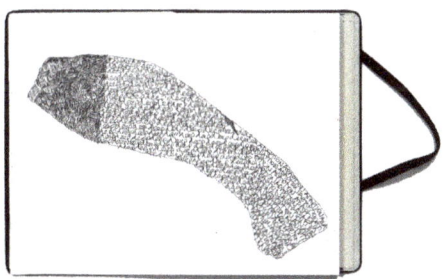

Sketch book pages, by James Soane, recorded at 'Kissing the Void' (a climate crisis retreat organised by Jem Bendell).

COLLECTIVE AGENCY

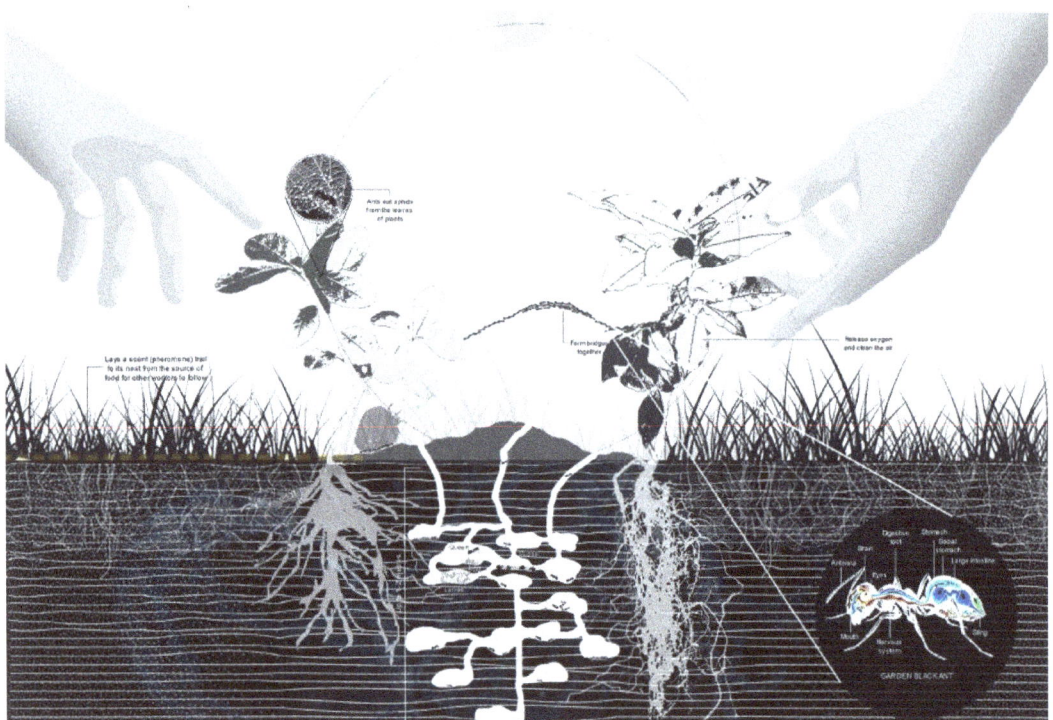

How can we consider the participation of not just human communities and their livelihood practices that intersect with natural processes, but also of beyond-human entities and forces such as other creatures whose paths intersect with them?

Top: Engagement by students from Marylebone Campus with students of Harrow Campus as part of the UniverCity brief by Christy Prothero
Bottom: Circularity diagram by Saima Rouf

ENGAGING PEOPLE+PLACE

MARIA KRAMER

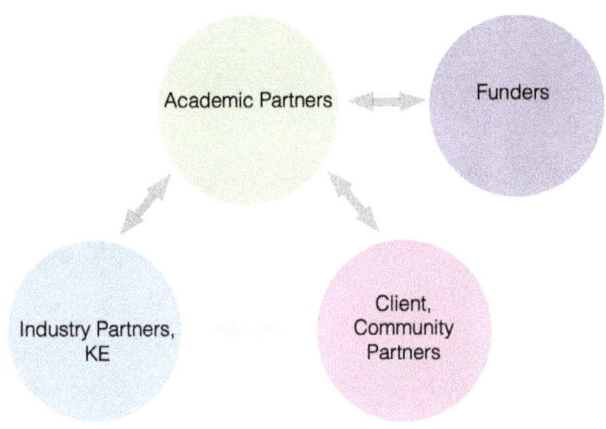

Diagram thowing different stakeholder groups and their possible relationships, with trust building amonst parties an important aspect

Engage with:
- Structural Engineers

Public Engagement

Live Projects provide a unique opportunity to gain first-hand insight into the complex and dynamic relationships between stakeholders - including clients, communities, users, operators, funders, and consultants. By facilitating hands-on, real-time involvement, Live Projects make participation exciting, empowering, and engaging. They allow students to experience the intersections of social, cultural, economic, technical and political interests that shape the built environment.

Through these projects, students gain an in-depth understanding of decision-making processes across all stages of design and construction. Learning to collaborate with consultants such as structural engineers, fabricators, and craftspeople - as well as community stakeholders—fosters a rich process of mutual learning and knowledge exchange. This collaborative approach helps bridge gaps between academic, professional and lived experience.

We engage with communities, the public, and stakeholders at every design stage. Early engagement begins with site visits, public interviews and informal conversations, where students are encouraged to talk to residents and local workers. These interactions help build a nuanced understanding of place, as

locals are the experts of their neighbourhoods.

The process is not only informative but also generative - initiating conversations that prompt communities to reflect on their identities, aspirations and concerns, which has value in itself. This can strengthen community ties and support the development of projects that are embedded, relevant and meaningful.

Community engagement gives access to on-the-ground knowledge that is otherwise inaccessible through maps, data, or desk-based research. Long-time residents often provide layered insights:

What are the area's pressing local issues?
How has it changed over time?
What are people proud of-and what do they wish could change?

Such insights foster a more empathetic, site-specific, and socially conscious design process, helping students connect personally and professionally to the context.

Local stakeholders are kept informed and invited to contribute throughout the project's development. For example, we have invited community group leaders to student design reviews at the university, an act that opened up conversations and disrupted the traditional academic bubble. These reviews demonstrated how architects must occupy multiple roles: as designers, facilitators, communicators, and collaborators. Conversely, we have exhibited student work in community centres and galleries with the goal of inspiring the next generation and creating a platform for mutual exchange between academia and local communities

Engaging with the public requires careful risk management and safeguarding and prepare students accordingly. Prior to any public interaction, students are briefed on risk awareness and appropriate behaviour in public spaces.

Live Projects offer a powerful model for community-engaged learning, cultivating a culture of listening, co-creation, and shared authorship. These experiences not only enrich the educational journey but also lay the groundwork for more ethical, inclusive, and responsive forms of architectural practice..

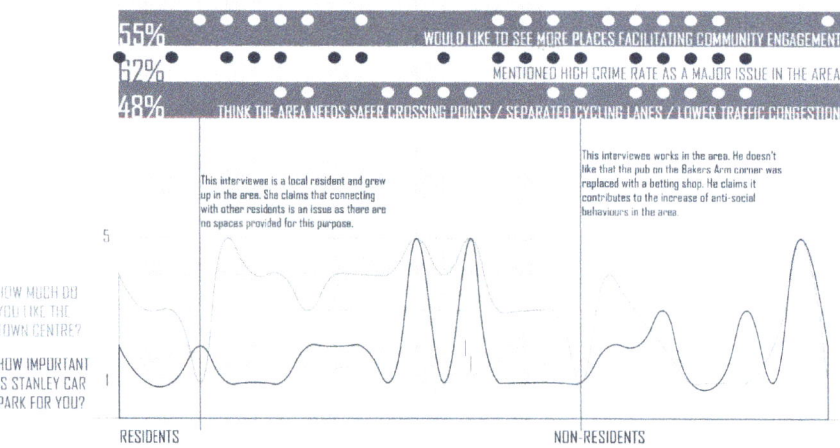

Top: One Hoe Street Gallery exhibiting student work and organising forums with locals by Wilfred Achille, Waltham Forest
Centre left: Community making workshops and public consultation as part of the London Festival of Architecture in Waltham Forest
Top right: Jointly developed questionnaire with Waltham Forest Council. Students asked locals to fill in the questionnaires and the council organised public engagement events.
Bottom right: Public Engagement visualisation of quantitative data from the questionnaires

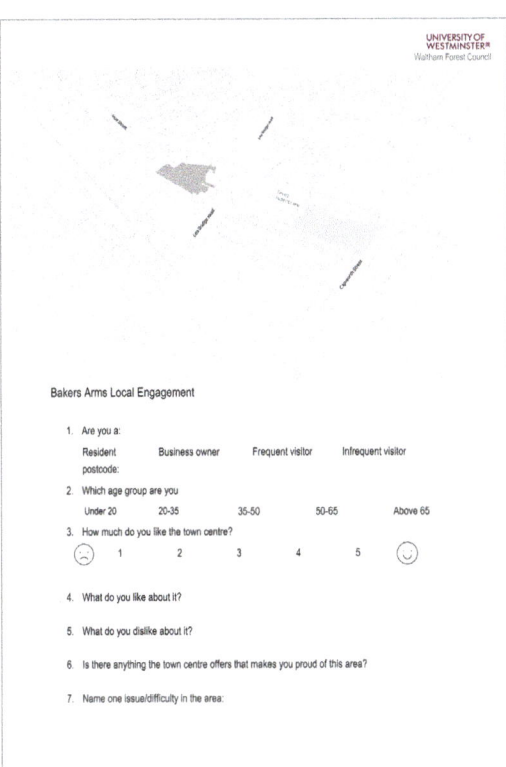
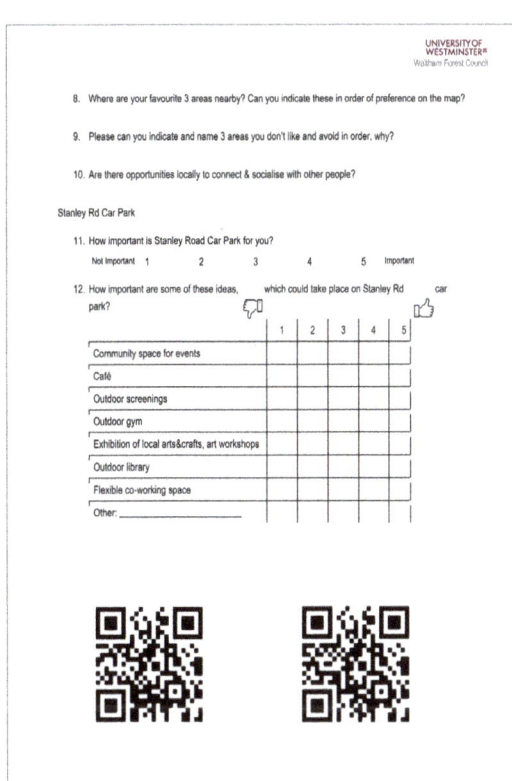
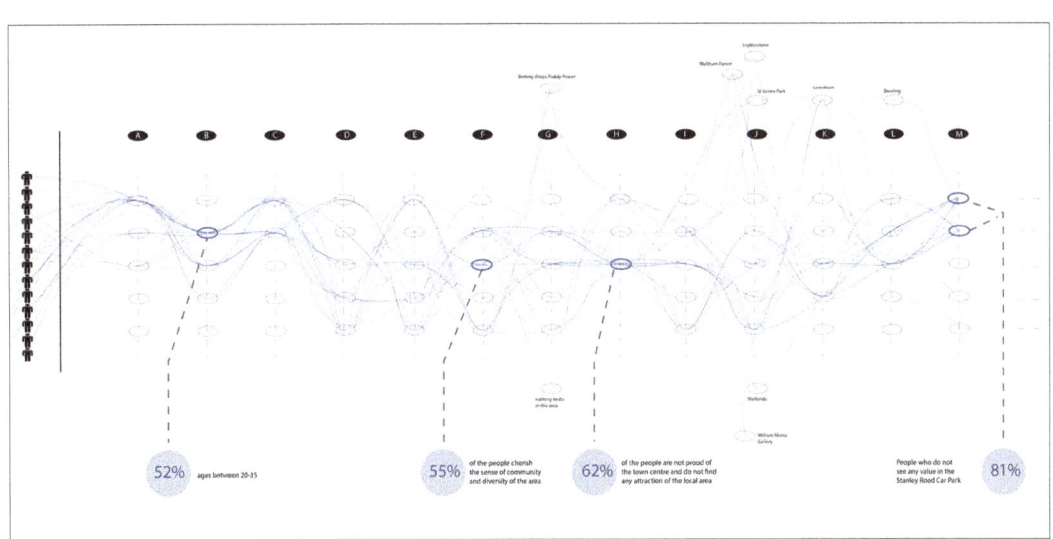

Initially we developed a questionnaire in collaboration with Waltham Forest council; crucial for the council was to manage expectations and not provide false expectations for a future community centre; students went and ask locals; the data was then visualised in infographics, see above and bottom right;

We exhibited students work locally in Waltham Forest initiated by Wilfred Achille, which included forums inviting the local community and our students. We actively brought together diverse stakeholders to share values, views, interests, cultivating listening and reaching a deeper understanding of needs and aspirations.

Left: Re-enacting guerilla botany labelling 'weeds'/street plants with chalk; Top: the re-inactment has impacted the final proposal's landscape concept; both by Will Lampert

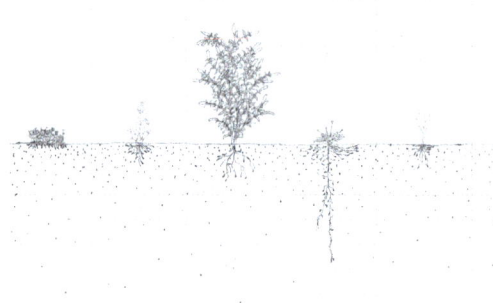
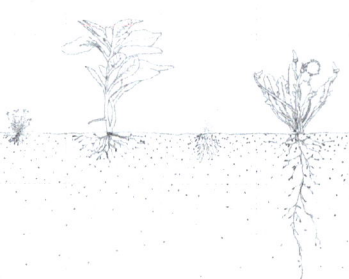

Diagram illustrating the maximum dimensions of these identified ruderal species when left to thrive and the fauna they typically support by Will Lampert.

Guerrilla botany, a term from Matthew Gandy's Natura Urbana, describes Boris Presseq's chalk labelling of street plants in Toulouse to raise awareness and respect for so-called "weeds" (fourth nature). As part of this project, the author practised guerrilla botany at Gillender Street warehouses, identifying resilient "ruderal" species that thrive in disturbed urban environments and support further ecological growth. This hands-on engagement deepened their appreciation of fourth nature and informed research on the species' growth potential, resilience, and the fauna they support.

The diagrams above shows the activity of endangered species throughout the whole year, showcasing when the creatures are breeding, nesting and migrating. The hunting diagram shows these creatures hunting their prey. These are the design factors to consider as my scheme and program needs to consider the different seasons and how these creatures behave and move throughout the year.

Left: Diagrams of different species at Cody Dock by Hamza Khan
Right: Public engagement sketches along the River Lea by Blessing Sulaiman

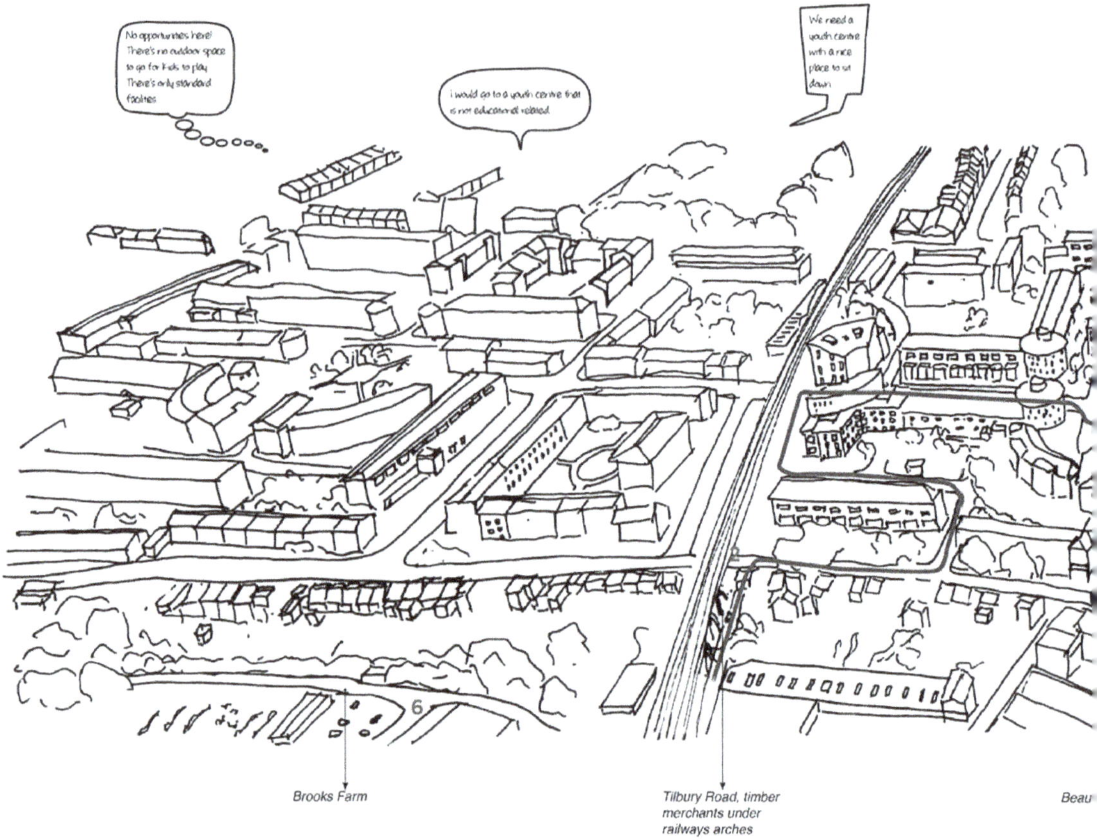

No opportunities here! There's no outdoor space to go for kids to play. There's only standard facilities

I would go to a youth centre that is not educational related

We need a youth centre with a nice place to sit down

Brooks Farm

Tilbury Road, timber merchants under railways arches

Beau

> "What makes mass society so difficult to bear is not the number of people involved, ...but the fact that the world between them has lost its power to gather them together, to relate and to separate them." Hannah Arendt, The Human Condition (1958), p. 52 (University of Chicago Press edition)

062

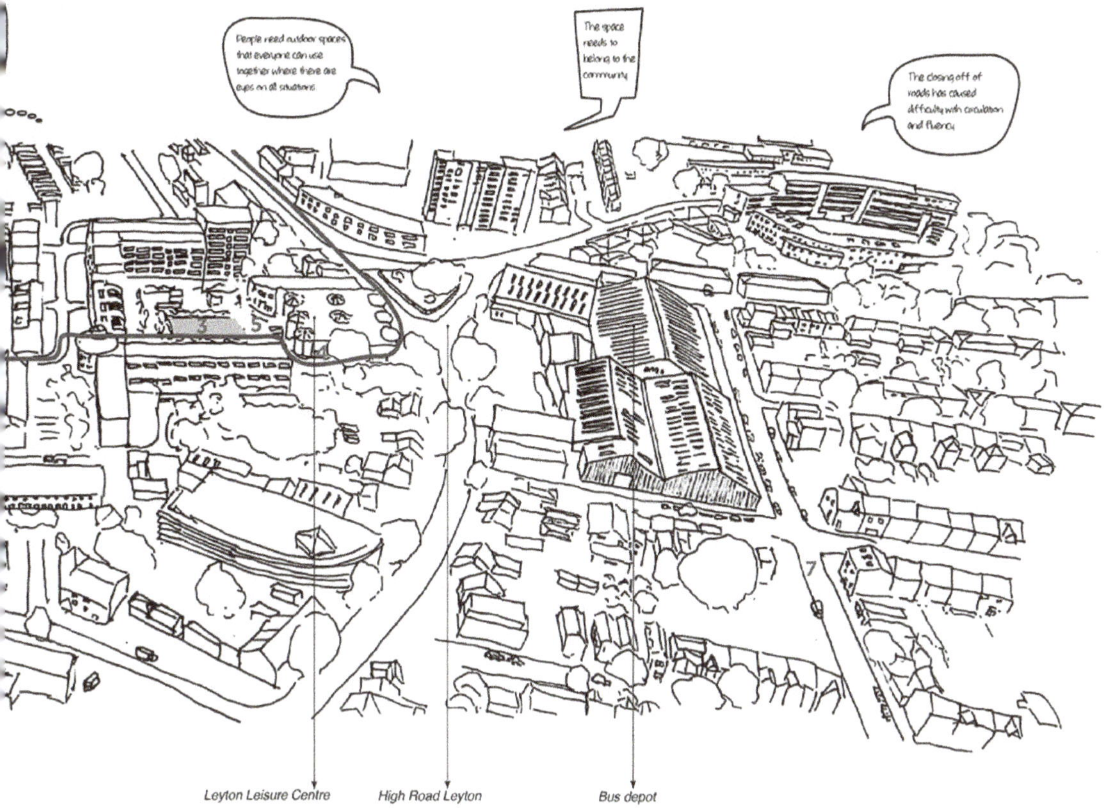

People need outdoor spaces that everyone can use together where there are eyes on all situations.

The space needs to belong to the community.

The closing off of roads has caused difficulty with circulation and fluency.

Leyton Leisure Centre High Road Leyton Bus depot

Top: Summary of Public Engagement Comment in Waltham Forest by Isabelle Reid
Right: Public engagement by architecture students from Marylebone Campus with students from Harrow Campus asking about what they appreciate about their campus and student living as part of the UniverCity project
Below: On site interventions at Harrow Campus make environmental factors, such as wind, visible and spark a conversation with local students including a photography student who was inspired by the installations;

0. Srategic Definition
1. Preparation & Brief
2. Concept Design
3. Spatial Coordination
4. Technical Design
5. Manufacturing & Construction

2021

May 2021
Westminster University Vice Chancellor visits the Botanic Gardens at Cambridge University and is inspired to implement a Botanic Garden at Harrow Campus.

June 2021
DS3.2 Studio Leader first approached by Sustainability Development Goal Coordinator about Botanic Garden Project.

July- September 2021
Sustainable Development Goal Coordinator puts together a Design Team to meet including Estate Manager, space planner, students interested in sustainability.

September 2021
Live Brief Introduction to DS3.2 students, who join the design team at start of term Feasibility Studies & Site Surveys begin.

October 2021
Stakeholder Engagement, Questionnaires with students and staff at Harrow Campus.

November 2021
Concept Design Begins

December 2021
Spatial Coordination begins: Design Studies, Engineering Analysis. Site Visits to Olympic Park with Vice Chancellor, The Marble Arch Mound, Frieze Sculpture Park.

December 2021
Concept Design Approved by Client,.

2022

Jan 2022
Further Stakeholder Engagement

Feb 2022
Brief (including programme, budget, spatial, sustainable, quality outcomes) agreed between client & design team.

Feb 2022
Architectural Concept & Spatial Design Approved by the Client: Vice Chancellor

Feb 2022
Detail Design Starts. Construction Phase plan started.

March 2022
Architectural Concept & Spatial Design Approved by the client.

March 2022
Planning Applicat

April 2022
Building Regulatio sucessful.

June 2022
Works begin on

June-Sept 2022 B
Design Team Mee principal contrac member & releva

Jun 2022
Live Project Pha Plan for use stra

Current Stage

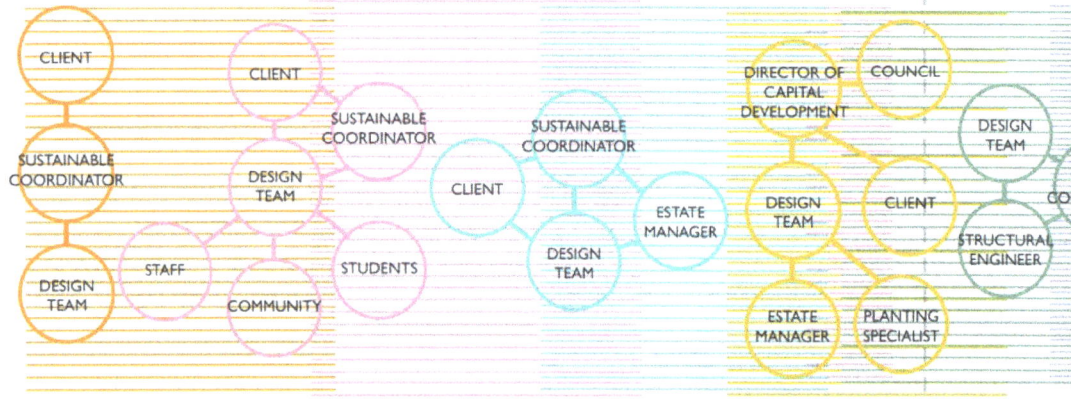

Stakeholder Engagement with students

Phoenix Community Garden Research Visit

Frieze Sculpture Park

Chelsea

RESEARCH

First Meeting & Harrow Campus tour

Meeting with the Westminster Clients, the Vice Chancellor, sustainability

Meeting with Sustainability Coordinator

Technical Design me

MEETINGS

2023

October 2022 - June 2023
Live Project in full use by student class of 2023.

Spring 2023
Post-Occupancy Evaluation & Feedback and environmental performance analysis.

June 2023
Design details altered in accordance with post-occupancy feedback and environmental performance.

2024

July-Sept 2023
Manufacturing and Construction over Summer period, when the campus is not in use by students.

Sept 2023
Live Project Phase 2 Completion
Plan for use strategy. Project is signed off and handed over to the client.

October 2023-June 2024
Live Project in full use by student class of 2024.

Spring 2024
Verify Project outcomes and sustainability outcomes.

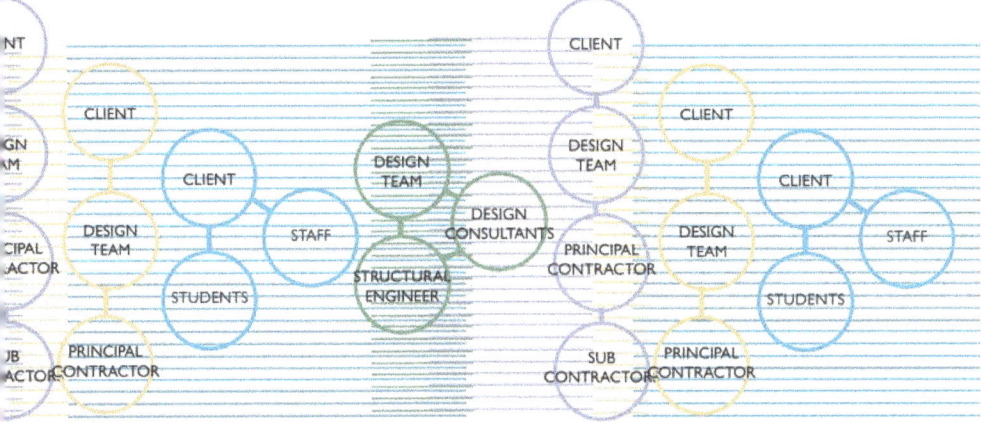

ment with director of Fine Art

Student survey & interviews.

Sensing Space Exhibition

Oxford University Tour.

cept Presentation to the Client.   Second Technical Design meeting with   Meeting with Collaborating Architect.

Visit to Building BLOQS Craft Community to

Diagram showing the many engagements done throughout the academic year as part of the Pavilion Prototype and UniverCity brief by Rebecca Welles

Image: Interview with a bench by Atefeh Arechfeh, DS3.2; A homeless person who regularly uses this bench near the site knew the daily routine of locals intimately

IN COMMON, REIMAGINE, VOICES
COMMUNITY ENGAGEMENT+LESSONS LEARNT FROM URBAN DESIGN PROJECTS

KRYSTALLIA KAMVASINOU

BEYOND THE PHYSICAL INTERVENTION

In April 2025, initiated by Maria Kramer, I and my MA Urban Design students participated with a poster in the Live Projects Exhibition on the occasion of the 'Shaping the Future of the Built Environment' event. The poster presented community-based project work from our MA Urban Design module "Place and Experience in Design of Urban Spaces", a first semester theory and project-based module for which I am Module Leader. The MA Urban Design approach to Live Projects is distinct to that of architecture and demonstrates that meaningful community engagement in urban design education extends far beyond the traditional boundaries of built interventions. Over three years of reimagining the public realm in the Church Street and St Mary's area of Westminster (2022-2025),

we have learned that Live Projects can be transformative and energising educational experiences even when they don't culminate in physical construction.

The power lies not in the building, but in the process of authentic first-hand engagement with communities and stakeholders outside the studio or classroom.

REDEFINING 'LIVE' IN LIVE PROJECTS

The conventional understanding of Live Projects often emphasises tangible outcomes-buildings constructed, spaces transformed, physical interventions realised. However, our experience in the Church Street ward has revealed that the 'live' quality of a project resides equally in its capacity to generate authentic dialogue and understanding between our students and different communities and create lasting relationships that extend beyond the academic semester.

Through our MA Urban Design public space and place-based work, focusing on St Mary's on Paddington Green, London W2, students have engaged with one of Westminster's most ethnically diverse areas, characterised by its complex social demographics and spatial morphology of modernist housing estates interwoven with Victorian housing and major infrastructure, and currently undergoing intensive regeneration. The 'liveness' of our public realm projects emerged not from construction activities, but from the choice of focus each year on inclusivity from the lens of a particular social group -disabled children, teenagers, College students – leading to deeper and more dynamic interactions and knowledge exchange between our students and local stakeholders such as the City of Westminster College, disability advocate Sara Momtaz, St Mary's church, and Westminster City Council officers.

WHY COMMUNITY ENGAGEMENT MATTERS IN DESIGN EDUCATION

Community engagement has become embedded in our teaching because urban design cannot be meaningfully practiced in isolation from the communities it serves. As David Harvey reminds us in The Right to the City (2003, p. 940) " 'There is', the old saying goes, 'nothing more unequal than the equal treatment of unequals'". This principle has guided our approach to working with diverse communities in Church Street, where exclusion can take many forms-physical disability, age, gender, ethnicity, cultural background, and socioeconomic status.

The collaboration with Sara Momtaz and her 'All Play' vision exemplifies this approach. Sara's tireless campaigning for the rights of children with disabilities in public space provided our students with direct access to advocacy in action, rather than studying inclusive design from textbooks. This engagement taught students that design is inherently political and that inclusive environments require active advocacy, not just technical solutions. In all iterations of the module, relationships with local stakeholders energised student cohorts making the work more meaningful.

THE PROCESS AS PRODUCT: LEARNING THROUGH COLLABORATION

Our three-year engagement with the Church Street area has evolved incrementally building on relationships established in previous years. The first year established connections through Sara Momtaz's initial approach to the university; this led to sharing the works with Westminster City Council's Inclusive Playgrounds Working group.

The second year deepened these relationships through collaboration with Reverend Andrew Norwood at St Mary's Church and expanded our network to include CitizensUK. By the third year, we had developed sufficient

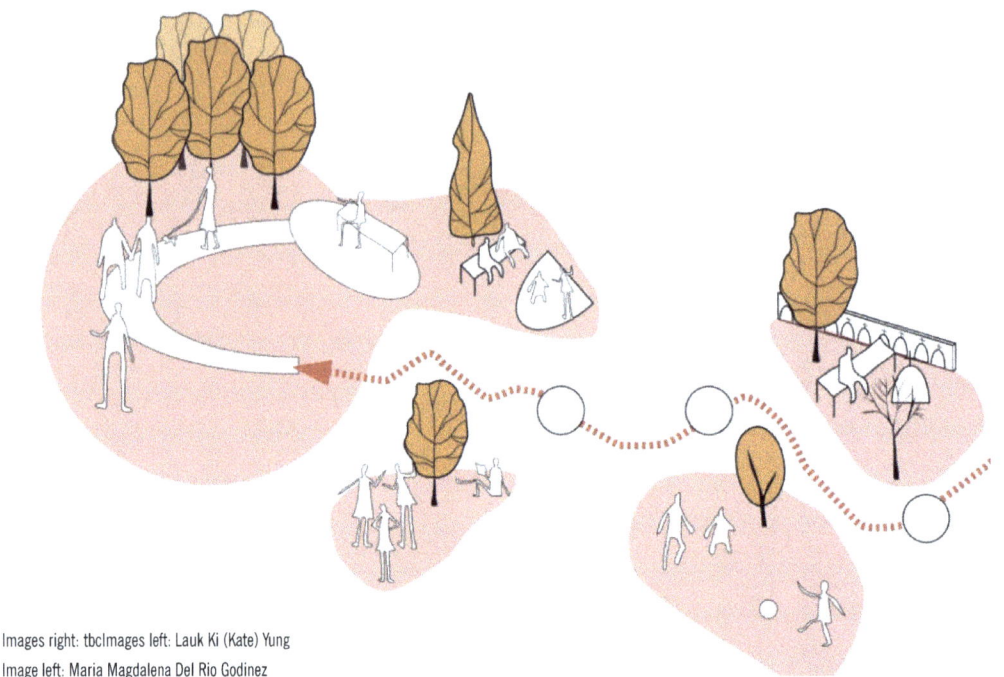

Images right: tbcImages left: Lauk Ki (Kate) Yung
Image left: Maria Magdalena Del Rio Godinez

trust to facilitate direct collaboration between our MA students and 6th form students from City of Westminster College and Westminster City Council's Placeshaping team.

This progression illustrates a key principle of community engagement in Live Projects:

relationships take time to develop and must be nurtured across multiple academic cycles.

The workshop in November 2024 where MA and College students walked together through St Mary's churchyard, conducting a "reality check" on safety, accessibility, and belonging, only became possible because of years of relationship building. The College students' voices were centred not as subjects of study, but as collaborators in reimagining public space, informing our MA students' proposals.

BENEFITS AND CHALLENGES OF COMMUNITY-ENGAGED LIVE PROJECTS

Through this approach students develop cultural competency and awareness of complex stakeholder relationships that characterise real-world practice. They experience the humility required to listen to communities whose lived experiences differ from their own. The collaboration with CitizensUK, for instance, introduced students to community organising and the intersection of design with broader social justice campaigns.

Students gain understanding of the temporal dimensions of community engagement. Unlike studio exercises with predetermined timelines, community-engaged projects operate on multiple timeframes simultaneously-the academic semester, the community's ongoing concerns, the council's planning cycles, and the longer arc of neighbourhood change.

However, this approach presents significant challenges.

Coordinating with external stakeholders requires flexibility that can conflict with academic scheduling. There's the ethical responsibility of ensuring that student learning doesn't exploit community time and expertise without reciprocal benefit.

The challenge of maintaining continuity across academic years while working with annual cohorts of students requires institutional commitment beyond individual modules. Our collaboration took off through the Cross-Disciplinary Exchange initiative led by Professor Lindsay Bremner in 2022-23, that introduced us to local stakeholders and acted as a springboard for the continuation of our work in the area - demonstrating the importance of institutional frameworks that support long-term community partnerships. Not everything can be planned though, and our work was also hugely enhanced by pure serendipity, when Sara Montaz independently contacted the University for support with her All Play vision, leading to our first meeting and ongoing work. This was

facilitated by the then Head of Culture and Inclusion, Andy Norris. Apart from the student projects, I was also invited to participate first in the Inclusive Playgrounds Quarterly Working Group of Westminster City Council and then the Alfred Road playground project group, broadening our access to the network of relevant actors involved in the area.

INTERDISCIPLINARY APPROACHES AND LIVE BRIEFS

Working in the public realm necessitates an interdisciplinary approach where urban design is informed by transport planning, architecture, environmental design, and landscape architecture. This mirrors the reality of urban development, where issues of public space intersect with housing, mobility, environmental justice, and economics.

The live briefs of our projects come not from predetermined design challenges, but from ongoing community concerns identified by our local partners. For example, Sara Momtaz identified the lack of play space for disabled children and advocated a vision for an All play flagship play area for St Mary's, which we explored in year one. The following year one of the council officers and member of the Inclusive Playgrounds Working group asked if we could explore issues of teenager space in the area triggered by concerns of antisocial behaviour. In parallel, the City of Westminster College students' safety campaign, organised with CitizensUK, provided a live brief that was simultaneously local and connected to broader urban issues. Through our connection with CitizensUK and Luch Gardner, in year three, we collaborated with the College on a workshop where our MA students worked in groups with College students to reimagine St Mary's park. Students learned to respond to community-identified priorities rather than internalised design problems.

LESSONS FOR FUTURE PRACTICE

Our experience suggests several principles for community-engaged Live Projects.

Relationship first, project second.

Successful community engagement requires prioritising relationship-building over project outcomes. The most meaningful learning often happens in conversations and collaborative processes rather than in final presentations.

COMMUNITY EXPERTISE

Communities possess expertise about their own needs and contexts that cannot be gained through observation alone. Students must learn to recognise and respect this expertise while contributing their developing design skills.

INSTITUTIONAL COMMITMENT

Meaningful community engagement requires institutional support for multi-year relationships and flexibility in academic structures. Community partners must gain value from collaboration beyond serving as learning opportunities for students. This might include advocacy support, design capacity, or amplification of community concerns.

CONCLUSION: THE ONGOING CONVERSATION – IN COMMON, REIMAGINE, VOICES

We have exhibited three times in the London Festival of Architecture, under the themes of 'In Common' (June 2023), 'Reimagine' (June 2024) and 'Voices' (June 2025). The latest exhibition "Reality Check: Re-imagining a park through student voices" represents not an endpoint but a moment in an ongoing conversation that continues to value local voices in the design process.

This cyclical feedback process embodies the essence of Live Projects as we understand them—not as linear progressions from brief to built outcome, but as dynamic engagements that generate new questions, relationships, and possibilities to update our briefs and thinking. In a world that seems increasingly divided, our commitment remains to listening to each other's voices, building local relationships between people and organisations towards a peaceful and inclusive future.

CO-CREATING JUST STREETS
LIBRARY PARKLET AS A SITE OF TRANSFORMATIVE PEDAGOGY AND PARTICIPATORY PRACTICE

ENRICA PAPA, SABINA CIOBATA, MARIA KRAMER

What is the role of academia, the university and live design studios in shaping participatory urban practices and transforming streets into spaces of not only mobility but also wellbeing, sociability and justice? How might university - community collaborations translate practice-oriented pedagogy into urban interventions that aim to transform streets into safer, more sustainable and more equitable places shaped by active mobility? This article reflects on the transformative possibilities of participatory pedagogy and civic practice in the context of street transformation interventions. It does so by examining one such intervention, the co-design of a parklet located in front of Marylebone Library in the London Borough of Westminster, a collaborative exercise carried out as part of the European JUST STREETS project.

Framing this reflection is a critique of the historically rationalised street, one configured around the logics of automobility and efficiency. As transport planning and mobility scholars highlight, *the 20th-century city saw a gradual but systematic 'taming' of streets for car use, marginalising other modes of movement (walking, cycling) and forms of occupation such as those centred around public life* (Norton, 2008).

These processes have contributed to patterns of exclusion and marginalisation, where certain mobilities and social practices are prioritised over others, shaping who feels welcome and who is left out of urban public spaces (Sheller, 2018). This transformation was not merely spatial but also ideological, embedding hierarchies of mobility and street use that continue to structure urban life. Yet, in the face of current overlapping crises including environmental and social, such paradigms are increasingly being challenged in academia, policy and practice.

It is within this context that efforts to reimagine streets have gained momentum over the past few decades, motivated by ambitions for urban sustainability, liveability and conviviality (Bertolini, 2023). Although contemporary interest and practice interventions have surged, research since the 1980s has explored street space reallocation through interventions like pedestrianisation, traffic calming, cycling infrastructure, and travel demand management (Tolley, 1990; Pharoah & Russell, 1991). Studies have examined economic effects (Hass-Klau, 1993), mobility behavioural change linked to reduced road capacity (Cairns, Atkins & Goodwin, 2002), and the social and spatial qualities that support vibrant public life on streets (Jacobs, 1993; Gehl & Gemzøe, 2003), influencing various design approaches and informing policy shifts (DfT & DCLG, 2007). Frameworks such as 'Link and Place' (Jones, Boujenko & Marshall, 2007) have been particularly influential, offering a model for balancing streets' dual roles as both transport corridors and vibrant public spaces conducive to community wellbeing and urban quality of life.

While the abovementioned research and practice shifts have been instrumental in reshaping approaches to street planning and design, critical perspectives have more recently drawn attention to who benefits from street changes, and who remains excluded. In this sense, emerging debates in transport and mobility justice (Sheller, 2018; Martens, 2016), and socio-spatial justice (Soja, 2010) emphasise that *without addressing entrenched power structures, interventions risk reproducing or deepening inequities.*

Justice in this context extends beyond the redistribution of physical space (e.g. reallocating street space from cars to people, providing good quality walking and cycling infrastructure in underserved areas etc.) to encompass procedural dimensions linked to whose needs are taken into consideration, whose knowledge is valued, and how decisions are legitimised (Sheller, 2018; Fricker, 2007). These academic perspectives highlight that street transformations are inherently political, often *exposing tensions between competing priorities such as car access and people-friendly design, and raising deeper questions over the right to the city, governance of public space, and the inclusion or exclusion of diverse social groups in mobility transitions* (Lees, 1998; Vitale-Brovarone, Staricco & Verlinghieri, 2023).

JUST STREETS emerges against this backdrop, and is an international research and innovation project funded through Horizon Europe, which started in 2024 and is represented at the University of Westminster by a team of researchers from the Transport and Mobilities Research Group. It seeks to reimagine streets into more just places that are shaped by active mobility and are safer, more sustainable and more inclusive for all citizens, through participatory processess particularly with marginalised communities. The project brings together 32 partners ranging from academia to municipalities, the private sector, and international organisations, and follows 9 European cities implementing transformations on the ground. At the core of the project is an inquiry into what justice means for streets and street transformations. Justice, in this context, is understood both through a distributive lens (Pereira, Schwanen & Banister, 2016), and through questions of recognition, participatory processes, and epistemology (Sheller, 2018; Fricker, 2007). In this regard,

one of the central ambitions of the project is to operationalise the dimensions of justice in practice, embedding them into concrete design, planning, and governance processes for urban street changes.

In the City of Westminster, one of the JUST STREETS partners in London, this ambition was materialised through the co-design and realisation of the Marylebone Library Parklet started in January 2025. Conceived as not only a street space reallocation exercise but also a situated experiment in operationalising justice on the ground, the project brought together architecture, urban design and planning students and researchers from the University of Westminster and a range of stakeholders including local communities, local associations, and London-wide organisations. The initiative is led by the University of Westminster in partnership with Cross River Partnership (one of the JUST STREETS London partners) and the Harley Street Business Improvement District (BID), within whose footprint the parklet is located. The initial decision to build a parklet funded through JUST STREETS was closely aligned with the BID's remit to enhance the public realm, deliver "streets for all", enhance the area's sense of place, increase biodiversity and mitigate the impacts of climate change (PUBLICA, 2025). In that sense, findings from Harley Street BID's public engagement highlighted an acute demand for seating as well as greener, more inclusive public spaces in the district for visitors, employees and residents. More broadly, the intervention also responded directly to Westminster City Council's broader strategic vision, with the Westminster City Plan 2019-2040 calling for enhanced pedestrian experiences, sustainable mobility, improved air quality, and expanded biodiversity (Westminster City Council, 2021). The parklet's positioning

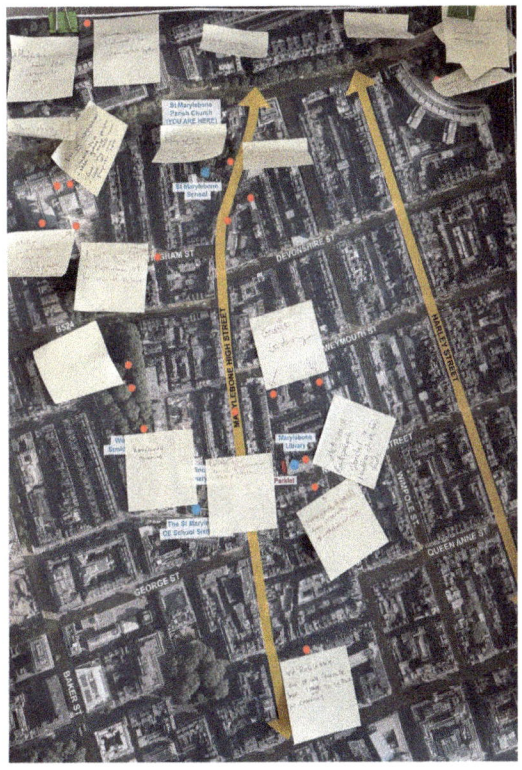

Top: Co-Design Workshop Invitation Poster (source: authors)
Bottom: Participatory mapping exercise (source: authors)

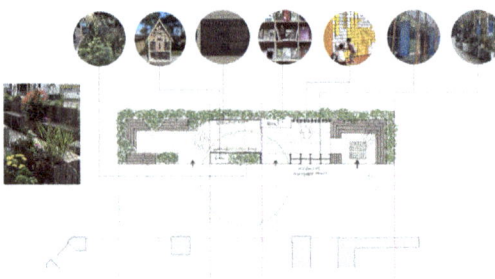

Figure 4. Proposed parklet design (source: authors)

Figure 3: Example of a parklet design collage result (source: authors)

outside the Marylebone Library responded to these multi-scalar ambitions, offering an integrated, low-impact solution within a constrained urban footprint.

The process began with street interviews and a community co-creation exercise led by UoW students, tutors and the JUST STREETS team in early 2025. While the student team was remunerated for their work, the exercise was carried out as part of *the Live Design Practice, a UoW platform fostering initiatives focused on action research, knowledge exchange, social value creation, and the exploration of alternative, innovative practices.*

www.openstudiowestminster.org/beyond-studio/live-design-practice/

Through participatory mapping, collage-making, and open dialogues, community members (including library users, residents, and local business representatives) were invited to articulate both needs and aspirations for the site. Outreach was facilitated via a network of established local organisations, including the Marylebone Forum, the Marylebone Association, and St Marylebone Parish Church, ensuring the process engaged a broad and representative cross-section of the community (Figure 1). The objectives were aligned with participatory and epistemic justice aspirations and were co-designing the parklet collaboratively, and ensuring that every participant's voice and needs were acknowledged, valued, and embedded in the final design.

The workshops combined spatial and narrative methods. Participatory mapping exercises prompted participants to locate and describe valued spaces, everyday routes, and points of disconnection or discomfort, alongside questions that unpacked emotional ties to place, sense of belonging, and personal stories or memories associated with the area (Figure 2). These activities revealed nuanced understandings of the site's social and spatial dynamics. The second stage of the workshop employed a collage-based design exercise, in which participants engaged with a curated set of parklet design features grouped into thematic zones (active travel, children and play, culture and civic spirit, and slowing down). Participants were tasked with selecting preferred features, combining them into their own parklet proposals, and prioritising elements in relation to locally identified needs (Figures 3 & 4). This iterative and co-creative process foregrounded epistemic justice by recognising local knowledge and lived experience as foundational to the design, while its open and deliberative format embodied procedural justice, enabling an inclusive authorship of space.

The student-led design outcome, a modular parklet situated outside Marylebone Library which repurposes two parking bays (Figure 5) embodies the multiplicity of uses articulated through the community co-design process. Structured around three programmatic zones, it combines ecological, recreational, and civic functions: a green oasis with planting and seating for 'slowing down'; a biodiversity module with insect habitats and educational signage; and a playful, children-oriented space with interactive storytelling elements and games (Figure 6). These included a chalkboard panel for public messages and a mini-library exchange, both shaped by ideas shared during workshops with families and library-goers. Materials such as timber and bamboo were chosen for sustainability, durability, and minimal disruption to the street infrastructure.

The parklet is on track to being constructed on a two-year temporary basis, with works projected to be completed by January 2026. Importantly, working with Cross River Partnership, the parklet also integrates air quality sensors and pedestrian counters to assess environmental and behavioural impacts. While such metrics cannot capture the full social and symbolic dimensions of the intervention, they will provide important data for decisions about making the parklet permanent, for informing future initiatives and for advocating for mobility and public realm policy changes locally and beyond. *In reclaiming space formerly dedicated to cars, the parklet challenges the hegemonic prioritisation of automobility in urban street planning and design, reasserting the value of streets as spaces 'for people'* (Bertolini, 2020).

Centre: Community co-design process at the Marylebone Centre (source: authors)

In that sense, the parklet experiment was not simply conceived as a spatial intervention but as a site of knowledge production, negotiation about space amogst different stakeholders, and an exercise for imagining alternative scenarios for urban streets. Crucially, students were central actors in this process, occupying the position between learners, facilitators, and designers. Starting in the classroom but far from being a controlled studio exercise, the project exposed students to the realities of urban transformation: ambiguity, compromise, and the complex dynamics of participation. As other scholars also argue, such an approach to pedagogy shifts architectural and urban design education away from a closed, atelier-based model towards a form of practice that is relational, situated, and socially responsive (Natarajan & Short, 2023). This way, creativity is not exercised in isolation but is embedded in collaborative responsibility, requiring students to adapt to emerging knowledge and remain accountable to those affected by their design decisions. This process fosters not only technical competence but also critical reflexivity, ethical sensitivity, and the ability to engage with shifting power dynamics in the shaping of urban space. In doing so, such an exercise

repositions the studio as a site of transformation and civic engagement and the university as an active participant in the process of co-creating more just and sustainable cities.

What emerges from this process is not only a street design which is more responsive to community needs and which challenges the prevailing logics of street space allocation, but a situated experiment in how justice might be enacted through pedagogical innovation, participatory practices, and co-creation (Lund, 2018). The university, in this configuration, is no longer simply a provider of education or a producer of knowledge, but a civic actor. It acts as a facilitator, a translator between different disciplines, sectors and stakeholders, and a platform for justice-oriented experimentation. This role challenges the traditional boundaries of academia, highlighting its capacity and responsibility in shaping more equitable urban futures (Fokdal et al. 2021).

Finally, the Marylebone Library Parklet project offers an example of how street transformations can be approached as both a spatial and political project. By engaging students and local communities in a shared process of reimagining different mobility futures and street scenarios, it resists the technocratic tendencies that continue to dominate urban design and planning. Instead, it demonstrates that justice in the street is not a predefined outcome, but an ongoing practice of negotiation, collaboration and co-creation.

For references, please see the end of the book.

STUDENT REFLECTIONS

""The Live Project offers a unique platform for designers to **step outside commercial constraints and reflect on the broader implications of their practice**. It encourages exploration of alternative approaches, fostering discussions around designers' role in society and the environment." MArch student

"… it is a fantastic **hands-on experience** to begin to understand a project's realisation and progression. The company of the studio, and **collaboration between the student and professionals was a great learning experience**." BA Y3 student

"Building the prototype was an invaluable experience; seeing how things are put together from the drawing, figuring it out and with things going wrong is a helpful process. It was useful **working together, the team building aspect is very beneficial.**" MArch student

"The Live Project provided a great opportunity to **experiment and explore materiality and making.** It stretched the whole work stages from engagement, design, making and construction and was a great opportunity to **learn in and from the real world**. Working with a wide range of specialist and consultants promote knowledge exchange and helped **develop my soft skills in communication…**"MArch student

"I must say it's very useful doing this, because you get a really good idea of when you put a 'number' on a drawing, what it means in real life. So if you can do it from the building perspective backwards, I think it will **make us better architects** and better 'detailers'." MArch student

"Building the community hub prototype helped me gain hands-on experience … used in real-life building projects, as well as a better understanding of the design and construction process. It provided a **practical context to the theories and concepts we learned in the classroom**. Building a prototype also allowed us to receive feedback on our design from real-world users. It was a proud moment to see how people were using the hub! I understand now how design decisions can impact the user experience and how to **iterate and improve the designs based on feedback**." BA student

CIVIC PERMEABILITY
BRENT CROSS

Z-01 INDUSTRIAL

The World Wars saw Brent Cross become a hub for industry as the needs of the time drove innovation and development. This rich history of making is slowly disappearing as the economy shifts towards retail warehouses and storage facilities as well as the introduction of new residential developments. These new developments are critiqued as being 'solution based' schemes, repeating a generic 'one size fits all' approach to urban, so failing to respond to local communities and context. Our projects have sought to enrich and diversify the existing industrial zone so that it can respond to a range of existing and emerging needs.

Z-02 RESERVOIR

The Welsh Harp Reservoir (Brent Reservoir), is a rare pocket of natural beauty in north-west London, nestled between West Hendon, Neasden, and Kingsbury. Built in 1837 for the Grand Union Canal, it is now a local nature reserve and Site of Special Scientific Interest. It is a refuge to great crested grebes and other diverse wildlife, it also offers activities like sailing and birdwatching within the city. Yet the reservoir faces pollution, neglect, and poor facilities. In response, we have imagined ways to restore and reconnect people with this fragile ecosystem, celebrating its beauty and ecological importance within the urban landscape.

Z-03 CONNECTION

In Brent Cross, major transport infrastructure has shaped the area's development. The North Circular ring road and its tributaries have subsumed the entire urban space. While the road network was designed to enable rapid road transportation into and across London, it has completely overpowered the landscape, resulting in a host of problematic impacts, from pedestrian navigation to sensory overload, to isolated and neglected parcels of land. Our projects seek to identify, assess and redefine these liminal spaces, and to re-establish a sense of identity, meaning and association within the local area.

Z-04 COMMERCIAL

The Brent Cross Shopping Centre was built in 1976 as the first American-style shopping mall in Britain. It introduced a new model of commercial space and public gathering to the Brent Cross community. However, as retail patterns change and the centre gradually loses its cultural and social significance, the vast car parks surrounding the site result in unused land and dereliction. In our projects we have sought to revitalise the areas and to propose new ways to repurpose these sites to create meaningful, socially and environmentally conscious spaces that better serve the evolving needs of the Brent Cross community.

Z-05 COMMUNITY

Community in Brent Cross, through its resilience and self-organisation, is vibrant in both the Whitefields Estate, and Clitterhouse Farm. The site of our Live Build project, Clitterhouse Farm was saved from demolition through grassroots action and has since become an important community hub. The Whitefield Estate residents have shown resilience in the face of demolition, navigating their changing environment. The projects in this zone uncover how architecture can support belonging, care, and local identity. It questions who buildings are for, and how places become meaningful when communities are empowered to shape them.

CIVIC PERMEABILITY

BRENT CROSS TOWN

2024-2025

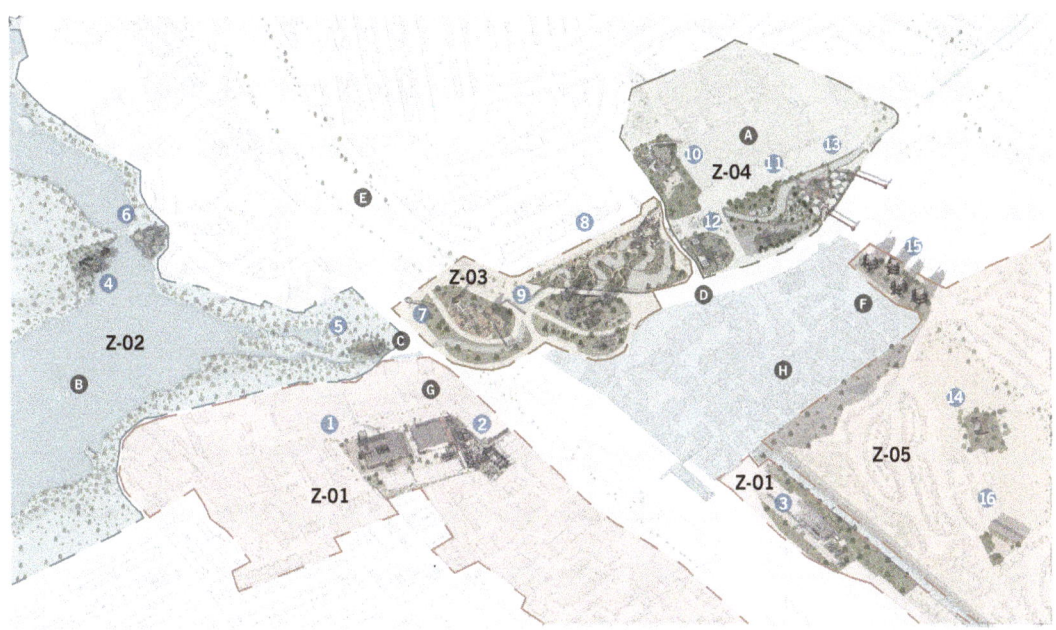

1. ALEX MARTON - INDUSTRIAL DOMESTICITY
2. HARDEEPAK SINGH PANESAR - THE ADHOC AGORA
3. ISABEL LIU - INFRA-ORDINARY EXCHANGE
4. YUELIN ZHOU - FEATHERED CONNECTIONS
5. YAMON PHU KYAW - RIPPLES OF RESTORATION
6. KAJANA CHAOUNTHARA GNANAN - ASYLUM OF GENTRIFICATION
7. MORGAN DOYLE - THE ISLAND RETREAT
8. KITTY EMERY RAINBIRD - THE HEARTH
9. ALISTAIR SEARCH - HY-WAY
10. YAEL SCHNITZER - RIPPLES OF INCLUSION
11. ANNA LONG - TEXTILE COMMONS
12. TUGCE YIGIT - MADE IN BRENT
13. JOSEPH KUFORIJI - CIVIC OF MANY VOICES
14. EMILY IVAN - OUR CHILDREN CENTRE
15. JAKE MILSOM - VERTICAL COMMONS
16. DS20 LIVE BUILD - CLITTERHOUSE FARM

A. BRENT CROSS SHOPPING CENTRE
B. THE WELSH HARP
C. RIVER BRENT
D. THE NORTH CIRCULAR
E. THE M1
F. WHITEFIELDS ESTATE
G. STAPLES CORNER
H. NEW BRENT CROSS TOWN

DS20's approach to architecture involves being active agents, or instigators, within the community, empowered to change a little of the world. We aim to explore the fullness and potential of architecture and how the power of design can be used to make a real difference. DS20 are also big advocates for applied making which helps us to bridge the gap between theory and practice.

Our work aims to encourage interaction, shared experiences, a sense of community, enhance ecology and most importantly, to foster a context specific, meaningful engagement with and experience of place. This year, we explored the area of Brent cross in north London, a complex part of the city where the Welsh harp reservoir, the Brent cross shopping centre, and major urban redevelopments meet local neighbourhood and community spaces. In this tangled mix of land uses, intersected by extensive road and rail transport infrastructures, diverse communities and economies are confronted by new scales of city making.

Through each individual project, DS20 has sought to engage with these social and urban conditions, as well as the thresholds and buffer zones across the area. We asked how these thresholds and borders occur across scales, from the urban, political, social to the personal and intimate. Our projects sought to enhance transition zones that we identified by creating civic spaces, moments, and experiences of permeability and translucency. The projects within DS20 propose new types and typologies of architectural, urban and civic space that challenge and oppose the existing ordering regimes of the city.

Axonometric Overview showing individual student proposals, the Live Project Our Canopy at Clitterhouse Farm and the Brent Cross Phase 1 development, including 6,700 new homes..Students could choose their sites within this complex area of north London around Brent Cross where the Welsh Harp Reservoir, the Brent Cross Shopping Centre and major urban redevelopments meet local neighbourhoods and community spaces including Clitterhouse Farm. In this tangled mix of land uses which are intersected by extensive road and rail transport infrastructures, established diverse communities and economies are confronted with a wholly new scale of city-making and visions of the future. We start with the question; what is the relationship between these communities and urban conditions and how do their current and future interrelationships impact the spatial, social and economic dynamics of the Brent Cross area?

BRENT CROSS TOWN PHASE 1 INCLUDING 6,700 NEW HOMES

OUR CANOPY AT CLITTERHOUSE FARM LIVE PROJECT

HOUSING AS COMMODITY, NOT COMMUNITY

Brent Cross Town, like many similar projects across London, re-imagines housing not as a right or a social necessity, but as an asset vehicle for private capital accumulation. The new homes are rarely designed with affordability or local need in mind. Even the few "affordable" units are often tenure-blind in name only, out of reach for many long-term local residents. This commodification of housing reinforces exclusion. By prioritising investor returns and market-driven metrics, such developments reproduce socio-spatial inequality under the guise of regeneration.

THE MYTH OF THE "NEW NEIGHBOURHOOD"

New developments often claim to be new neighbourhoods, yet they fail to embody the fundamental principles of what makes a neighbourhood meaningful: a strong local identity, diverse socio-economic representation, multi-programmatic functions, and inclusive spaces that grow organically from the lived experiences of communities. Instead, what is offered is a generic spatial product - a series of high-density residential blocks with lifestyle-driven amenities that cater almost exclusively to middle-class and investor demographics. The language of the development reads like a copy-paste formula used across dozens of global cities. This branding decouples place from history, and detaches architecture from social responsibility.

LACK OF MULTI-PROGRAMMATIC AND INDUSTRIAL INTEGRATION

There is a lack of programmatic diversity in these developments, which are overwhelmingly residential, with the only non-housing functions being retail (often chain stores) and leisure amenities (gyms, cafés, wellness hubs). There is little to no provision for light industry, craft or informal economic activity - all vital components of a living, breathing urban economy. Cities need places to work, make, repair, teach, share, and collaborate. This erasure of production in favour of consumption reflects a larger trend in urban planning: cities becoming containers for lifestyle rather than ecosystems for livelihood.

SOCIAL SUSTAINABILITY

Developments often describes themselves as a green neighbourhood, yet its sustainability is framed in terms of surface-level aesthetics and energy performance metrics - not social sustainability. There is no integration of community land trusts, co-operative housing, or any models that democratise land and empower residents to shape their environment. Without community co-design and shared ownership structures, sustainability becomes yet another tool of exclusion, dressed in a green cloak.

BRENT CROSS TOWN: A £7 BILLION PROMISE - OR ANOTHER DEVELOPER DREAM?

"Experience luxury living in London's newest green neighbourhood — just 12 minutes from Central London. Brent Cross Town is a bold £7 billion regeneration development offering a remarkable lifestyle only a short train ride to St Pancras. This visionary project will feature: 6,700 stylish new homes. A vibrant community focused on health, well-being and exceptional amenities. Welcome to a new standard of urban living!"

This is how the new development is being marketed.

LOCAL IDENTITY AND PLACE-MAKING

Developments often flatten the rich, at times messy textures of local culture into an abstract vision of urban life that could be anywhere - and nowhere. What does Brent Cross Town say about Brent? About the histories, struggles, and triumphs of its people? "Placemaking," in the hands of developers, often becomes a branding exercise rather than a truly participatory process with long-term cultural embeddedness. What is created is not a place, but a product - a modular, repeatable, and exportable urban unit. These are not London's neighbourhoods - they are nowhere-villes.

RECLAIMING URBAN FUTURES

Urban regeneration cannot be driven by real estate logic alone. It must be grounded in community-led development, inclusive planning processes and economic diversity. This means creating spaces for light and creative industries, for making and production, and for people being able to live and work affordably, and to stay when they start families. It requires viewing cities not as markets first, but as complex, multi-layered communities - investing in a wide range of small and local businesses to support sustainable growth.

Photo of the large scale model of the new development of Phase 1 at Brent Cross

AN ARCHITECT'S DILEMMA IN THE AGE OF CAPITALIST REALISM

**AN EXTRACT FROM MARCH DISSERTATION
KITTY EMERY RAINBIRD**

IF ONE LOOKS AT THE EMERGING BUILT ENVIRONMENT IN LONDON, COUNTLESS NEAR IDENTICAL DEVELOPMENTS, PRIORITISING DEVELOPER PROFIT, ARE REPLACING ESTABLISHED SOCIAL HOUSING DEVELOPMENTS, AND DISPLACING THE COMMUNITIES ROOTED THERE. THE NEW BRENT CROSS TOWN DEVELOPMENT IS NO EXCEPTION. THESE EXTRACTS FROM MY DISSERTATION EXPLORE THE COMMODIFICATION OF HOUSING, THE EVER CHANGING ROLE OF THE STATE, AND THE COMPLICITY OF THE ARCHITECT WITHIN THIS SYSTEM.

LARGE SCALE PRIVATE DEVELOPMENTS - THE COMMODIFICATION OF HOUSING

Large Scale Private Developments (LSPDs), are defined here as any major development of over 40 units delivered by the private sector. In the 2022/2023 financial year, 60% of all homes completed in London were in large scale private developments, a proportional increase of a third in the decade since the 2012/2013 year, when they accounted for just over 41% of completed homes These developments are usually distinguishable by their 'New London Vernacular' style, which has been championed by private developers due to its 'reducing of sales risk' and 'quicker planning decisions'[1]. This has left the capital peppered with developments showing little originality, and few features giving them any sense of local identity. Many of these schemes have been developed as regeneration projects through joint ventures with local councils, such as Brent Cross Town (Related Argent and Barnet Council), and High Road West (London Borough of Haringey and Lendlease), and Woodberry Down (Berkley Homes and Hackney Council).

Housing in the UK has become increasingly commodified, meaning "that a structure's function as real estate takes precedence over its usefulness as a place to live. [...] the subordination of the social use of housing to its economic value."[2] This commodification of housing has increased exponentially since the 1980s under Margaret Thatcher's government and continues to increase today. In 1975 when 54% of houses were being built by the government, housing was a right, today[3] with 80% being built by private developers[4] and a housing shortage pushing up prices. The commodification of housing has also led to a noticeable fall in quality, with a third of people in the UK reporting that they would not buy a new build home due to fears of poor quality[5]. When housing is produced by developers as a commodity, it is not built for the end user, but rather as a product from which profit can be made: they are not designing with the highest quality or longevity in mind. In 2020, an audit of large-scale residential developments in England found that three quarters of all new build properties had a build quality rated 'mediocre or 'poor', with a fifth of such poor design that they should never have been approved for planning[6]. This demonstrates that in relation to both build quality and social function, the commodification of housing has had a negative impact on the built environment.

In an age when social and environmental concerns are becoming more and more prevalent in the decisions we make as consumers, it makes sense that these companies wish to appear to align with these values: appearances have great power in the capitalist system, and this appropriation of ethical practice increases the exchange value of the development. "To a degree unprecedented in any other social system, [capitalism] ... both feeds on and reproduces the moods of populations."[7] When examining a brochure for any one of the large scale developments appearing throughout London, you will be bombarded with the development's environmental and social credentials, buzz-phrases such as 'sustainable development', providing 'green space', and 'flourishing community' are splattered over glossy brochure pages and social media ads. "In capitalism, that is to say, all that is solid melts into PR, and late capitalism is defined at least as much by this ubiquitous tendency towards PR-production as it is by the imposition of market mechanisms"[8].

It can be observed however, that these principles are only implemented to the level that is required to increase value: in a capitalist system ethics could never be allowed to limit profit. For example, building a neighbourhood which can foster a healthy multigenerational community is clearly not a leading factor of design, as only 14% of units meeting the needs of a family are built in favour of the more profitable one- and two-bedroom units.

When we unpack private developers' specious statements of social and environmental sustainability, systematic greenwashing and morally questionable practices are revealed. Greenwashing, described as "... misleading information about how a company's [...] projects are more environmentally friendly than they are when analysed from a more critical and careful perspective"[9], is rife within London's LSPDs.

One such example is Brent Cross Town, in which misleading claims about the production of greenspace are made (when in practice a net loss is observed), alongside blatant disregard of the consequences of demolishing the existing estate. "The greenest building is the one that already exists"[10] - a well-known fact in the construction industry, yet a total demolition of the Whitefield estate was chosen over refurbishment or incorporating it in future development.

These demolitions also expose inconsistencies in developers' social claims. Many schemes such as this one are being brought forward in collaboration with local councils. Developers use this to laud their social credentials, yet they are almost exclusively demolishing existing council housing estates, and the flourishing communities within. Whilst it is claimed that all those living on land earmarked for demolition will be rehoused in the new development[11], this is often masking the fact that only those with secure tenancies will be rehoused[12]. Those without have no rights to remain in the area and can be relocated anywhere in the country. They have no say in this decision: if they refuse to move, they will be declared 'intentionally homeless' and lose any further support for housing[13].

Examples such as these expose the disparity between the stated goals of developers and their actions. Yet individual developers cannot be held wholly responsible. Poor quality and superficial socio-environmental practices are symptomatic of a wider neoliberal system which equates value only to profit.

THE POSITION OF THE STATE – THE IMPACT OF NEOLIBERAL POLICIES ON THE BUILT ENVIRONMENT.

Since the 1980s, neoliberalism has been the dominant economic ideology in the UK. Characterised as a stage of capitalism deeply tied to financialisation[14], neoliberalism has reshaped the role of the State, particularly in how public services are structured and delivered. Where the post-war era saw the State playing an active role in protecting the welfare of its citizens—most notably through the establishment of social housing, the NHS, and other public services—the Thatcher era marked a shift toward market primacy. Under neoliberal ideology, it is assumed that the market is the most efficient mechanism for organising society and driving productivity[15]. Consequently, the State has transformed from an entity prioritising social welfare to one that increasingly exists to support market

The looming sight of New Brent Cross Town between existing housing in the area

interests.

This ideological shift has deeply affected the UK's approach to housing. One of the clearest manifestations of neoliberal influence is the adoption of a "business ontology," whereby all public services, including housing, healthcare, and education, are managed as if they were private businesses. Within this framework, success is measured by financial efficiency and market competitiveness rather than social outcomes or public good[16].

In the post-World War II period, the UK government played a central role in housebuilding, with over 100,000 homes constructed annually by state bodies. However, the 1980s saw a rapid decline in this practice. By the 1990s, local authorities were building as few as 400 homes per year[17]. While the State dramatically reduced its role in housing provision, private developers failed to fill the gap[18]. The number of new homes built annually has remained substantially below 1970 levels[19]. Importantly, developers have little incentive to ramp up supply, as increasing the availability of homes would reduce prices and cut into their profits[20].

The Right to Buy policy, introduced under Thatcher, had a profound and lasting impact. This policy gave social housing tenants the right to purchase their homes at a discount, dramatically reducing the social housing stock. While the scheme helped many people become homeowners, it also restricted local authorities from reinvesting the proceeds into new housing construction[21]. As a result, the homes sold were not replaced. Furthermore, nearly half of the homes sold through Right to Buy are now privately rented[22], many leased back to councils and housing associations at significant cost to the taxpayer[23].

The decline in social housing was not just a matter of reduced building and sales policy but also one of perception and rhetoric. Under New Labour in 1997, a negative narrative around social housing was institutionalised. The term "sink estates" gained currency, encouraging the demolition of large social housing projects and their replacement with mixed-use private developments. Despite higher densities in these redevelopments, the result was often a net loss in homes available for social rent[24].

Compounding this problem has been the

increasingly misleading use of the term "affordable housing." Traditionally, this was used interchangeably with social housing—homes rented out at significantly below market rates. However, the term now encompasses a broad range of housing tenures, many of which are not affordable to low- or even middle-income families[25]. The 2011 Affordable Homes Programme under the Conservative-Liberal Democrat coalition redefined the term to include options like shared ownership and intermediate rent, which offer far less affordability.

This semantic shift has allowed policymakers to claim progress in providing affordable housing while masking the actual decline in social rent properties. For example, London's planning policy requires 35% of new housing in major developments to be "affordable," but only around 11% must be low-cost rent, and even then, there is no firm requirement that it be traditional social rent[26]. Consequently, the proportion of genuinely affordable homes being built—especially those for social rent—has declined sharply since 2011[27].

In line with neoliberal ideology, UK state policies have increasingly supported private developers and market interests. This shift has pushed local authorities into closer partnerships with private sector developers, often through the depletion of public assets, including the widespread sale of public land—around 50% of which has been sold since the 1970s[28]. One of the most significant outcomes of this trend is the financialisation of housing, whereby homes are treated as investment assets rather than essential dwellings intended to provide long-term shelter[29].

This broader economic context directly affects the architectural profession. Although state regulations exist to ensure quality in areas such as safety, energy efficiency, accessibility, and space standards, the bureaucratic rigidity of these rules often stifles architectural creativity and flexibility. Architects have limited freedom to tailor designs to the specific needs of a site or client brief. The tension between market-driven development and regulatory oversight frequently results in housing schemes that, while compliant, lack identity, character, and a true sense of place. Despite meeting all formal requirements, architects often struggle to justify alternative or more context-sensitive designs, given the dominance of developer priorities and regulatory constraints.

THE ROLE OF THE ARCHITECT – COMPLICIT OR COMPLIANT IN A CAPITALIST SOCIETY?

In contemporary society, architects find themselves in a morally and professionally conflicted position. Despite being trained to design socially responsible, sustainable, and high-quality environments, much of the housing they help produce is of poor quality. This contradiction arises from the structural constraints imposed by neoliberalism and the pervasive influence of what theorist Mark Fisher calls capitalist realism—the belief that capitalism is the only viable socio-economic system. This world view has permeated not just politics and economics, but also culture, creativity, and individual agency, making it nearly impossible to imagine or realise alternatives[30].

Under this framework, architecture is deeply embedded in market-driven forces. Architects must rely on private sector clients—particularly large-scale private developers—for commissions, as public sector opportunities have dwindled[31]. Local councils, once major employers of architects, now offer only a handful of roles nationwide[32]. This near-total dependence on private capital means that architects must conform to the expectations and priorities of clients who are largely focused on profit, not public benefit or design quality.

Financial control within this system restricts architects' agency. The structure of contemporary capitalism equates survival with participation in the labour market, and architecture is no exception. Refusing to work within the prevailing market conditions means losing professional relevance or even livelihood. As a result, architects often produce buildings that conflict with their personal values or theoretical positions. For example, some architects known for their critical discourse on capitalism produce commercial work that conforms precisely to the system they critique[33]. This paradox reflects how capitalism absorbs and neutralises opposition[34].

Attempts to resist these conditions collectively have been largely ineffective. Architecture, as a profession, promotes individualism and competition over collaboration. Nonetheless, there are exceptions that suggest alternative approaches are possible. Environmental advocacy groups like the Architects Climate Action Network (ACAN) and Architects Declare have shown that collective action can occur, especially in response to ecological concerns[35]. These movements challenge industry complacency and push for meaningful systemic change, exposing the potential for solidarity around shared values despite the isolating pressures of capitalism.

The role of the architect today is shaped by a system that prioritises capital over people and design. While many architects remain critical of this system, they are often forced to comply with its demands to maintain their careers. The current economic and political framework not only limits what architects can design but also undermines the imagination of alternative ways to practice architecture. This results in a profession caught between ethical ideals and market realities—where true agency is severely constrained, and meaningful resistance remains difficult but not impossible.

> "Architecture at every stage of its existence […] is buffeted by external forces. Other people, circumstances, and events intervene to upset the architect's best-laid plans. These forces are […] beyond the direct control of the architect. Architecture is thus shaped more by external conditions than by the internal processes of the architect.[36]"- Jeremy Till

1. Design for Homes, 'A New London Housing Vernacular' (Design for Homes, 2020).
2. David Madden and Peter. Marcuse, In Defence of Housing: The Politics of Crisis Figures taken for 2022
3. Office for National Statistics (UK), 'Number of Houses Built in the UK 1949-2023, by Tenure', Statista, 2024.
4. Seamus Doherty, 'Over Half of Brits Wouldn't Buy a New-Build, with Almost a Third Blaming Poor Quality', London Property News, 2024.
5. M Carmona et al., 'A Housing Design Audit for England' (London: Place Alliance, 2020).
6. Mark Fisher, Capitalist Realism: Is There No Alternative? (Zero Books, 2009). p. 35
7. Ibid. p. 44
8. Adele Belitardo, 'Greenwashing in Architecture: Identifying False Sustainable Strategies', ArchDaily, 6 November 2023.
9. Will Hurst, 'The Greenest Building Is the One That Already Exists', The Architects' Journal, 27 February 2020, 6.
10. 'Relocated Homes', Transforming Brent Cross Cricklewood
11. 'Frequently Asked Questions for Non-Secure Tenants on Regeneration;Estates', Barnet Homes.
12. Anna Minton, 'Policy Paralysis, Financialisation, and the Politics of Facadism: Housing Policy Post Grenfell', The Journal of Architecture 27, no. 1 (2022): 13–20.
13. Kate Bayliss et al., 'Reports of My Death Are Greatly Exaggerated: The Persistence of Neoliberalism in Britain', European Journal of Social Theory 27, no. 4 (2024): 540–60.
14. Nelly Stromquist, Education in a Globalized World: The Connectivity of Economic Power, Technology, and Knowledge (United Kingdom: Rowman & Littlefield, 2002). p. 25
15. Fisher, Capitalist Realism: Is There No Alternative? p.16.
16. Peter Apps, 'Have the Conservatives Really Built Twice as Much Council Housing as Labour?', Inside Housing, March 2017.
17. Minton, 'Policy Paralysis, Financialisation, and the Politics of Facadism'.
18. Alex Lord, 'No Government in Half a Century Has Built 300,000 Homes Every Year, but That's What Labour Wants to Do Now', The Conversation, 13 August 2024.
19. Minton, 'Policy Paralysis, Financialisation, and the Politics of Facadism'.
20. Brian Milligan, 'Right-to-Buy: Margaret Thatcher's Controversial Gift', BBC News, 04/2013.
21. Alex Diner and Hollie Wright, 'Reforming Right to Buy' (The New Economics Foundation)
22. Tom Copley, 'Councils Fork out Millions Renting Back Right to Buy Properties' Simon Elmer, 'Rioting, Legislation and Estate Demolition: A Chronology of Social Cleansing in London, 1999-2019', Architects for Social Housing (blog), 16 October 2019.
23. Affordable Housing Commission, 'Making Housing Affordable Again: Rebalancing the Nation's Housing System' (London: The Smith Institute, 2020).
24. Greater London Authority, 'The London Plan' (Greater London Authority, 2021). p. 181
25. Barton et al., 'Affordable Housing in England'.
26. Brett Christophers, 'If This Public Land Sell-off Continues, There Could Be None Left by 2050', The Guardian, 5 March 2019
27. Miriam Axel-Lute, 'What Is the Financialization of Housing?', Shelterforce, 8 August 2022.
28. Fisher, Capitalist Realism: Is There No Alternative? p. 2.
29. Chris Foye and Edward Shepherd, 'How Big UK Housebuilders Have Remained Profitable without Meeting Housing Supply Targets', The Conversation, 28 November 2023.
30. In 1976, 49% of architects worked in the public sector. See: Simon Elmer and Geraldine Dening, For a Socialist Architecture Under Capitalism
31. Nic Clear, 'The Architecture of Capitalist Realism' (Conference Presentation. Capitalist Realism 10 Years on, University of Huddersfield, 16 February 2020).
32. Fisher, Capitalist Realism: Is There No Alternative? p. 69
33. 'The Regenerative Architecture Index', Architecture Today, 1 February 2024.
34. Jeremy Till, Architecture Depends, Architecture Depends (MIT Press, 2009). p. 1

Existing Whitefields estate properties and established trees demolished in favour of new for-profit development.

OUR CANOPY AT CLITTERHOUSE FARM

LIVE PROJECT
2024-2025

TUTORS: MARIA KRAMER AND SHAHED SALEEM
STUDENTS: KAJANA GNANAN, MORGAN DOYLE, EMILY IVAN, JOSEPH KUFORIJI, YAMON KYAW, ANNA LONG, JAKE MILSOM, TUGCE YIGIT, KITTY EMERY RAINBIRD, ISABEL LIU, ALEX MARTON, HARDEEPAK SINGH PANESAR, YAEL SCHNITZER, ALISTAIR SEARCH, YUELIN ZHOU
FUNDER: CETI + CLITTERHOUSE FARM
PARTNERS: NICHOLAS ALEXANDER, WEBB YATES ENGINEERS

Top: Drone view of the construction process of the 7 wing modules with students helping to install the wings; Left: Construction of one of the wing modules

"The studio brief explored challenges of urban regeneration, gentrification, and how these forces can be made more equitable. The Canopy Live Project is a physical response to those larger questions."

Our Live Project: "Our Canopy at Clitterhouse Farm" in Brent Cross is a multifunctional structure which was co-created a vibrant grassroots community and our making partner (Nicholas Alexander) and structural engineering partner Steve Webb with students from DS20.

Clitterhouse Farm serves as a beacon of local engagement, saving the heritage building from demolition and providing space for workshops, growing and social activities, encouraging and promoting a wide range of voices from the local community. Our Yard's mission is to foster resilient, sustainable communities in and around Clitterhouse Farm and Northwest London. The aim is to serve as a community-led exemplar for embedding social value into regeneration projects.

By conserving and enhancing this significant heritage site, Our Yard strives to create a vibrant, inclusive space where communities and small businesses can come together to address social and environmental challenges locally and nationally. Our Yard celebrates local history, promote sustainable living, and support the arts and culture. Their goal is to offer opportunities, events, services, and facilities that are welcoming, engaging, and financially accessible to all.

Initial funding for the Live Project came from CETI, while the community secured most of the construction funds themselves. The project is integrated in our Master's studio brief, which explored challenges of urban regeneration, gentrification, and how these forces can be

**PAULETTE SINGER
FOUNDING DIRECTOR**

CLITTERHOUSE FARM PROJECT

"It's easier to ask for forgiveness than permission"

"I would be heartbroken if our campaign failed. It's one of the only pieces of history Barnet has left"

"We want to keep it alive. When you come down here, you realise it's got an energy of its own"

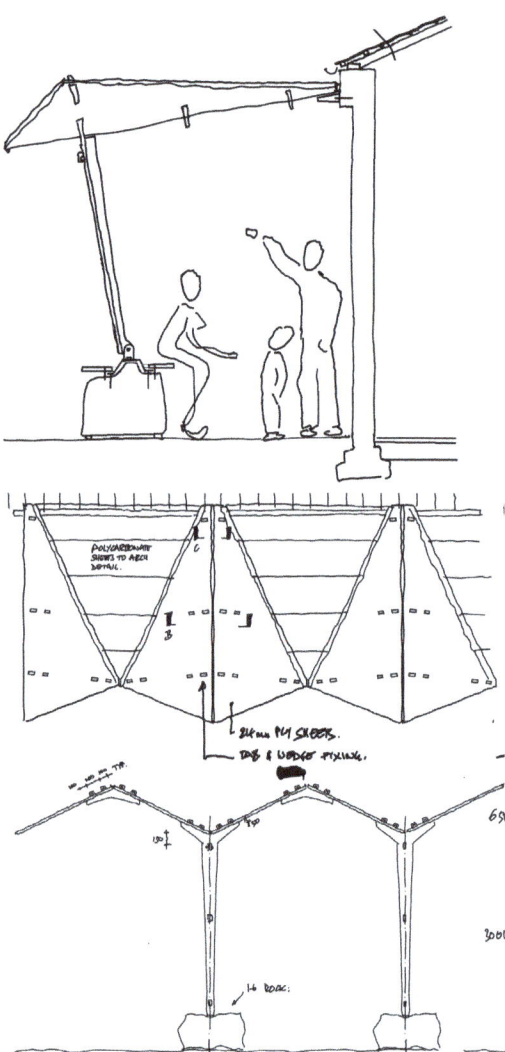

Above: Sketches by Steve Webb

Above: Steve Webb sketching in the studio with students; the initial cardboard sketch model by students was translated into a stiff wing-like light weight structure
Top Left: Quote summary from Paulette Singer by Hardeepak Panesar

The Canopy structure is based on simple folding origami by folding paper creating a rigid form which could be applied to a larger scale. Tree like structural support columns provide a slender frame at the bottom and larger at the roof connection point to support the 18mm ply roof.

Public Engagement at Clitterhouse Farm

Public Engagement at Clitterhouse Farm as part of the spring community event also showcasing students proposals

As part of the engagement process, public feedback on the canopy design indicated that the concrete foundation stones appeared too bold. In response, they were modified by adding timber seating panels;

Students developed a workshop for and with local children, which also inspired the individual proposal; organised by Emily Ivan with Joseph Kyforiji

made more equitable. It's a physical response to those larger questions. Through projects like this, we contribute to the social fabric, civic engagement, and the green transition of neighbourhoods.

Our Canopy provides shelter to host large events with a large covering from weather. The construction is made out of CNC-cut plywood and has 7 modular bays. The folded triangulation of the canopy provides a stiff wing-like structure with translucent cut-outs towards the rear giving light to the existing barn.

Our Yard's supports resilient, sustainable communities in and around Clitterhouse Farm, championing local heritage, sustainability, arts, and culture. The aim is to create an inclusive space where communities and small businesses collaborate to meet social and environmental needs.

This Live Project is more than a temporary intervention - it leaves a lasting legacy, both in the built environment and in the people involved. Participants not only develop practical construction and design skills, but also gain a deeper understanding of social responsibility and the power of co-creation. By engaging directly with the communities we serve, we learn to listen, adapt, and respond with empathy - shaping spaces that reflect shared values and local identity.

The process fosters mutual learning: communities share their lived experiences, and participants contribute their creativity, energy, and problem-solving. This reciprocal exchange strengthens trust and encourages long-term thinking about how we build and who we build for. As we reflect on the outcomes, it becomes clear that the impact goes beyond physical structures - it's about empowerment, capacity-building, and inspiring new approaches to design education and practice. The Live Project becomes a model for future work: grounded in collaboration, committed to care, and shaped by the people it's meant to serve.

"I believe that design and making are part of the same process. It's important that you're not just coming up with an idea or a drawing for something, but that you're physically resolving all of the issues. A lot of design happens in the final moments of production, that's where the fixings are. So I believe very strongly that this is important." Nick Runeckles Specialist designer.

Top: Building a 1:1 prototype with Nic Runeckles, Nicholas Alexander, at his warehouse in Kent; students help weld the brackets; the prototype made us realise that the structure requires additional bracing;
Right from top to bottom: Preparing the CNC cutting of the canopy wings; students welding brackets for the canopy joints; Installing the wing substructure

"The Live Project is a project that arguably bridges the gap between academia and the real world. We work with real clients, reaching out and making real interventions. It's all about authentic learning, that's at the heart of it. You have such an amazing world in academia, and then you go out into the real world, and it's so different, the constraints are so different. There is a lot of knowledge out there, and that's what we want to tap into and help nurture."

"The Live Project is mainly based on group work and teamwork, but there's a lot of learning that feeds into individual work as well for example, in technical studies and vice versa. Students do their own analysis and engagement with local communities, and that can feed back into the Live Project.

We record the group work, the process, the engagement We ask students to take a lot of photos of what's happening, and then reflect on that process and there's a lot of learning in the reflection itself. That reflection is something that's also really easy to assess. It's about being involved from the very beginning, through all the work stages, right through to the build. Normally, an architect isn't involved in the construction itself, but when you do this, you learn so much and you become a better designer."

"The process is so important because normally you just see the end result. As an architect, you might draw a line and then see the final product, but you often don't see the process in between, and there's so much knowledge and important design in Stage Four. When you collaborate with makers and fabricators, you gain that site knowledge and that informs your designs in a really meaningful way.

Students who include the Live Project and its process in their portfolios when they go to interviews and present it, the employers really value that. It feels empowering, it feels like people can come together, and we have people power. You come out of something like this and you feel like you can make a difference and I think you learn and support each other. So I think it's a huge privilege, on one level, because we can make a difference, and the students really understand that." Maria Kramer.

"It's usually enriching. It gives students a much broader and more holistic sense of how design works, alongside construction, fabrication, and implementation. I think the key thing is to consider the capacity of the students, what you can realistically expect them to do within their coursework, and within the level of skills they have, which will vary across the group. Then, it's about positioning the work the students are going to do within a realistic framework of the overall project." Shahed Saleem.

'Having experience of that relationship and that kind of back and forward is really similar to what we'd be doing in reality as well.' - Kitty Emery Rainbird

'You actually get to speak to people and if you're stuck inside a studio, you don't really get that opportunity. But this is live you go out, you interact, and then you take their input and possibly apply it to your design. So it becomes even more meaningful for the projects you work on.' - Kajana Chaounthara Gnanan March student

'You're actually going to build something that you've designed. But there are also a lot of issues that come up, and then you work through them with the contractor, which is really good.' - Jake Milton March student.

'It's really good being able to communicate with the clients, they're more willing to talk to you and understand why you're doing what you're doing, and I think that personal experience in that, I think it's really fulfilling.' - Joseph Kuforiji March student.

Values: *Connecting & Collaborating*: Bringing people together across generations to build community resilience.
Cultivating: Promoting sustainable living through organic and permaculture practices.
Creating: Supporting accessible arts, crafts, and skill-sharing opportunities.
Caring: Restoring heritage spaces with care for people and the environment.
Celebrating: Honouring local history and community achievements to foster pride and belonging.

Clitterhouse Farm has a rich history dating back to at least the 14th century, with its name believed to originate from "clite," an old English word for clay. Over the centuries, the site evolved from farmland serving the local manor into a working farm supporting the surrounding communities of what is now North West London.

By the 20th century, the farm had become part of the expanding urban landscape, falling into decline as development encroached. But in 2013, a group of local residents came together with a shared vision: to rescue Clitterhouse Farm's historic buildings and repurpose them as a vibrant community hub. This vision became Our Yard, a community-led social enterprise dedicated to restoring and revitalizing the farm. Through grassroots activism, partnership-building, and tireless volunteer support, Our Yard has transformed the site into a centre for social enterprise, sustainable living, and community cohesion.

Top: Students installing the precut wings and installing the column onto the foundation
Left: Photo with students after a day of installation sitting on the integrated benches of Our Canopy

ALEX MARTON

YUELIN ZHOU　　　HARDEEPAK SINGH PANESAR

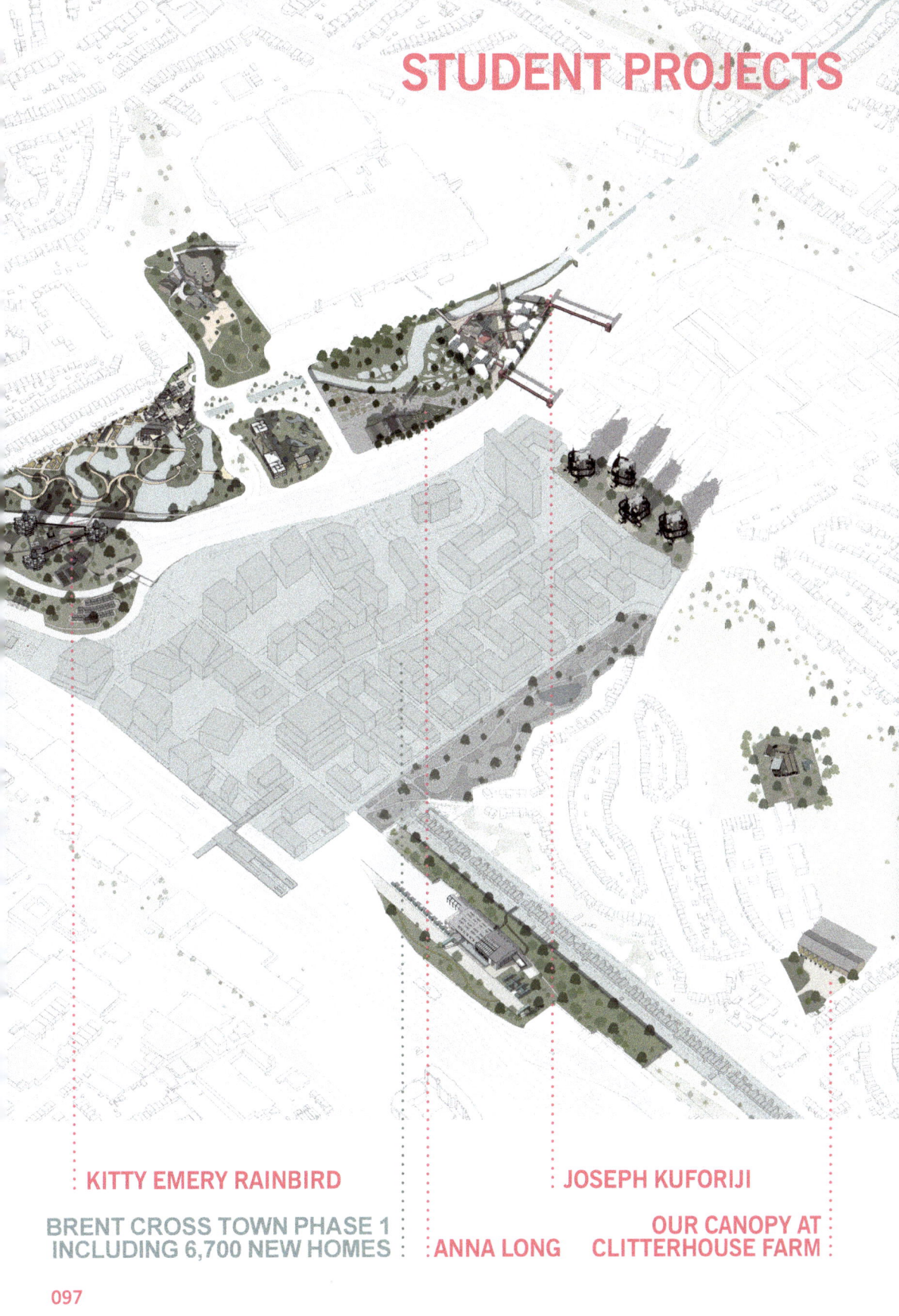

STUDENT PROJECTS

KITTY EMERY RAINBIRD
BRENT CROSS TOWN PHASE 1 INCLUDING 6,700 NEW HOMES

ANNA LONG

JOSEPH KUFORIJI
OUR CANOPY AT CLITTERHOUSE FARM

Beaver Timeline and Site Evolution

Year 0: Diverting River Brent, planting native wetland species. Releasing water voles (one of the fastest declining land mammals).

Year 1: Release beaver pair into fenced areas of the river and sponge wetland/woodland zone. Initial monitoring.

Year 2: Small dam constructions built along the river, shallow lodges built. Sedges and rushes begin to colonise wetland zones.

Year 3: Beaver kits born. Reed beds expand along the river and wetland zones. Water voles sighted along the river. Year 5: Expansion of dam network along river, extending into the sponge wetlands. Floodwater storage increases and flash-flooding downstream is reduced by 30%. 2-3 beaver populations. Diverse mosaic of wetland types provide refuge for wildlife.

Year 10: Sponge ecosystem is fully functioning, filled with diverse and rich land and water species. 2000% increase in aquatic habitat, with an increase in previously declining species.

BRENT CROSS TEXTILE COMMONS
WEAVING SLOWNESS INTO THE URBAN FABRIC

ANNA LONG

Aerial visual

In 2021, 90% of storm overflows discharged at least once, with 5% discharging over 100 times, including into or near 'high priority' nature sites, such as Brent Reservoir. We need to find more natural approaches to storm water management, rather than overwhelming the sewage systems which ultimately damage natural water bodies. Brent Cross Textile Commons focuses on slowing down the River Brent, stormwater absorption, and the community.

Jonathon Bell's book 'Carchitecture: When the Car and the City Collide' discusses the beginnings of the automobile, and how it has reconfigured cities and landscapes to accommodate the human desire for speed, movement and freedom. The proximity of the motorway to the site, which was an underused overflow parking lot for the adjacent Brent Cross Shopping Centre, led to a concern that we humans have grown to accept this normality of traffic noise, pollution, acres of tarmac and motorways, but we need to remember the importance and benefit of slowing down.

Additionally, climate change has had a huge impact on cities, with flash floods becoming more normal. However, our storm overflows are unprepared for these events, and the shortcut to removing water quickly is to discharge it into natural water bodies. Last year, the Met Office stated that we should expect future flash floods to be four times as frequent, meaning that we must begin to repair the ground surfaces to make them permeable, to absorb the stormwater. The existing site sits with the canalised River Brent flowing alongside it, and Textile Commons proposes to meander the river into the site, to slow the river flow down, as flash floods also lead to a quicker flow, and thus, a higher risk of flooding downstream.

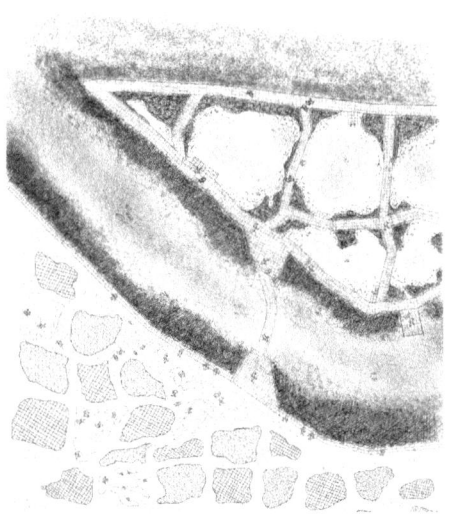
Layers of landscape

The site will introduce a Eurasian beaver pair to the diverted River Brent, to create a successful mechanism for flood prevention. Wetland trees, such as Alder, Poplar, and Willow, will have been planted around the river and the wetland zones, to be used as fell trees for the beaver dams. These trunks will slow the river flow, spread floodwaters across the sponge zones, as well as provide habitat for biodiversity to form. The slower water flow allows for heavier sediment to sink to the bottom, meaning that cleaner water can continue downstream to the Brent Reservoir. Wetland specialist species, amphibians, fish, insects, and plants, have more opportunity to flourish in clean water conditions.

The wetland zones in the site act as a floodplain to hold excess water during heavy downpours, slowly absorbing it into the ground and slowly releasing into the river. The site sponge will retain stormwater up to a few weeks. Allowing the ground to soak up water naturally is the key concept of sponge cities - copying nature rather than fighting it with traditional hard solutions of concrete and canals. The site acts as a large sponge, storing stormwater, reducing the risk of flooding downstream and alleviating drought conditions.

Micro-scale: Gabion Habitats
Excavated material from site will be recycled into the gabion cages, reducing the need to take it off site, and gaps in the gabion cages allow for biodiversity to flourish, providing habitat for invertebrates and native wildlife.

Meso-scale: Reedbeds
The reedbeds contribute to a healthy river system through their natural filtration methods, removing pollutants from the water, providing oxygen for the water, and providing excellent habitat for fish, invertebrates and birds to live in.

Macro-scale: The Beaver
The beaver's ecosystem engineering develops complex waterscapes along the river and wetlands to slow down the river flow, reduce flooding downstream, remove pollutants from the water, and provide important habitats.

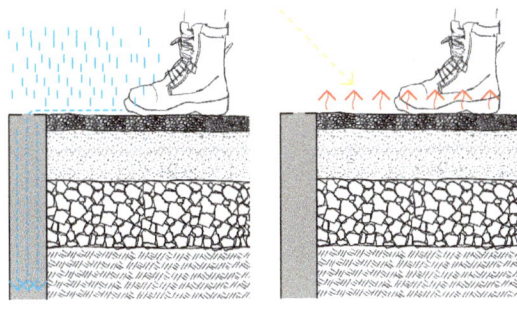

Section Diagram of Existing Asphalt

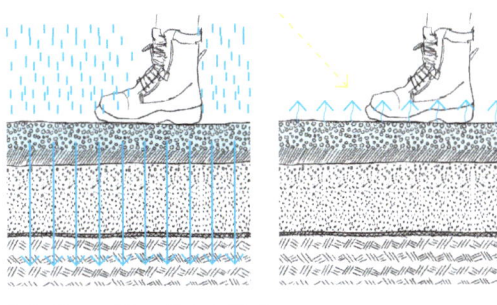

Section Diagram of Permeable Asphalt System

Asphalt was used across the whole existing parking lot. During heavy rain periods, the asphalt cannot absorb the stormwater. The surface water runs off into drainage pipes, often overwhelming the sewage systems, leading to floods and overflows into natural bodies of water. Asphalt also contributes to the urban heat island effect by absorbing solar energy, released as thermal energy, thus increasing heat gains.

Textile Commons depaves the asphalt and reuses it in a permeable asphalt system. During heavy rain periods, stormwater can filter slowly through the permeable asphalt layers, releasing into the earth. Tarmac's system allows for insitu flow rates of 8,000mm per hour. The permeable asphalt system mitigates the urban heat island effect through localised cooling, as water held within the voids of the asphalt evaporates, creating a cooling effect.

The theme of circular material reuse continues in the production building that grows from the landscape itself, where locals engage in hands-on brick production, made from recycled materials such as demolished construction material, combined with bio materials grown on site, such as corn stalks and hemp. These 'rebirth bricks' would then be used in small-scale construction projects across site, as well as the wider community sites, reinforce the project's ethos of reuse, slowness, and regeneration.

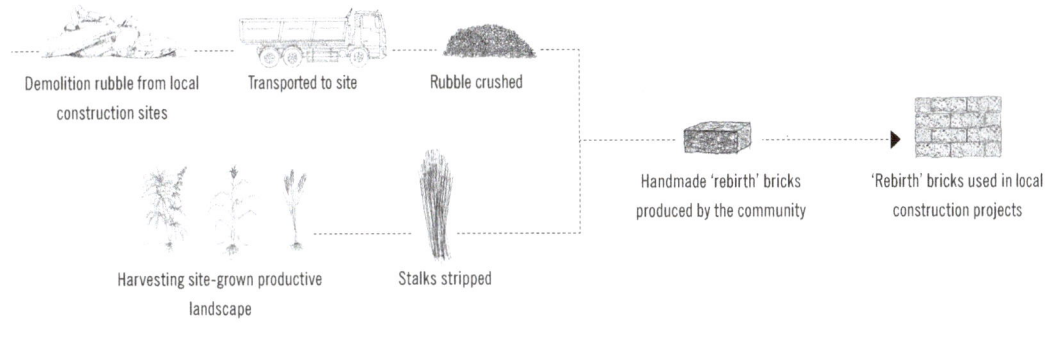

Demolition rubble from local construction sites

Transported to site

Rubble crushed

Handmade 'rebirth' bricks produced by the community

'Rebirth' bricks used in local construction projects

Harvesting site-grown productive landscape

Stalks stripped

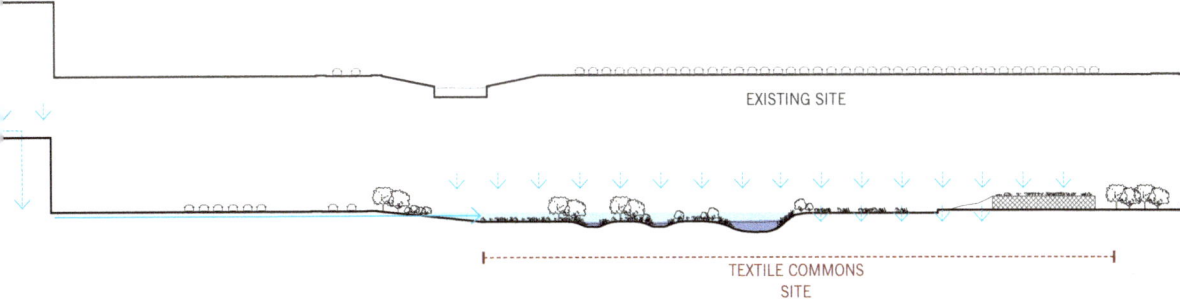

EXISTING SITE

TEXTILE COMMONS SITE

9.7 million litres of Brent Cross Shopping Centre surface water run-off per year is redirected to the site. The 26,000m² converted site will save the drainage systems 6.3 million litres of stormwater per year.

During a flash flood, the sponge wetlands can retain up to 15,000m3, with the river level increasing to up to 3.5m in depth, allowing 22,000m3 of river water to flow slowly through the site during heavy periods. The site will significantly ease flood pressure from the River Brent through the sponge wetlands.

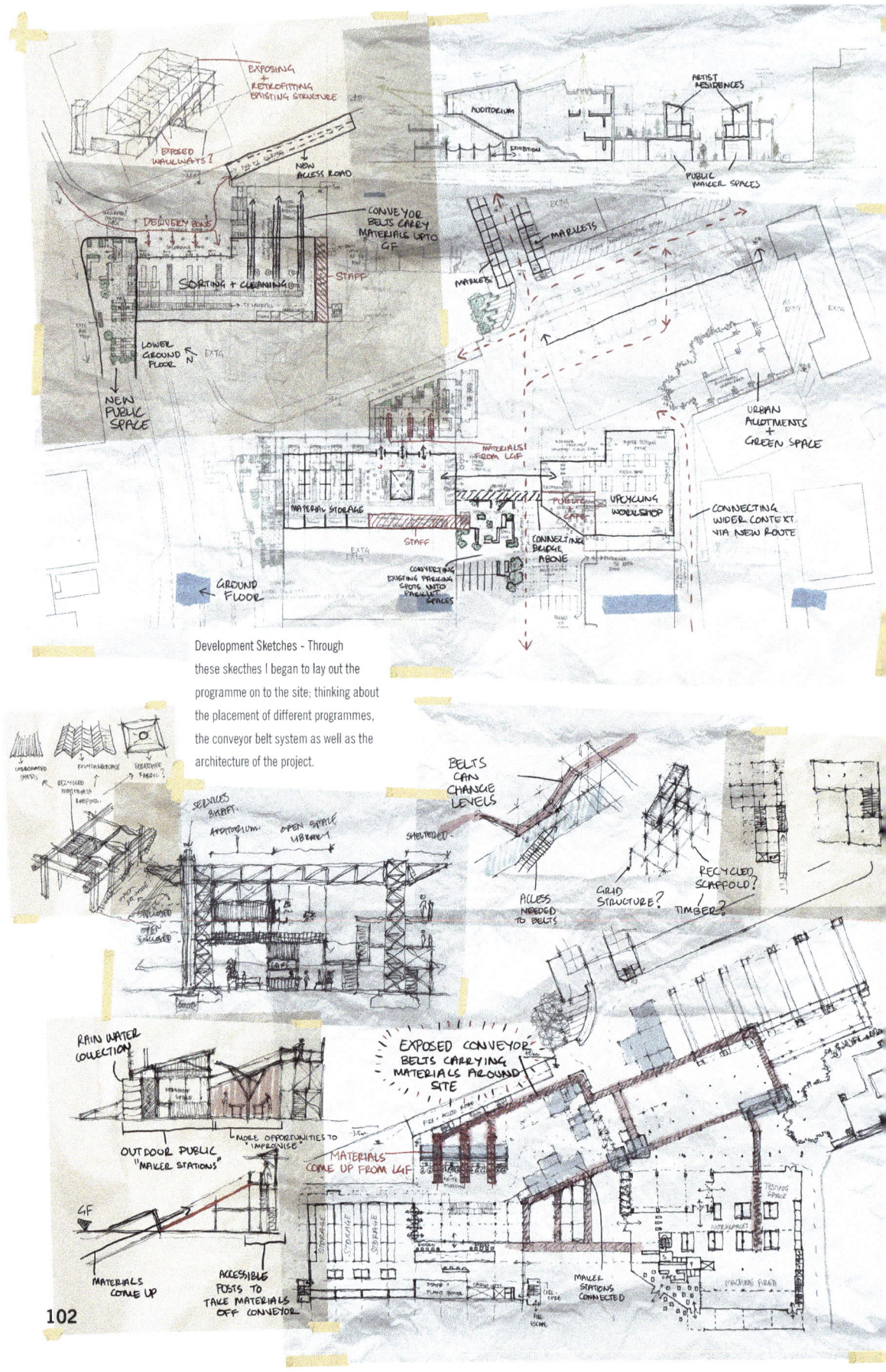

Development Sketches - Through these sketches I began to lay out the programme on to the site; thinking about the placement of different programmes, the conveyor belt system as well as the architecture of the project.

THE ADHOC AGORA
UPCYCLING, IMPROVISING AND FREE LEARNING

HARDEEPAK SINGH PANESAR

Aerial perspective of site

Our cities are slowly starting to be governed not by people, but by masterplans - rigid frameworks that prioritise efficiency, uniformity and profit over lived experience, spontaneity and community. In the face of these sanitised developments, acts of improvisation emerge as quiet resistance. From guerrilla gardening to self built cafes, people repurpose waste and reclaim space to meet real, immediate needs. Rather than a fixed architectural outcome, my proposal is a framework for continuous adaptation - encouraging the public to take part in the evolution of their environment.

Brent Cross is changing - fast. New developments are rising across the area, guided by large-scale masterplans that often overlook the informal, everyday ways people already shape their surroundings. Between industrial sites, houses, and redevelopment zones, traces of this resourcefulness remain: improvised gardens, self-built structures, reclaimed materials put to new use.

The AdHoc Agora grows from this spirit. It is not a finished building, but a framework—open-ended, evolving, and participatory. The Agora is a proposal for a building waste storage, up-cycling and fabrication centre, alongside a material passports database and material withdrawal centre. These facilities form the core basis for a dynamic site that connects people with resources and skills.

A network of conveyor belts moves construction waste around the site, connecting sorting zones, maker stations, green spaces and public spaces. Along the way, people take what they need, make what they want. Some stay, some build, some just pass through. Nothing is fixed. Everything is in progress.

The Agora proposes a civic architecture shaped by circular economy, care, and collective authorship.

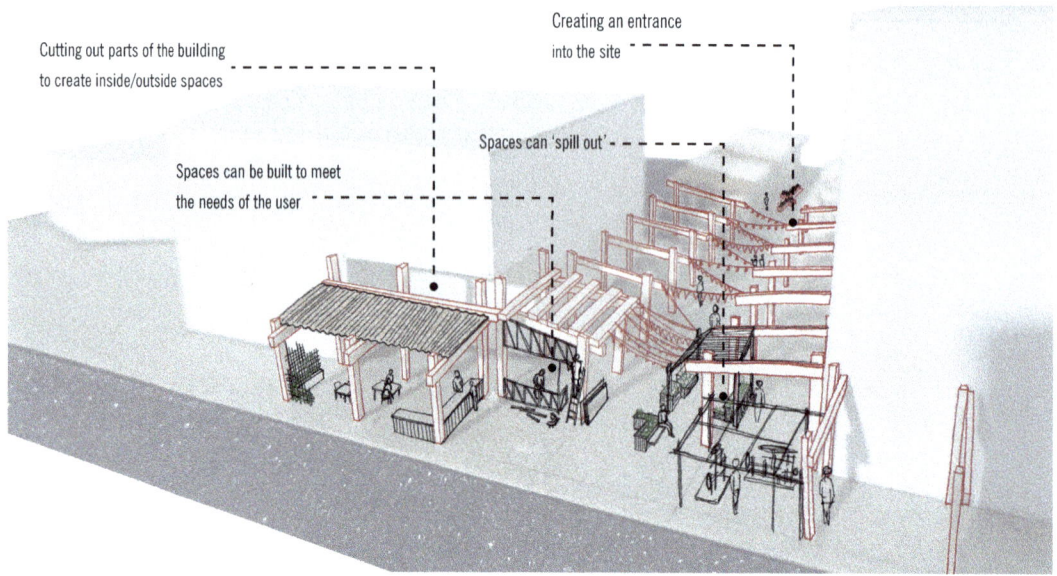

This development model proposes the use of a pergola like structure which works with the 'rigid architecture' on site while also creating an entrance into the site. The aim is for the spaces within the structure to be used in creative manners by the public. Spaces such as markets, local businesses, exhibitions/installations could be created by upcycling the materials stored on site.

The Agora is shaped by the spirit of Adhocism. Coined by Charles Jencks and Nathan Silver, Adhocism is a philosophy of working with what's at hand - solving problems through creative improvisation and resisting rigid systems. It values spontaneity, resourcefulness, and agency. At its core, it is deeply human. The AdHoc Agora embodies this in both form and function. Facades made construction waste, performance spaces formed from scaffold and fabric, conveyor belts not just for transport, but for transformation. These elements are not afterthoughts; they are the architecture. Structures are designed to adapt - growing, shrinking, or disappearing as needed. The Agora is never finished. It's a test bed for new ways of building and being.

Improvisation here is both ethos and method. Scrap becomes signage, land becomes garden, walls become canvases. The site encourages users to bring their own skills, collaborate, and teach through action. No credentials required. The process is the pedagogy. This hands-on, informal learning challenges conventional architectural models. The Agora offers a participatory approach, where education and agency are shared. Volunteers, professionals, and local makers pass on skills in fabrication and repair. People are encouraged to test ideas, build temporary structures, and learn by doing - free from the barriers of formal planning systems. The managing body supports rather than restricts, shaping proposals with the community to keep the space open and adaptable. The architecture of the project is formed by retrofitted warehouses. Their industrial shells are softened with greenery and public additions, their facades textured with reused materials. These walls do not hide waste; they celebrate its transformation. Architecture becomes evidence of cycles, not obsolescence. Early in the design, the focus was on permeability. The site, once enclosed by roads, warehouses and zoning, is now more accessible. New entries are carved into old edges. Paths criss cross and blur the lines between programme and encounter. No space is fixed. No border is absolute.

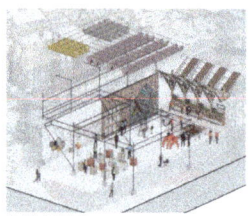
Public Exhibitions

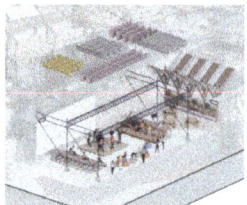
Performances

Upcycling Workshops

Pop Up Markets

One Space, Many Uses - The images aim to show how a single space can be 'improvised' in different ways to meet the needs of users.

Creating adaptable and resilient spaces.

Improvising with building waste to form the facades.

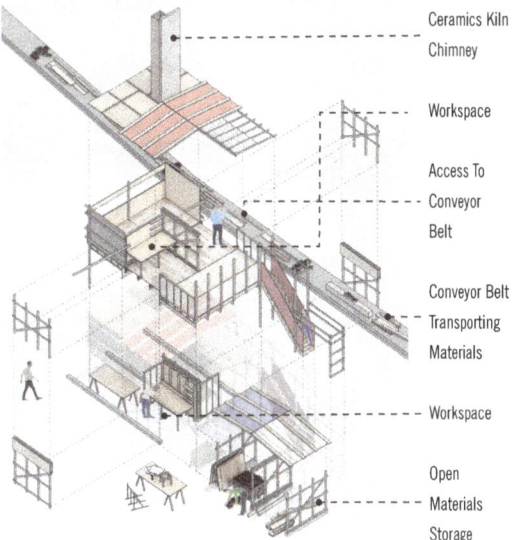

Ceramics Kiln Chimney

Workspace

Access To Conveyor Belt

Conveyor Belt Transporting Materials

Workspace

Open Materials Storage

The sustainability strategy is not an add on - it is the project. The AdHoc Agora establishes a physical circular economy through a network of conveyor belts and an open-access digital material database. Construction waste is delivered to the site, cleaned, sorted, and either stored or circulated via conveyor belts. Smaller materials - such as timber offcuts, sheet goods, bricks, and metal are transported around the site via the system of conveyor belts, while larger items are catalogued with material passports and held in storage for later use. Along the conveyor paths, 'maker stations' invite users to collect materials and fabricate on-site, encouraging hands-on reuse. This system offers a free and accessible way for people to source materials, promoting resourcefulness and reducing reliance on new products. Leftover materials are stored and made available to the public and contractors at reduced cost, supporting both environmental sustainability and local economies. The process embodies the ethos of Adhocism—making with what's available and adapting creatively to need.

Exploded axonometric breaking down the maker stations found along the conveyor belts. The maker stations are multi disciplinary which would allow people to 'improvise' through making. These maker stations would also allow access to the conveyor belts, allowing people to take materials off them in order to use.

Fundamentally, The AdHoc Agora is born of a personal ambition: to design places where architecture is more than form. Where it becomes a medium of exchange—between people, materials, and futures. Where innovation grows not from capital but from constraint. And where the city is not delivered, but made - repeatedly, with care, with others.

Top: Artist Impression Eye Level Perspective of the Industrial Domesticity project
Bottom: Initial Concept Sketch

INDUSTRIAL DOMESTICITY
SURVIVING AN IMPENDING SYSTEMIC COLLAPSE

ALEX MARTON

Aerial Overview of Industrial Domesticity, showing the first phase, the converted Big Yellow Self-Storage warehouse.

Industrial Domesticity reimagines urban development by embracing existing heritage and reusing overlooked industrial spaces. Set in the Staples Corner Industrial Estate, the project retrofits underused self-storage and warehouse units into hybrid residential-making spaces. It promotes a resilient, mixed-use urban fabric and reconnects the area to Brent Cross through a green, pedestrian-focused walkway.

Industrial Domesticity is a radical reimagining of city-making in the face of systemic failures in housing, economy and ecology. Set within the Staples Corner Industrial Estate in Brent Cross, North-West London, the project seeks to transform an overlooked and underutilised industrial zone into a socially resilient, self-sustaining urban district. Rather than erasing the past, it embraces the site's industrial fabric and layers in new programs of living, working and making.

The project challenges the top-down, profit-led approach typified by contemporary regeneration schemes, instead proposing an alternative rooted in adaptive reuse, community empowerment and incremental change. It avoids the 'tabula rasa' erasure of place, focusing on the careful retrofitting of existing warehouses, currently used for self-storage and light industry, into hybrid, multifunctional spaces that serve both current and future residents. Strategic phasing of the project allows for minimal displacement and maximum flexibility.

At its core, the proposal envisions a new urban logic: one where residential typologies, productive spaces, hydroponic farms and public amenities coexist within retrofitted industrial structures. The intervention is structured at three scales, the macro, meso and micro.

Warehouses are converted into mixed-use hubs that

A new biodiverse path through Brent Cross

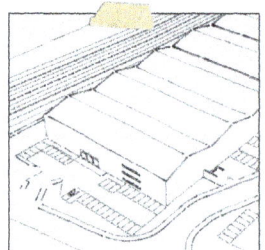

The Industrial Estate in its current condition. It's bare, vehicles dominate the area and it's transient.

The 'Landmark Tower' begins construction, using prefabricated CLT/GluLam elements.

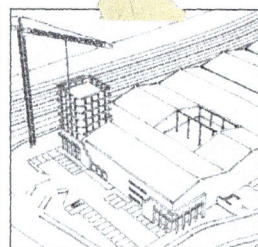

The middle courtyard is adapted for the greywater garden, the tower grows further.

The public realm undergoes transformation, vegetation is planted, softening the site.

A warehouse is converted to a makers' space and prefabrication hub, where internal partitions are made.

Users begin moving in, occupying the converted warehouses. The tower is completed and occupied.

Industrial Domesticity is bustling with diverse uses and activities, all making the area lively.

In 20 years, the project is not demolished, it is transformed. Spaces are reworked for future users and activities.

Perspective Cross Section drawing of the converted warehouses

blend domestic and productive programs, streets within the estate are softened and pedestrianised, supporting shared use, pop-up markets and community events and a new biodiverse pedestrian walkway reclaims lanes of the A406 North Circular, linking disconnected neighbourhoods and stitching the site back into the city.

Three prototype conversions explore the proposal's ambitions: one warehouse becomes a high-density landmark block with new housing built above retained office and storage spaces, another follows a monocentric model, arranged around a greywater courtyard that serves as both growing space and environmental modifier and the last takes a polycentric approach with dispersed courtyards and transparent workshop zones that invite public engagement. Rainwater harvesting and hydroponic systems support on-site food production and reduce external dependencies. Inspired by projects like Studio Bark's U-Build and ViviHouse, lightweight prefabricated components, assembled locally, allow for efficient, low-impact and low-carbon construction and future adaptability.

Stakeholder interviews, from builders and engineers to self-storage workers, offer grounded insights into the everyday realities and aspirations of people living and working in Brent Cross, which directly inform the design.

Industrial Domesticity is not a static masterplan, but a constantly evolving framework. It offers a counter-narrative to the homogeneity of speculative development by layering memory, infrastructure and culture. The project

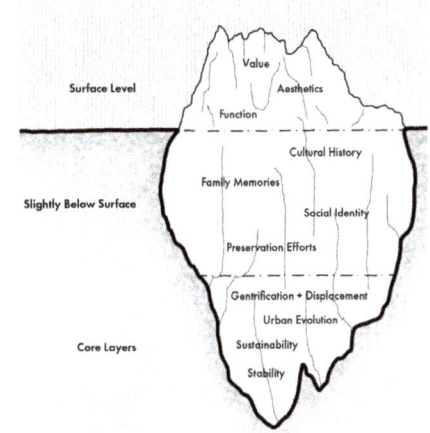

Top: Diagram of the 'Iceberg Theory' indicating what is visible is based on many invisible factors, such as cultural and social parameters

treats architecture as both a memory holder and a catalyst for interaction. The metaphor of ice, melting and losing form, becomes a powerful lens for understanding how urban histories are erased and how design can resist this

The project is an act of urban stewardship. It seeks not to perfect the city, but to make it layered and alive. It shows how architecture, through thoughtful reuse and engagement, can create environments where communities do not merely survive collapse, but thrive beyond it.

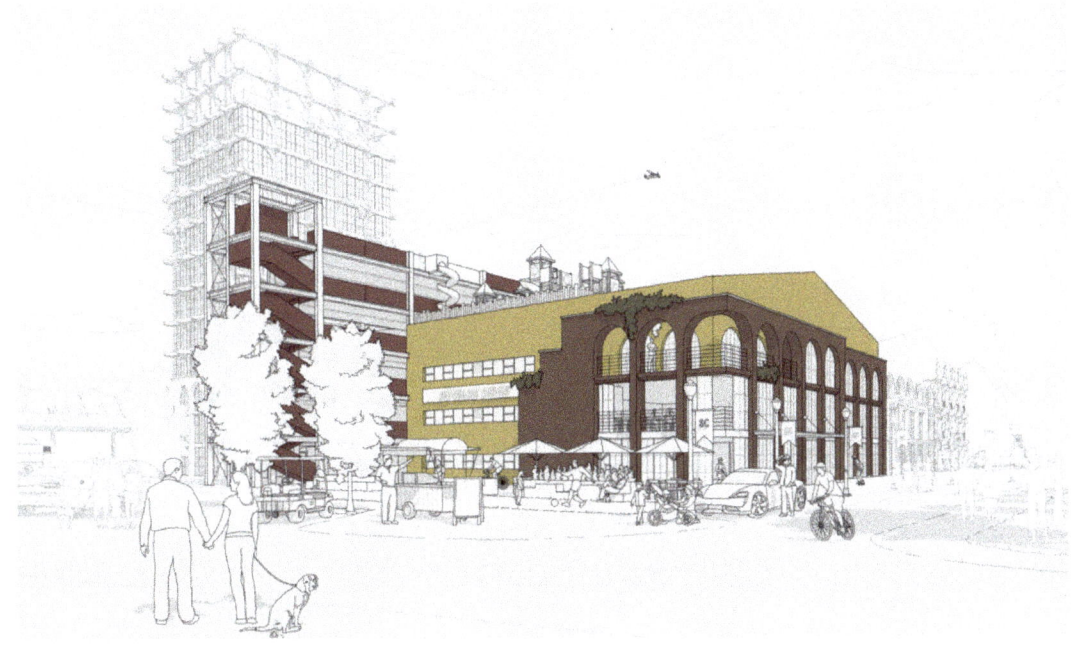

Artist Impression of transforming the existing warehouse into the multi programmatic proposal, including production, living and community facilities

Aerial Overview of The Hearth showing the entrance from Brent Cross shopping centre, the connections to the residential street adjacent, and the site's position within the context of the wider area and infrastructure

THE HEARTH
YOU MIGHT BE SUFFERING FROM CAPITALISM?
KITTY EMERY RAINBIRD

Final aerial axo render showing the relationship between the Hearth, the adjacent residential street, and the rewilded landscape.

We live in a time when we are no longer citizens of a nation, but a nation of consumers: our public services are being privatised at an alarming rate, and our lives are dictated by profit. - Through investigating the links between consumerism, late-stage capitalism and the mental health crisis, I have developed a proposal for a centre for Social Prescribing. This project explores the benefits that hand crafting and self build have on both physical and mental health, along with the impact of being part of an active and thriving community on our collective wellbeing

'All that is solid, melts into PR' Our minds are bombarded by advertising and propaganda. Individualism is lauded, community is dying. How can we escape? What can we escape to? Stop. Breathe. Take a seat. Don't worry, we're not going to charge you anything. Let's have a chat, we're in this together.

Based in Brent Cross, North London, 'The Hearth' explores the DS20 studio themes of Civic Permeability, examining how architecture can foster inclusivity, accessibility, and social connection within urban environments. Social Prescribing, a relatively new approach within the NHS, allows healthcare professionals to refer individuals to community-based support. Guided by a link worker, patients are connected to non-medical services and activities to improve their physical and mental well-being. Instead of relying solely on medication or clinical interventions, social prescribing recognises the wider social, emotional, and environmental factors that influence health. By emphasizing the importance of communal relationships, craft, and nature, the centre seeks to counteract both the isolating effects of consumerism, and the built environment's increasing detachment from nature.

The wider site seeks to embed itself into the local urban fabric, weaving into the surrounding residential area through accessible public routes, shared spaces, and permeable thresholds. Expanding outwards, land bridges connect the landscape with the fragmented natural habitats of the Brent Cross area, enhancing biodiversity, and encouraging a sense of integration and continuity between the built and natural environments.

At the heart of the landscape development is the re-meandering of the River Brent, a process which enriches biodiversity, and reintroduces wetlands and keystone species such as beavers. It slows the flow of water, reducing flood risks and enhancing the ecological health of the area. This intervention gives the community direct access to green spaces, widely recognised for their therapeutic benefits. The urban wetlands which form provide numerous benefits, including reducing flood risks, and improving water quality through the filtration of pollutants. They act as ecological sponges, absorbing excess rainwater and helping cities adapt to the increasing impacts of climate change. In addition to the benefits they provide humans, wetlands support rich biodiversity, offering crucial habitats for birds, insects, and aquatic life within the urban fabric.

The architectural composition consists of multiple buildings interconnected through a network of walkways. This arrangement encourages movement and interaction, while maintaining a permeable boundary between built and natural elements. The programme includes workshop spaces, allotments, greenhouses, a community kitchen, a swap shop, a centre for multi-generational care, an art trail, and an ecology walk, ensuring a diverse range of activities that cater to different social needs.

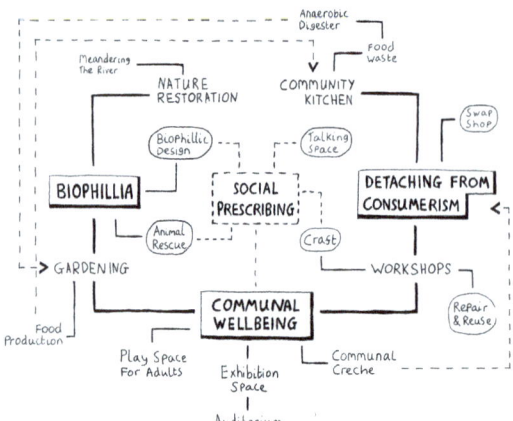

Initial Programme Diagram

As community needs evolve, the ability to modify or expand the buildings ensures relevance and longevity without the need for costly redevelopment. They have the resources to shape their own environment, reinforcing a sense of local ownership and collective agency, and deepening the community's relationship with the architecture. Skill-sharing and involvement in construction build local knowledge and confidence, fostering a sense of pride in the space.

East/West site section showing the relationship between the Hearth and the shopping centre to the east, and the new path of the River Brent with wilded landscape to the west.

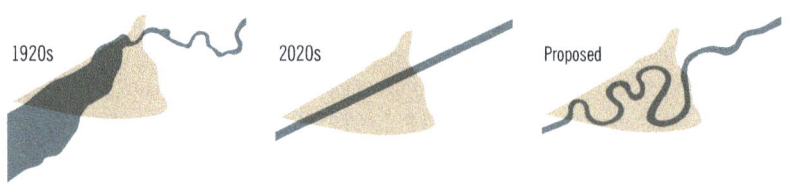

Evolution of the River Brent, showing the Brent reservoir in the late 19th century/early 20th century, the shrinkage of the reservoir and canalisation of the river in the mid 20th century, and the proposed re-meandering of the river.

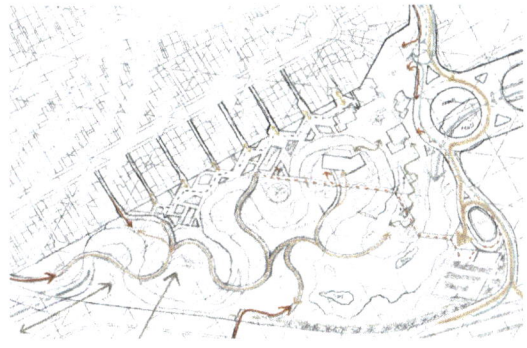

Early sketch of site-wide landscaping, and a concept strategy for access, and movement

Sketch diagram of material reclamation.

Sustainability is a key principle of the project, embracing a circular economy by integrating recycled materials, and taking a flexible, adaptable, approach to development. The project will repurpose construction waste from the demolition of post-war housing estates in the local area to create waste bricks. Manufactured on site, these bricks are made by breaking down the waste materials into component parts, separating the glass and concrete, and crushing it up so it can be mixed with hydraulic lime, sand, and calcium carbonate, and then formed, pressed, and cured. These bricks will be used during the initial phase of construction, which consists of the foundations and ground floors of the structures. This is provided by the local NHS foundation trust, and delivered by local tradespeople, providing a structure from which The Hearth can grow, and establishing the presence of holistic mental healthcare in the local area. During the second phase of construction, the timber frame which makes up the first floor and roof of the buildings will be constructed from Glulam timber beams made from scrap timber. This part of construction is a guided self build, led by the NHS trust in collaboration with the local people. This stage develops the knowledge and skills of the community, and over time, the project will expand into the third phase, which will be led by them.

Building de-constructed.

Demolition Waste Taken to Site.

Waste concrete and glass broken down into aggregate.

Mixed with hydraulic lime, sand, and calcium carbonate

Gardening has been shown to reduce stress, anxiety, and depression through physical exercise, exposure to nature, therapeutic structure, and increased self esteem.

Brick mixture poured into moulds

Bricks pressed into form under high pressure.

Bricks cured for two weeks in a humid environment.

Bricks air dried - mineral carbonisation strengthens them.

Recycled waste brick process

Community workshops offer hands-on, purposeful activities that foster connection and wellbeing. They provide safe, inclusive spaces where individuals can develop new skills, build confidence, and engaging with others, and improving mental health.

Visual - Café and outdoor birdwatching platforms

FEATHERED CONNECTIONS
BIRDWATCHING SCIENCE AND COMMUNITY CENTRE

YUELIN ZHOU

Aerial perspective from reservoir

Under the rapid development of modern metropolises, form-driven high-rises have become the dominant force in cities, severing the relationship between architecture and its surroundings, placing buildings in a position of dominance. Using the two existing nesting sites by the reservoir on the site as a starting point, I propose a "Birdwatching Science and Community Centre." The project does not take form as its priority but instead explores the vanishing boundary and the interconnected relationship between architecture, people, and the environment.

Losing Architecture. It doesn't mean losing. It means architecture not being in a leading position. Forms disappear but spatial connections appear. The people become the subject. ---Kengo Kuma

Feathered Connections is a wetland centre dedicated to bird observation and research. To explore the theme of "Civic Permeability" of DS20 Studio, the architecture deliberately avoids a form-driven approach, instead employing tree-like columns to create a "forest-like" structure. The boundaries between façades and forms are dissolved, allowing the building to blend seamlessly into its surroundings and fostering a connection between humans, nature, and birds.

Beyond providing enhanced opportunities for bird research and observation, the scheme offers additional nesting and breeding spaces for birds and waterfowl, attracting more migratory species. Additionally, the project incorporates a workshop, a community hub, and educational and exhibition spaces. While drawing visitors, it also aims to revitalise and stimulate the surrounding Brent Cross area, which is undergoing active development.

Situated on the shores of the Brent Cross Reservoir,

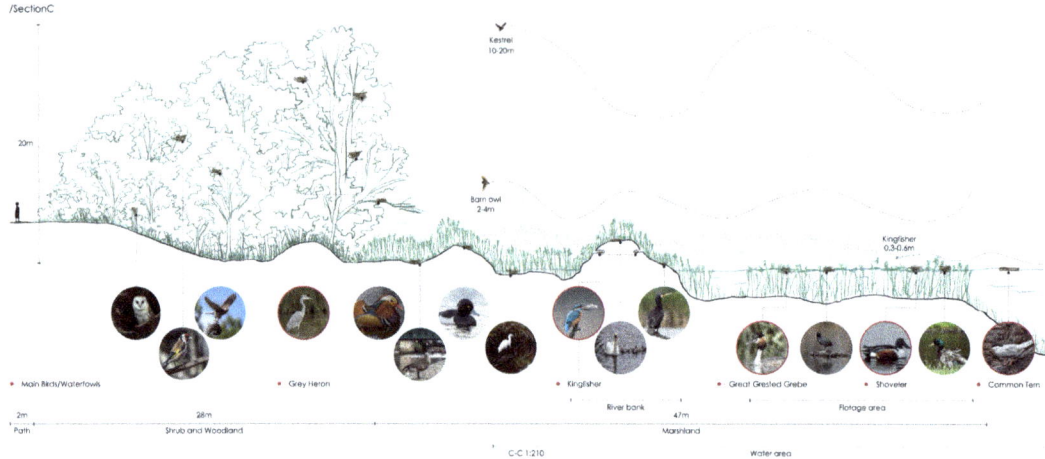

Section of buffer area - The main living areas and nesting sites of birds and waterfowl

the site is flanked by two existing nesting sites to the north and south. The primary migration, nesting, and breeding seasons occur in winter and summer. However, the reservoir faces challenges such as shrinking buffer zones due to urban expansion, as well as environmental and water pollution. The project necessitates effective management of existing trees and wetlands, mitigating the impact of urban development on the reservoir's natural surroundings. By safeguarding these ecosystems, it aims to protect biodiversity, particularly for bird species and other wildlife dependent on this habitat.

The project is located in the entrance area of the main road in the northern part of the reservoir, connecting the eastern and western sides of the reservoir. Based on research into the local buffer area and waterfowl, the project primarily focuses on five species of migratory and nesting waterbirds as the main subjects of study. Their nesting locations, habits, and the resulting artificial nesting

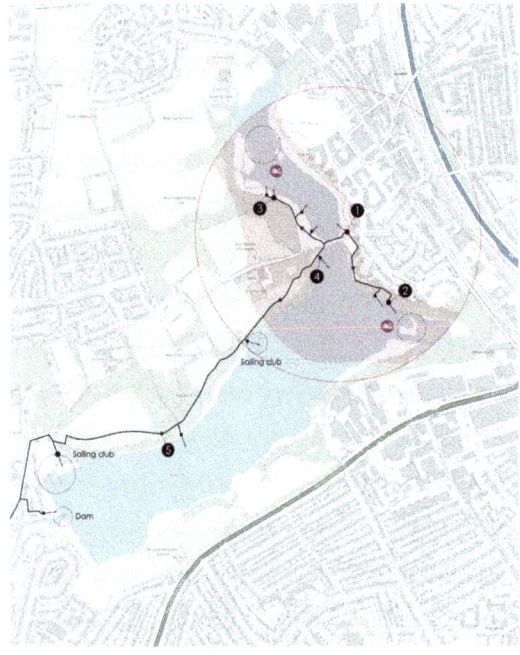

Route in site - The two existing nesting sites are situated on the northern and southern banks of the reservoir's western section, constituting important local biological resources. Surrounding them are several deteriorated viewpoints that were originally constructed for observing these nesting sites.

Core concept - The columns form a forest-like structure, while the curved roof mimics mountains, seamlessly blending the architecture into its surroundings. The building's boundaries dissolve and blur, fostering a stronger connection between birds, nature, and humans.

structures inform the logic behind the architectural design.

The goal of the landscape design is dedicated to protecting local biodiversity—by creating an artificial wetland at the centre of nesting sites, which not only provides more nesting and habitat opportunities for waterfowl but also offers people more chances to observe birds up close. The artificial wetland is divided into pond and land areas, forming a buffer zone that transitions from the forest area to the water. Their shapes are inspired by the natural wetland landscapes of the UK.

The main architectural complex is arranged in a triangular configuration around the artificial wetland, minimizing ecological disruption while enhancing opportunities for nature immersion. Rather than being form-driven, the design derives its fundamental hexagonal module for wooden columns from local woven thatch patterns. The planar layout establishes basic building boundaries through hexagonal arrangements, which are then dissolved by the introduction of curved glazed facades. Ultimately, the undulating green roof system camouflages the structure within its environment - eschewing definitive formal expression in favour of rich spatial experiences. Here, architecture recedes as the protagonist, giving way to intensified spatial interconnections.

The project embodies environmentally conscious and sustainable construction principles. Utilizing locally sourced British timber for primary columns and roof structures, the design mimics arboreal habitats - the treelike wooden columns incorporate vegetation and artificial nesting boxes at their tops, much like birds would naturally nest in tree canopies. Visitors can ascend through the building to the rooftop observatory for close-range birdwatching or to enjoy sunlight on the green roof terrace. At the same time, it activates and drives the development of Brent cross and surrounding area.

Visual of roof structure

Basic pillar model - shows the relationship between two sizes of pillars

Visual - It is divided into 1 Indoor pillars and roof structure 2 Outdoor pillars structure 3 Artificial wetland

Conceptual Collage - exploring what a new civic could represent for the Brent Cross Community.

CIVIC OF MANY VOICES
ENVISIONING A NEW CIVIC FOR BRENT CROSS

JOSEPH KUFORIJI

Civic of many voices - Site Axonometric

Inspired by the increasing loss of civic buildings as spaces for cultivating community and cultural identity in our increasingly digital age, The Civic of Many Voices proposes what a new civic could look like for the Brent Cross region. Rooted in the perspectives of local communities and their responses to ongoing changes in their built environment, the project aims to create shared spaces where people can come together to celebrate their cultures, histories, and futures.

Based in Brent Cross, North London, The Civic of Many Voices builds upon the themes explored in the dS20 Studio of Civic Permeability. It investigates how architecture can serve as a means to explore and promote connection and permeability within the shared spaces of our built environment.

The project responds to the growing loss of civic buildings in the 21st century and highlights their crucial role in fostering community engagement and cultural identity. Increasingly, these spaces are underused or undervalued within many communities, as people often choose to gather digitally rather than physically. However, despite this shift, we continue to see rising loneliness, isolation, and a decline in community engagement and cultural belonging in modern society.

This project aims to explore the importance of civic spaces as places that can nurture the traits we are losing—connection, belonging, and shared identity, asking ; What could a new civic look like for different communities?

Focusing on the Brent Cross area, the region currently undergoing major urban redevelopment intended to benefit the wider community, the project acknowledges how such transformations can significantly impact the social and built fabric of the region. Community engagements meetings were conducted with various Brent Cross communities to understand what "civicness" means to them, their history with Brent Cross, and their concerns on how the new developments might affect their local and wider communities. A recurring theme emerged: a fear of cultural erasure and the loss of shared spaces and histories. To address these worries, the project proposes a design centred around the voiced needs and aspirations of local communities. Selected uses included healthcare facilities, archives, learning spaces, allotments, and places for gathering and community expression. Together, these elements form a civic hub that can cultivate a stronger sense of belonging and celebration amid the changing landscape.

A key design strategy to achieve this vision was the use of polycentric civic cores across the site. These multi-use civic cores act as spaces where local residents can gather, celebrate, and voice their concerns. By creating several cores rather than a single central hub,

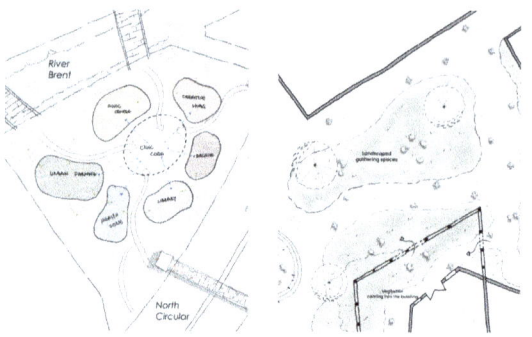

Design Sketches - Exploring strategies to create multiple points of gathering and enhancing vegetation.

the proposal allows for multiple events and gatherings to happen simultaneously, creating opportunities for organic interactions as people move through the site.

Vegetation was also explored as a way of enhancing connection and permeability within the scheme. Each hub is connected to surrounding green spaces that flow into the architecture itself, creating natural points of gathering and relaxation both inside and out. This integration softens the built environment, reinforcing the project's civic and social aims by encouraging interaction and relaxation.

Polycentric civic cores surrounding the civic buildings, creating spaces for gathering and celebration as multiple events co-occur. As community members move between different uses, they can organically encounter these events, fostering spontaneous interaction and engagement.

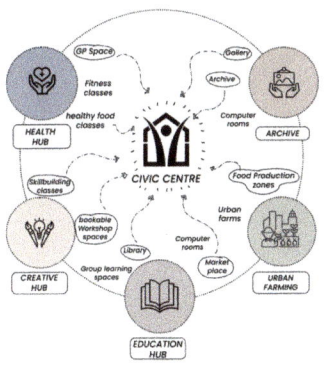

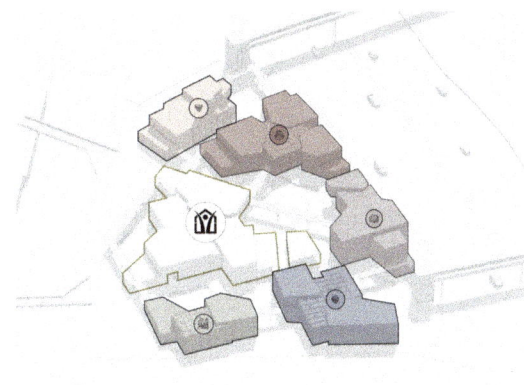

Initial Program Diagram - created from community consultation meetings.

Initial proposal of all uses separated in hubs located around the site.

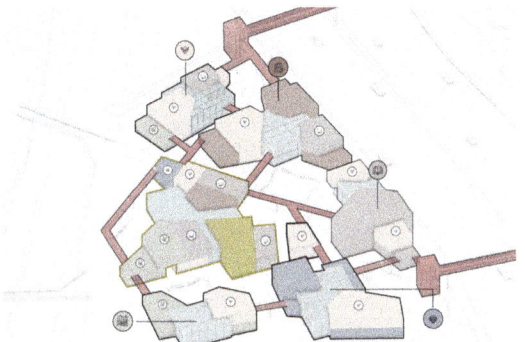

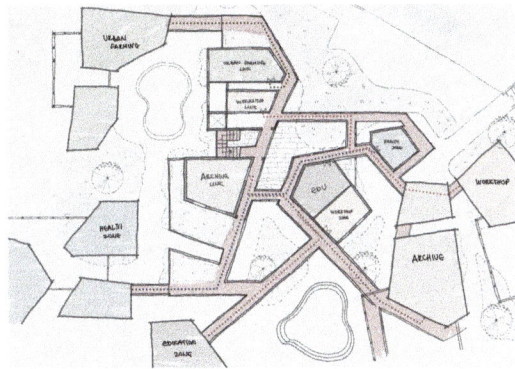

Visualisation of interconnected uses around the site, connected via walkways.

Design Sketch - initial explorations of the connected uses spread across the site.

Civic centre internal civic cores - creating an area of community gathering within the building, where those accessing the walkways can interact with the events taking place.

Connected walkways - allowing connecting community members to the different uses spread around the site, while providing areas to gather and watch events taking place on the civic cores below.

Interconnectivity between programs was also central design strategy. Initially, each program proposed through community consultation was planned within separate hubs. However, this adapted into a model where each hub is interconnected by sharing different functions. This blending of uses breaks down segregation and reflects the increasingly mixed character of the communities who will use the civic hub.

This idea is embodied in the central civic centre located at the heart of the site. Each of its programs is directly connected to the surrounding hubs, making the building an important point of gathering where community members can flow organically in and out, interacting with the events taking place within its internal civic core.

Walkways were also a key design implementation seen around and within the site, further reinforcing these connections. These pathways not only link different programs and hubs but also traverse many of the civic cores, enabling community members to engage with the activities taking place below. In this way, the walkways become key points of interaction and visibility, fostering a richer sense of community engagement and permeability.

OPEN 2025 Launch party
Below - DS20 students and tutors at the OPEN exhibition launch evening

OPEN 2025

DS20 END OF YEAR EXHIBITION

OPEN 2025 - DS20's end of year exhibition space.

It was important to us to celebrate the work we produced throughout the year, and that our end-of-year show was a culmination not just of individual design work, but of the collective spirit and collaboration that defined our unit. In DS20, the design and curation of the exhibition is student-led, and we pushed ourselves to create something that truly captured the ethos of our work. This allowed us to create a space that not only showcased our architectural proposals but also celebrated our shared experiences, particularly the live project we delivered together.

This process of designing, fabricating, and curating together became an extension of our architectural thinking, materialising not just the end product, but the collective journey behind it. Along with a film of our live project build, we exhibited a 1:1 prototype we made in Kent with Nick our fabricator. Placing this in the space highlighted the real-world testing and hands-on making that grounded our academic work.

We carefully considered how to use the wooden panel system constructed for the wider exhibition. By alternating panels, we introduced depth and allowed for glimpses of light and external views, while also forming niches to display physical models. The exhibition was divided into five thematic and geographical zones, helping contextualise each project within its site and narrative. Central to the exhibition was a collaborative Brent Cross site model, which brought together all of our individual schemes. This consisted of a unified axonometric plan, which we CNC cut and rigid media printed onto a plywood base. Our individual projects were represented by 3D printed models atop laser-cut and engraved plinths, mounted on transparent acrylic legs.

APPLIED MAKING
THROUGH COMMUNITY + ECOLOGY AT THE RIVER LEA

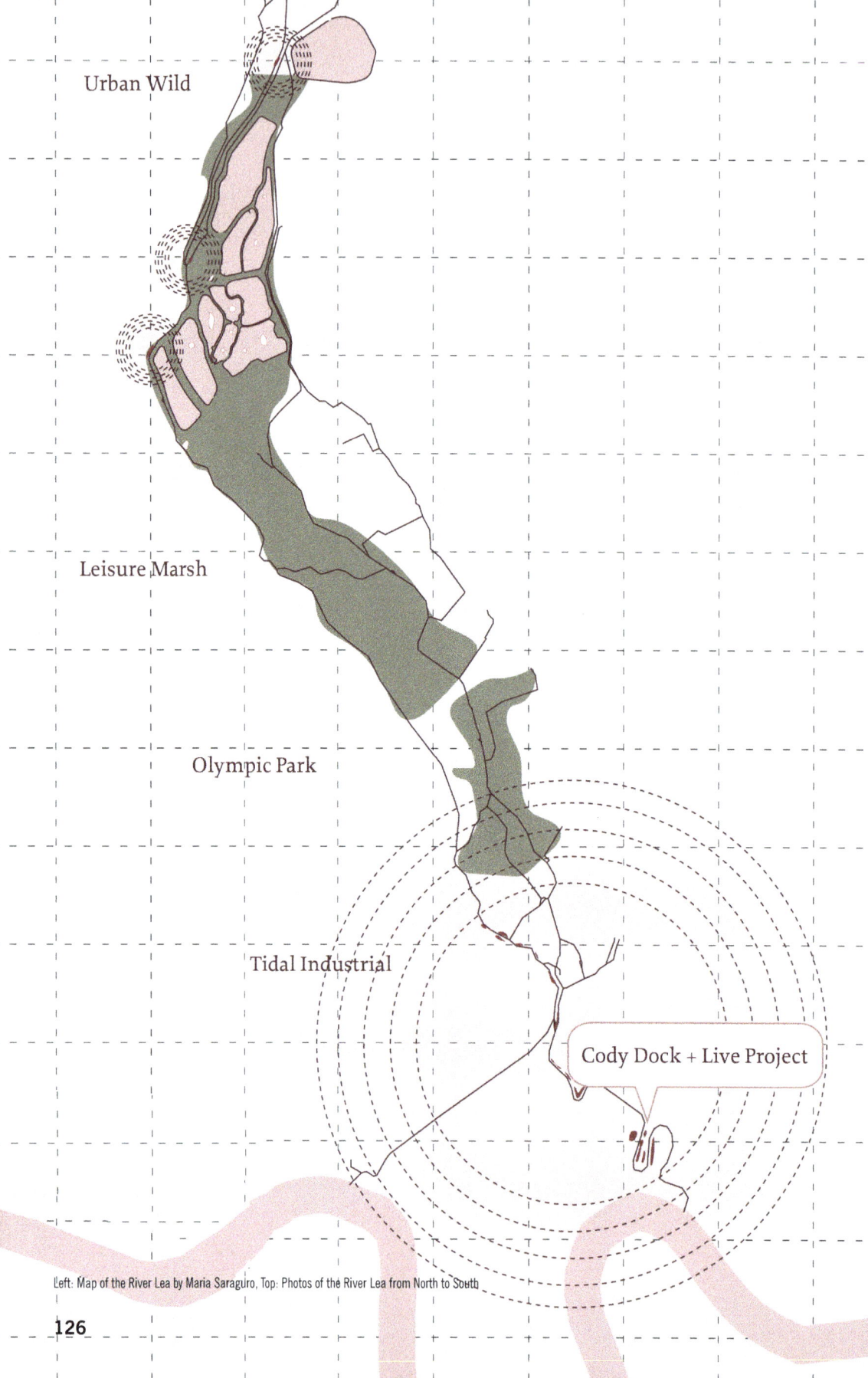

Left: Map of the River Lea by Maria Saraguro, Top: Photos of the River Lea from North to South

THE RIVER LEA

The River Lea is one of 210 chalk rivers in the world. The more agricultural economy in the North contrasts with the shifting former Post-industrial sites and city back-up services in the Lower Lea, which leads to London's hard core financial district at Canary Wharf on the Thames and the adjacent underdeveloped Royal Docks.

Historic global events on the macro scale have had an impact on the micro scale, such as the river being the border between Anglo-Saxons and the Danish, Cody Dock being a major coal distribution centre and now cleaning up the polluted dock with volunteers, citizen scientists and Live Projects whilst major housing developments are taking place of more than 50,000 flats in the surrounding area, which is the highest developmental activity in the UK.

We explored how water-both as infrastructure and designed landscape-has played a central role in urban modernisation, shifting its view from a rural, organic element to a biophysical resource. This shift created new nature-culture relationships, prompting us to question whether there is still room for an understanding that imagines a more empathetic watery future. The tensions within sensitive ecologies cannot be resolved through conservation alone: How can we include the intricate and intimate relations between nature and culture? How can we respond to changing terrain and include not just human practices but also non-human entities and natural forces? How can we work with shifting weather, waters and soils in more accessible ways?

We examined water in multiple roles-tidal systems, drainage, harvesting, and biodiversity-in designing new ecological landscapes amid the climate crisis. With droughts and floods creating extreme conditions, climate urbanism now demands attention to soil health and water decontamination. We focused on experimenting with individual materials at scale 1:1, based on low embodied or recycled materials, which also helped inform the Live Project at Cody Dock. The initial material investigation and experimentation were extended into studying the River, in regard to multiple relationships such as between social, political and cultural factors, running through different ecologies and economies. Proposals emphasise the power of slow placemaking in shaping spaces collaboratively, fostering organic growth, addressing ecological challenges, and demonstrating resilience based on a circular understanding of natural processes including seasonality and tidal cycles.

Touching the reeds from The Floating Forest Live Project, photo by author

THE FLOATING FORUM

LIVE PROJECT

2023-2024

**TUTORS: MARIA KRAMER AND CORINNA DEAN
STUDENTS: ELISA DEFRIES, KITTY EMERY RAINBIRD, JENNY FOSTER, MARIA GLEED ELINA, LOTTIE GREENWOOD, ALEX MARTON, SHANNON MCCADDON, STEVEN OP, GBEMISOLA OSINAIKE, HARDEEPAK PANESAR, NATALIA PETROVA, JONATHAN RAFFRAY, YAEL SCHNITZER, ALISTAIR SEARCH, ATHETHAN VARMAN, BENJAMIN WONG, GALINA DIMOVA, MARIA FERNANDA SARAGURO PALTIN
FUNDER: UNIVERSITY OF WESTMINSTER QHT FUND
PARTNERS: WEBB YATES ENGINEERS, NICHOLAS ALEXANDER**

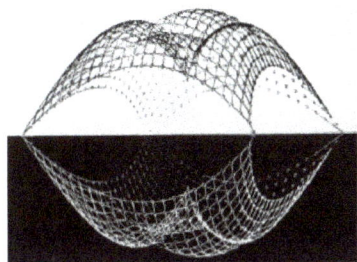

A form-finding experiment by Frei Otto illustrates Hooke's principle of inversion. Photo: Schanz

Isler's process of hardening an inverted surface (left) and then carefully measuring the resultant form (right). Photos: Chilton

'The Floating Forum' Live Project adds to the existing cluster of buildings making up Cody Dock's community hub. The Floating Forum accommodates for exhibition, workshops and bird watching and helps the community to widen their offer and become self sufficient.

The pavilion was co-designed and co-constructed the pavilion from the conception, briefing and making in collaboration with Webb Yates Engineers and Nicholas Alexander.

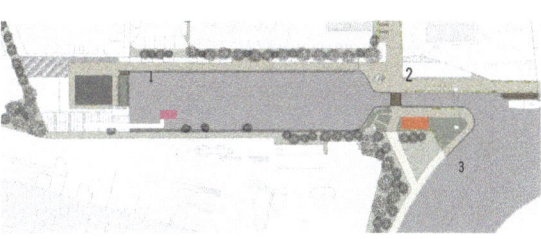

1 Location of the Floating Form   2 Location of the Growing Space   3 River Lea

"The disused coal barge dock lies at the heart of Cody Dock - not only in geography, but as a living space, vibrant and unexpected amidst the surrounding industry. Its brick cavities host nesting Sand Martins, returning each year from North Africa. Beneath the water's surface, Roach, Carp, Three-spined Sticklebacks, and Smooth Newts find refuge, while in summer the reedbed trembles with the voices of Reed Warblers, House Sparrows, and Goldfinches. Twelve species of dragonfly and damselfly hover and dart, their presence mirrored by the flash of a Kingfisher diving for prey.

The Floating Forum draws us into this abundance. No longer passive onlookers, *we find ourselves among the reeds, on the water, woven into the dock's ecosystem. To step onto it is to shift our perspective: from separation to belonging, from observers to participants. In this reclaimed corner of the city, we encounter not just wildlife but the reminder that we are part of the same living fabric"* Gino Brignoli, ecologist and biodiversity Officer at Cody Dock

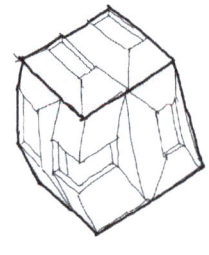

Top: Photo of heron at the River Lea with kind permission by Zuzanna Rydz
Top right: Artist Impression and material experimentation by author
Right: Interior Artist Impression and sketch by Alex Marton; bottom
Right: Model of pavilion proposal by Lottie Greenwood
Above: Internal and external reed elevations by Maria Saraguro

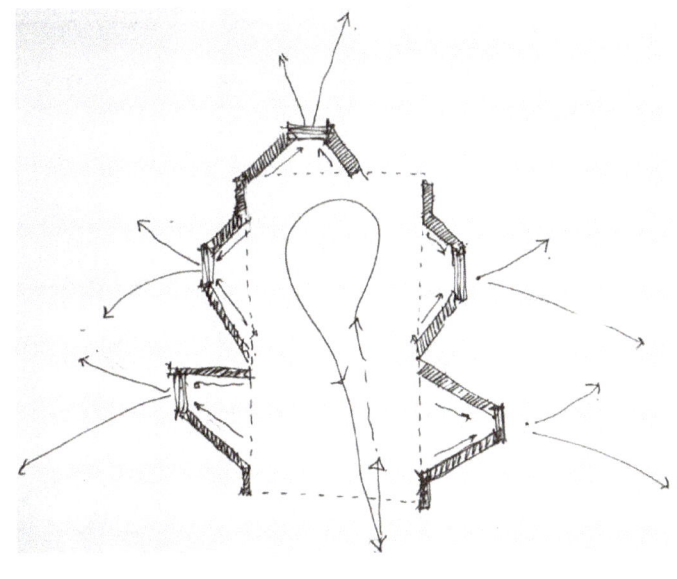

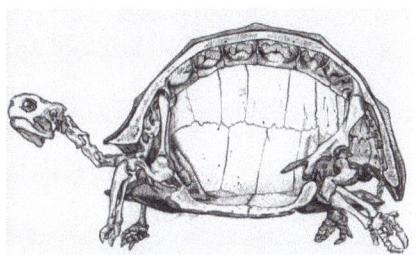
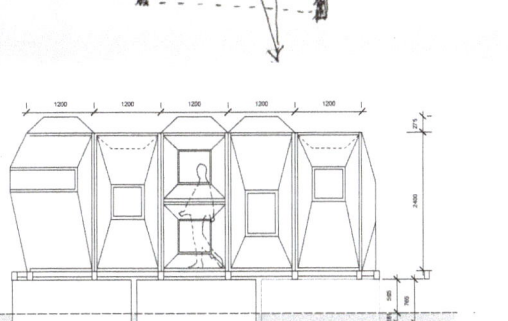

Initially, students developed individual proposals (see opposite page), also based on material explorations. Rather than designing a simple 'flat box,' the initial concept focused on framing specific views of the dock, as the space was also intended to serve as a bird-watching pavilion. A key anecdote from the local ecologist, Gino Brignoli, during our site visit to Cody Dock strongly influenced this approach. He showed us the spot where a heron regularly bashes fish against the dock wall to kill them while standing on a particular maintenance ladder. We wanted to frame this moment, and that's where the idea for the openings first emerged.

The desire to frame views led to the need for a more sculptural, three-dimensional façade that projected outward (see plan sketch above). Rather than constructing this spatial concept from plywood (see 3D sketch at the top), we worked with Steve Webb to develop the idea of using hessian fabric and gravity to find the optimal structural form under tension for the sculptural view-framing panel system.

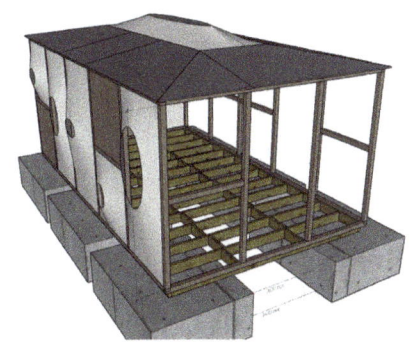

Top: Plan sketch and elevation by Alex Marton; Right from top: the design follows the tortoise shell principle of scutes; Hainz Isler Form Finding; Nic Runeckles standing on the first test panel to check its strength; Digital 3D model by Nicholas Alexander;

Top: Making of the panels at the warehouse of Nicholas Alexander
Top right: Sketch by Jenny Foster
Right: Photos of the making of the panles by Kitty Emery Rainbird and Maria Kramer

The ~20 sqm structure sits on reclaimed pontoons and is constructed from cedar timber with modular light weight hessian panels treated with gypsum and acrylic resin that have been prefabricated using the principle developed by the engineer Heinz Isler using flexible textiles. Allowing the fabric to hang downward under gravity, results in shapes which are naturally efficient as the hanging structure because it is in pure tension under gravity and does not resist any bending.

We explored new techniques based on manipulating materials to understand their innate properties and environmental properties to develop an architecture that embodies the fluidity of the world, where borders are not rigid divisions but dynamic, responsive membranes. Leveraging gravity creates forms that are in pure tension, naturally efficient and structurally sound.

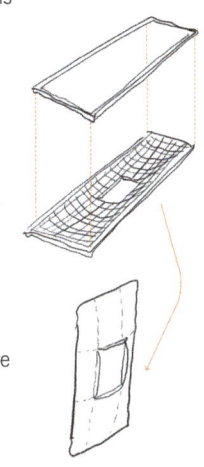

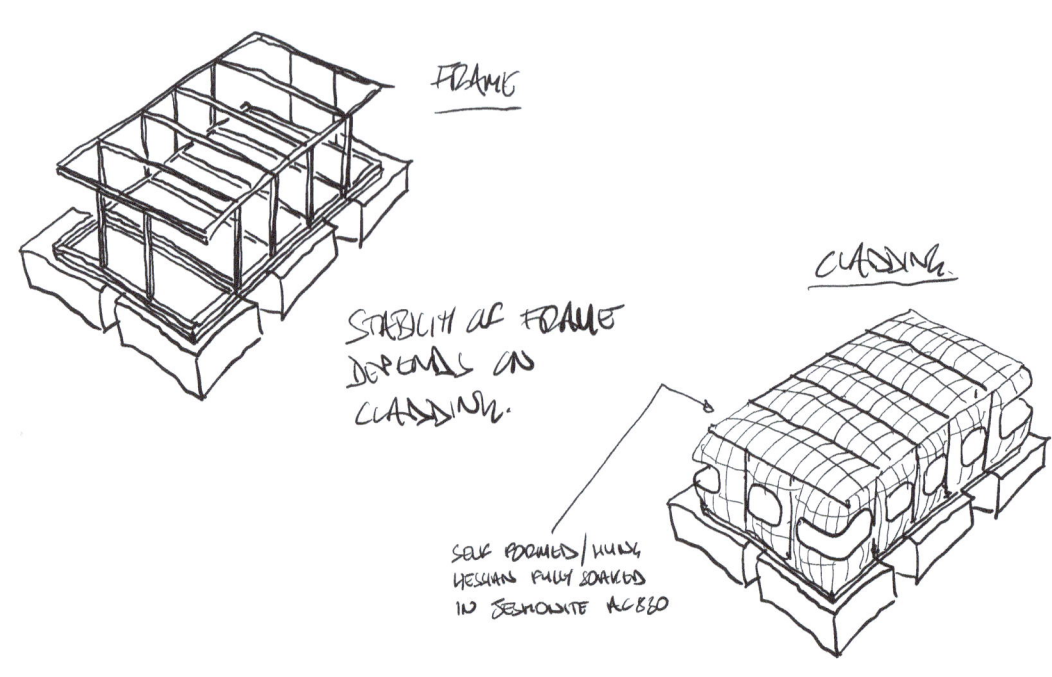

FRAME

STABILITY OF FRAME DEPENDS ON CLADDING.

CLADDING.

SELF FORMED/HUNG HESSIAN FULLY SOAKED IN SESMONITE AC860

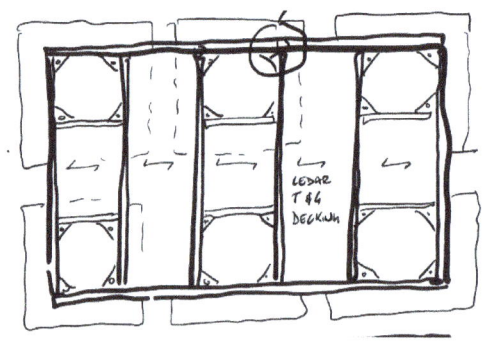

CEDAR T&G DECKING

Top left: Sketches by Steve Webb
Bottom left: Photo carrying timber columns down to the pontoon at the dock
Right: Building the structure of the Floating Forum, photo by author

Left: The openings frame specific views, photos by Simon Meyer
Right: The finished panels delivered on site to Cody Dock, photos by author

Left: Interior views showing the differently sculptured openings, photos by author; top right: Floating Forum external view surrounded by reeds, photo by Simon Meyers

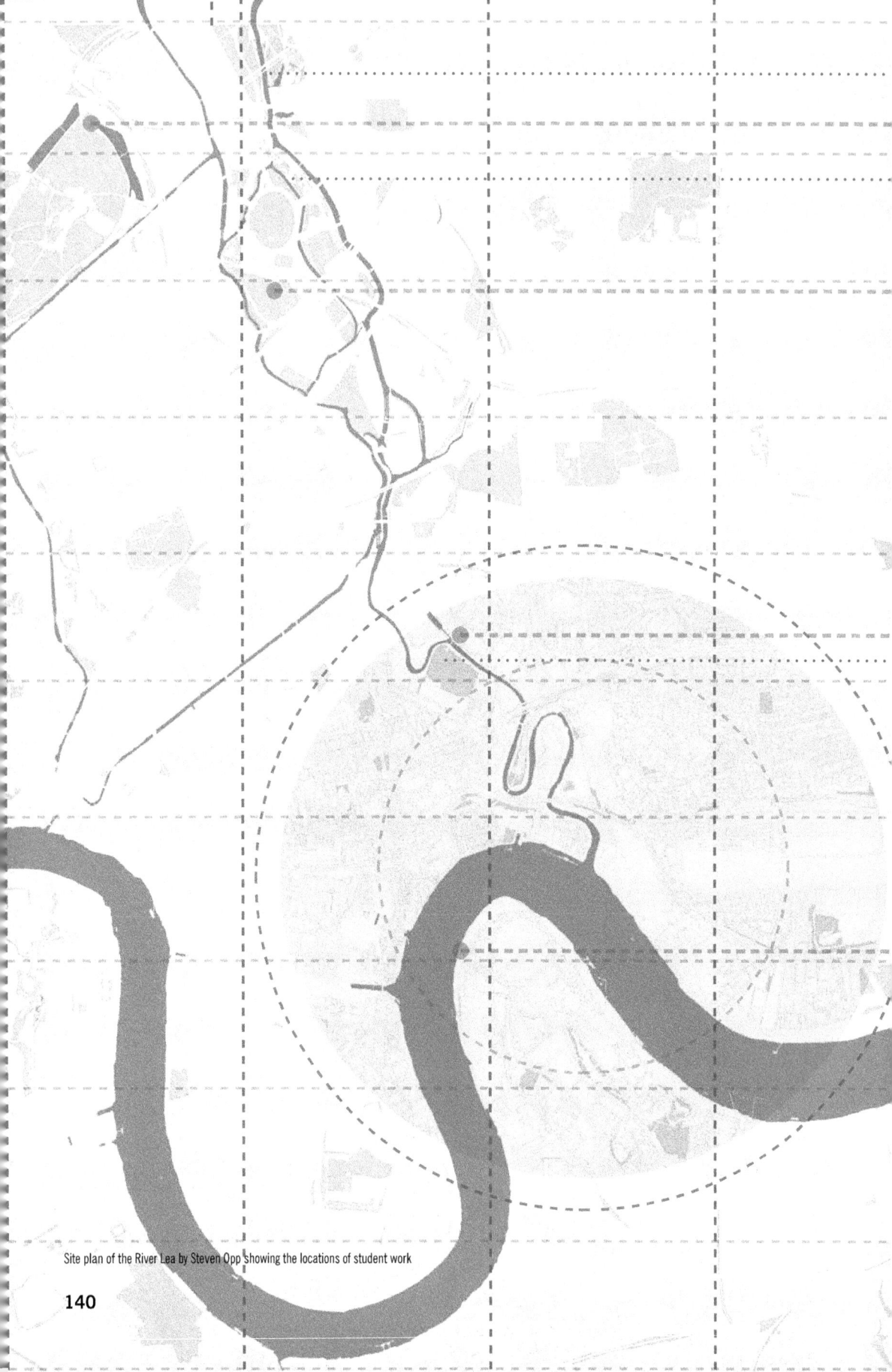

Site plan of the River Lea by Steven Opp showing the locations of student work

STUDENT PROJECTS

STEVEN OPP

Victoria Park
It is the largest park in Tower Hamlets and one of London's most visited green spaces with ~9 million visitors every year.

JENNY FOSTER

Olympic Park
The Olympic park covers 560 acres, 6.5km of waterways, 15 acres of woodland and hedgerow habitat with more than 6,000 new trees.

Cody Dock
Cody Dock and Cody Wilds project seek to promote greater awareness of this amazing asset, strengthen the existing wildlife habitats and ensure that this wildlife continues to flourish alongside the emerging regeneration that is set to line the river's banks.

MARIA SARAGURO

River Thames
River Lea flows for 46 miles (74 km) east and then south to enter the River Thames near Bromley-byBow

Removing Silt from the River Lea and Collecting Raw Material Samples

MUSSEL MEADOW
SHELLSCAPES OF HACKNEY

STEVEN OP

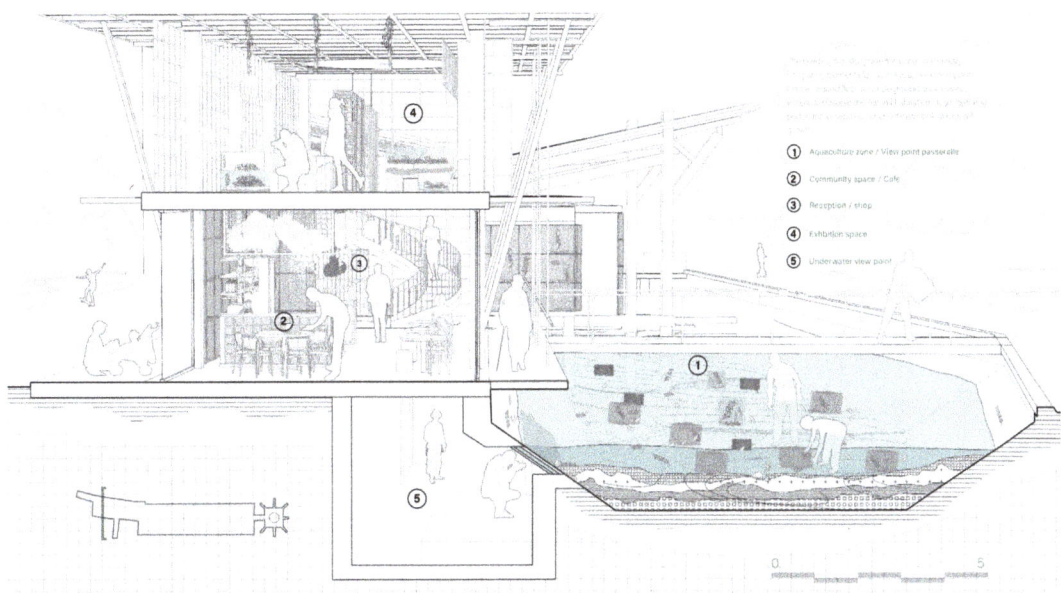

Top: Section through the mussel processing workshop
Left: Steven Opp collecting sediment samples from the River Lea, from which he discovered mussels.

The journey began along the banks of London's River Lea, with an investigation into silt as a potential building material. On a return visit, unexpected fragments emerged scattered shells embedded in the mud. A closer look revealed they belonged to freshwater mussels. This quiet discovery shifted the project's trajectory. What started as a study of sediment transformed into an exploration of mussels as makers of material, leading to a design narrative where waste becomes resource and ecology meets construction.

Since 2014, Quagga mussels, a species of fresh water mussel, have been growing and thriving in London's water pipe system. Each year, 10,000 tons of these mussels are removed and sent to waste fields, costing water companies millions of pounds since the removal treatment began. However, the material properties found in mussel shells are valuable for sustainable approaches that can be applied to products used in our daily lives. This building initiative seeks to revitalise the abandoned Middlesex water beds of Hackney in London, dormant since the 1800s, re-purposing them into a secondary habitat for mussels to thrive. As the mussels reach maturity and naturally perish, their shells are gathered and processed to create authentic materials which can be used for building construction. Moreover, the program advocates for outdoor pursuits such as mussel-based aquaculture, fostering community involvement and sustainable practices.

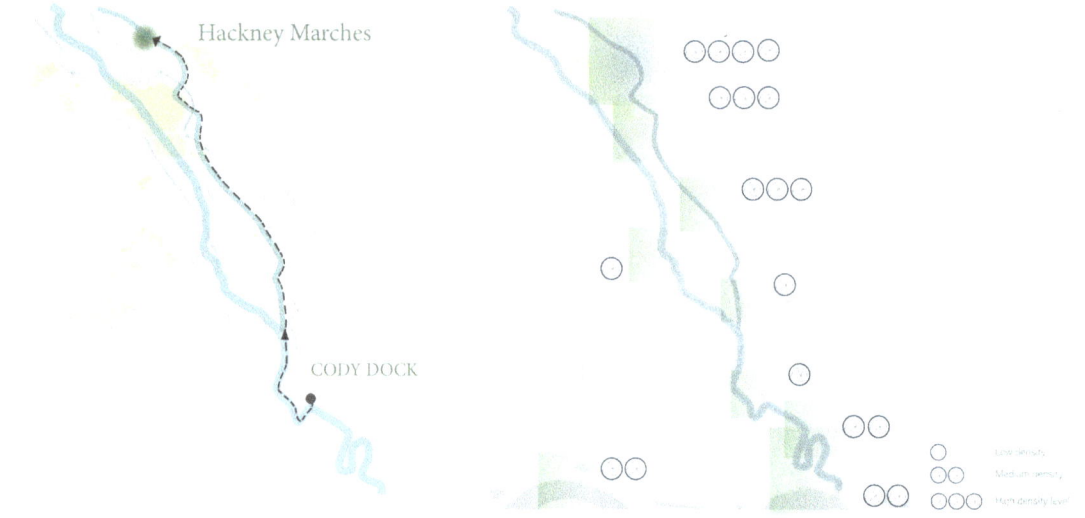

Site Plan with site indicated in relation to Cody Dock   Locations of where mussels can be found around the River Lea

Quagga mussels, a species of fresh water mussel, have been growing and thriving in London's water pipe system. Each year, 10,000 tons of these mussels are removed and sent to waste fields.

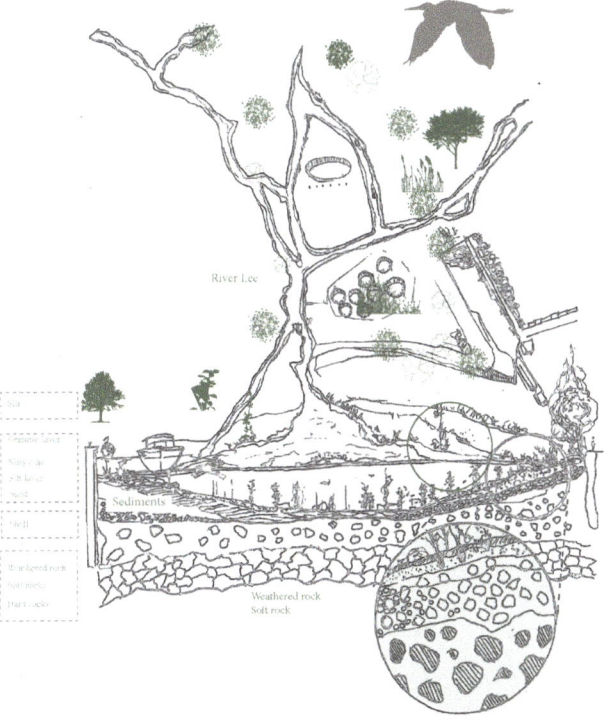

Right: The River Lea offers a whole range of raw material underneath its water level. A mix of residue from natural and human chemical waste. Underneath the organic layer and water plants we can find silty clay, sand, weathered rock and many and lots of embodied carbon material impacted by industrial activities.

Top: Material samples made out of mussels and eco resin

Getting silt out from the River Lea: after researching how to test silt, I went back to the site equipped with a local and a scoop to extract a sample of raw material from a location near Cody Dock. The River did not have the same look when I came back to site compare to the first time we went on site visit. The water level went up and the silt was no more visible from the side river walk.

A few weeks after the first site visit I decided to explore another part of the river towards north. Hackney Marches has an extended branch of the River Lea which offers a entirely different appearance and feel to the river. While picking up a sample of the silt on this part of the river I discover that the river had shell under the layer of silt. My research journey changes trajectory towards testing with shells as a new material.

DS20
BUILDING DESIGN

DS20
The Mussel Meadows
2023-2024

① Show case mussel ponds
② Open green space with outdoor furniture
③ View points to the River
④ Kids play ground
⑤ Interactive Mussel Gardens
⑥ Crane mussel cage lifter Zone
⑦ Mussel bridge (NEW ACCESS TO SITE)

THE BUILDING & LANDSCAPE

Creating garden pockets

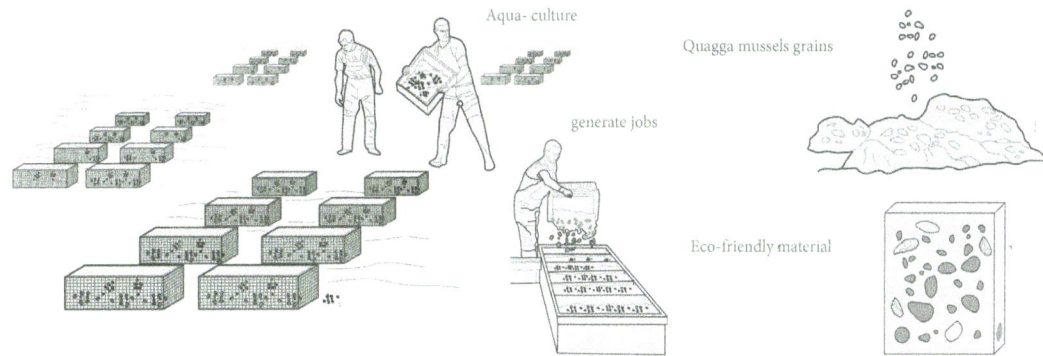

Top: Growing Mussels as an eco friendly solution Mussels are a problem for water pipes. About eight years ago, an invasive species called Quagga mussel shells started clogging up London's water pipes and tunnels. Since then, Thames Water, the utility company that's responsible for the city's public water supply and wastewater treatment has spent millions of pounds to remove them.

Right: Creating pocket garden - the mussel cages are spread between the un-flooded area to create connection paths. The mussels are growing inside the cages which is protecting it from predators

Top left: Site plan, reviving the Middlesex water beds
Bottom left: Artist Impression External View
Bottom right: Artist Impression harvesting mussels

The building's spacious workshops will significantly enhance the capacity for recycling mussel materials, aiming to reduce London's mussel waste in landfills by 70%. The program also seeks to bring limnologists, aquaculture enthusiasts, local craftsmen, and visitors together for an intimate experience with the mussels, providing opportunities to learn about their natural habitat and the potential for recycling mussel materials. with the mussels, providing opportunities to learn about their natural habitat and the potential for recycling mussel materials. The architectural design seamlessly blends natural elements with eco-conscious principles. Elevated on stilts, the building not only gains structural stability but also fosters a thriving ecosystem for mussels, offering a symbiotic relationship that champions environmental sustainability and biodiversity.

The indoor space brings the mussels' natural habitat indoors, creating a living exhibit for visitors and limnology enthusiasts. Water basins with native aquatic plants allow for close observation of mussel ecosystems, offering an educational environment that bridges science, landscape, and architecture The urban proposal for the Middlesex Waterfront revitalises the surrounding waterbeds, providing numerous opportunities for public engagement and exploration of the unique ecosystem, including the life of the quagga mussels. Visitors will have access to the water beds through carefully designed pathways above the water level, allowing for immersive experiences with nature. The building is nestled within the historic water beds, fully surrounded and partially submerged to create an immersive experience for visitors. Mussel cultivation takes place beneath and around the structure, allowing the production process to unfold in real time. As visitors move through the space, they are engaged with the aquatic environment blurring the boundary between architecture and living systems.

View of the site near Cody Dock on the River Lea, photo by Maria Saraguro

WEAVING GENDER

THE WOMEN'S RHIZOME VILLAGE

MARIA SARAGURO

Site Location – River Lea. Once neglected and stripped of nature by industrial use, the site now becomes a point of ecological restoration.

Aerial View of The Women's Rhizome Village diverting the tidal river into the site to create idea conditions for reed beds as ecological infrastructure and as landscape

In the context of today's housing crisis, gender remains a critical yet often overlooked factor shaping vulnerability and exclusion. We live in a time where housing is increasingly treated as a commodity rather than a human right where systemic inequalities, including gender, determine who has access to safe, secure living conditions. As the housing crisis deepens, its impacts fall disproportionately on women, revealing a critical need for spatial responses that address this imbalance.

In the United Kingdom, a staggering 17.5 million people, nearly a third of adults, are affected by the housing emergency, living in unsafe or insecure housing conditions (New Statesman, 2021). Among them, women face a disproportionate burden. According to Shelter, six in ten homeless people in temporary accommodation are women, despite women making up just over half the population. Shelter has described women as "some of the biggest losers in England's broken housing system" (Shelter, 2021). The situation is even more acute for single mothers, with 65% living in insecure housing, alongside 57% of Black adults, further highlighting how housing insecurity intersects with race and family dynamics (New Statesman, 2021). Set with this context, this project responds to the DS20 studio theme *Applied Making through Community and Ecology*, developed during the 2024 MArch final year. The studio

Left: Photo of the site at its current stage

focuses on the complex relationships between human and ecological systems in the Tidal Industrial area of the River Lea. DS20's ethos centres on designing resilient, inclusive urban environments through hands-on engagement, community-led processes, and deep ecological awareness.

This project underscores the urgent need for spatial interventions that address structural inequalities and contribute to the security, visibility, and empowerment of all individuals particularly those most impacted by systemic failures.

Nested within the Tidal Industrial Area of the River Lea, The Women's Rhizome Village blends ecological restoration with female empowerment. Historically affected by industrial pollution, the River Leas has faced significant environmental degradation. The village serves as a sanctuary for women and single mothers facing

Match-girls' strike 1888

PAST PAST PAST PAST PRESENT

Half of women in UK fear equality is going back to 1970s – survey

Homelessness isn't a 'lifestyle choice'

"I was never sure I'd make it through the night": inside the hidden homelessness crisis

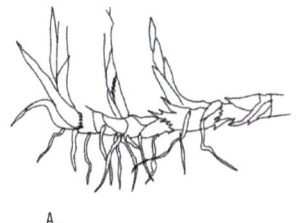
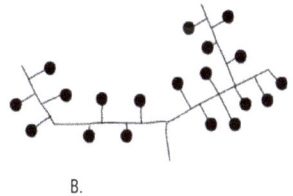
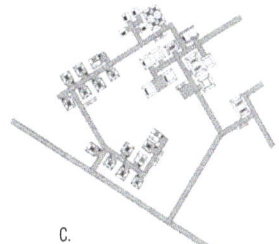

A. Rhizome; B. Rhizome nodes abstract representation; C. Rhizome applied concept - The Rhizome Village.

In the smoky haze of 1888 London, the Bryant and May match factory in Bow, near the River Lea and Cody Dock in East London, became the unlikely epicenter of a pivotal moment in the fight for workers' rights and social justice. The Match Girls' Strikes, led by predominantly young women and girls, were sparked by the oppressive working conditions, meager wages, and the hazardous use of chemicals like white phosphorus in matchstick production. This historic event not only marked a turning point in labour movements but laid the foundation for a broader conversation on gender equality and societal change. As the echoes of the Match Girls' Strikes reverberate through time, the struggles faced by the underrepresented communities, particularly women, persist in different forms in the contemporary world. From the gritty streets of East London to the broader global landscape, the challenges that these women confronted in the late 19th century find echoes in the ongoing battles against domestic abuse, homelessness, and the pursuit of gender equality. In this narrative, the arc from the match factory floors of 1888 to the present day, exploring how the resilience of these women continues to inspire and inform the modern fight for justice and empowerment.

Hand-drawn sketch of the Women's Rhizome Village, illustrating the integration of reeds, living spaces, and natural systems designed to foster community and ecological connection.

Top: Axonometric View of the Polycentric Proposal of the Rhizome Village
Bottom: Eye-level View showing the proposed Reed Landscaping and Rhizome Village in the Background

Common Reeds (Phragmites Australis) vertical flow wetland treatment systems.

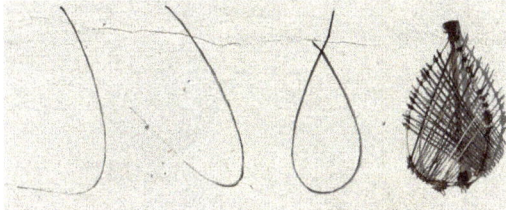

Making a reed panel by soaking the stalk for three days to make it bend sufficiently

The use of locally harvested common reed known for its water-purifying properties through its roots, plays a role in the Women's Rhizome Village. Serving as both a primary construction material and a means to cleanse the surrounding water, this dual-purpose approach significantly enhances the village's environmental sustainability, resilience, and self-sufficiency. Sustainable native reeds purify the contaminated river and serves as a resource for local crafts and construction. The Women's' Rhizome Village empowers women, fostering new beginnings and economic opportunities where individuals connect and support one another, creating a resilient and sustainable communal and ecological fabric.

The project location is a site that becomes the catalyst for women empowering by connecting it to a wider London. A place where women and single mothers can create new opportunities for their families, a community that empowers and educate women, helping them establish economic independence for themselves. The overall intention is to create a therapeutic bond between users and nature, thus minimising the feeling of isolation in women and their children. The Women's Rhizome Village adopts a strategy inspired by the natural growth of common reed rhizomes (Diagram A, previous page), underground stems that spread horizontally, sending out roots and shoots from their nodes to create a resilient and interconnected system. Similarly, the village envisions a community where women, like nodes (B) in a rhizome, connect and support each other, fostering strength and unity. Just as rhizomes establish a widespread and robust network, the village (C) aims to cultivate a cohesive and empowering environment for its residents.

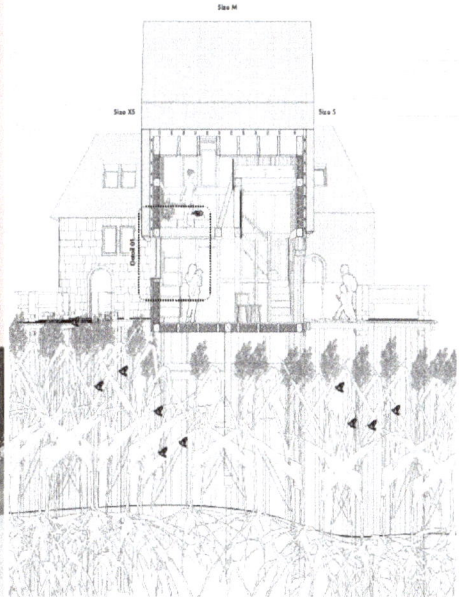

Above: Section through the proposed Rhizome Village; Right: Detailed Cross Section; Left: Artist Impressions of the village with reed beds as ecological infrastructure and as landscape strategy

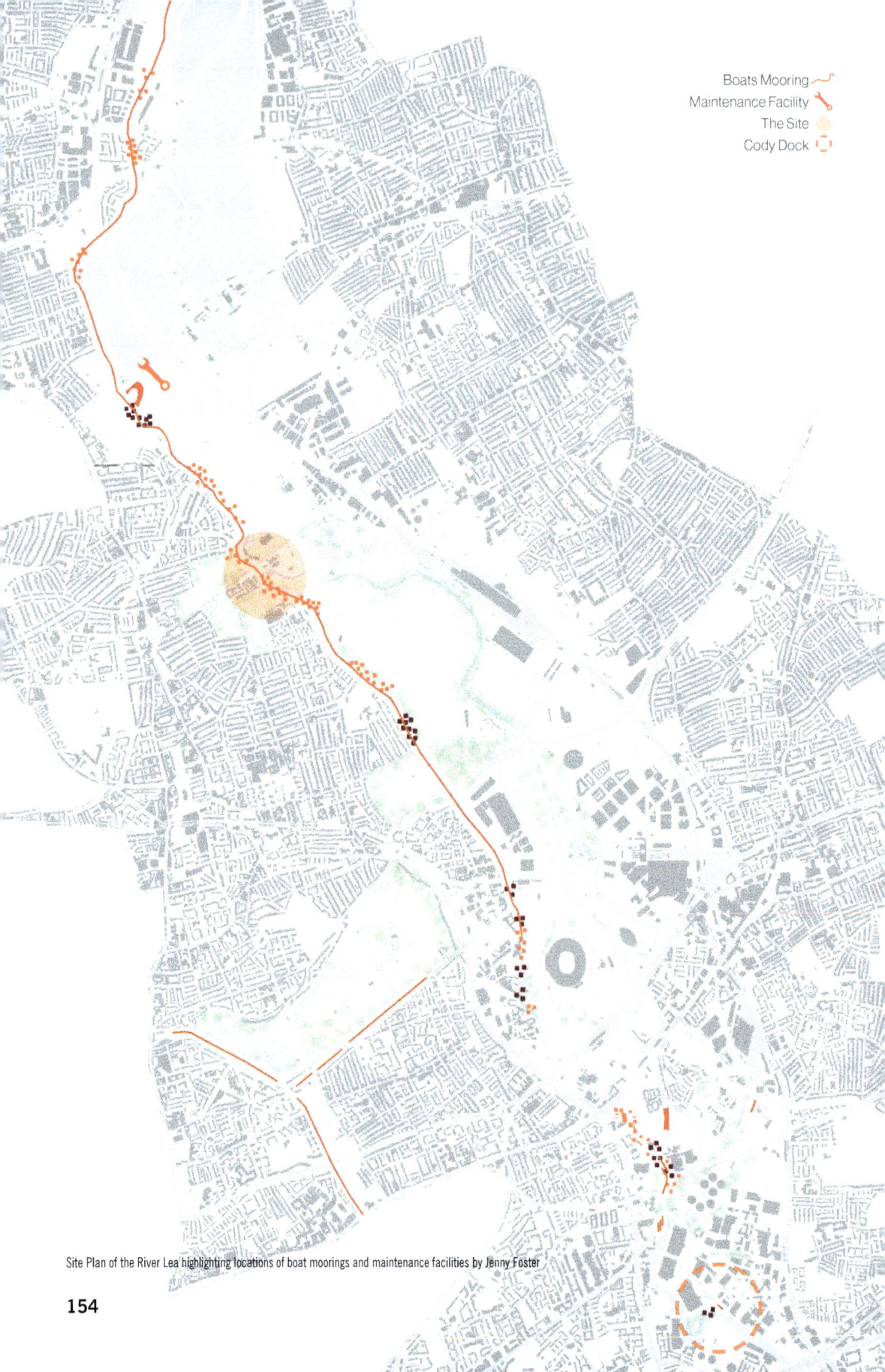
Site Plan of the River Lea highlighting locations of boat moorings and maintenance facilities by Jenny Foster

RIVER REPAIR

ADAPTING THE HARSH RIPARIAN

JENNY FOSTER

 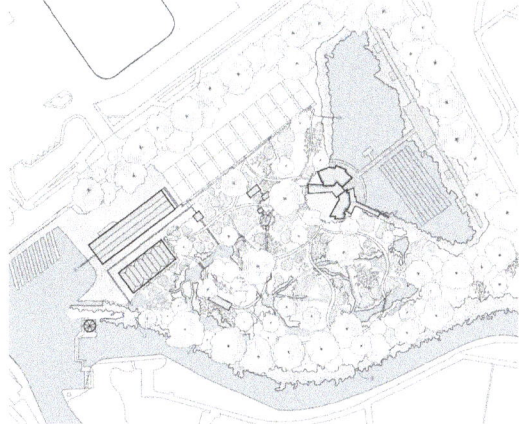

Strategic Plan demonstrating how water is being collected, cleaned and slowly released to the River Lea   Strategic Site Plan

Located in East London, River Repair seeks to tackle problems of water pollution in the River Lea through carefully considered drainage solutions. Driven by the cleaning qualities of rhizome root filtration and community-led research, this project identifies opportunities to store rainwater and slow the rate of surface run-off while also filtering water pollutants before they reach the river.

The project began with a walk down the River Lea, amongst the vibrant communities of East London, water pollution was prominent on a number of sites. Be it large collections of litter or culverts depositing harmful substances from industrial sites, the water and wildlife of the River Lea was suffering.

One solution to the problem, spearheaded by local charity groups, is the introduction of new man-made reedbeds. Despite being considered a weed, the common reed is incredibly effective at filtering water pollutants. Their rhizome roots help to oxygenate water, turn toxic ammonia into nitrates and remove carbon from wetlands before it is exposed to the air. An ethnobontany class held at Cody Dock on the Lea provided more inspiration for working with reeds but in a physical capacity alongside other foraged, natural elements. Inspired by the rhizome filtration of reeds, a number of early material explorations were carried out - collaging with reed stems, woven together with bind weed lashing knots.

In addition to reedbed qualities, another strong driving factor behind the project was a prominent community that occupy the water's edge - narrowboat dwellers. As significant, everyday stakeholders in the condition of the River Lea, it was important to understand the daily routine of narrowboat dwellers and the water cycle of their homes. If chemical products are used inside the boat, they can end up in the river and be harmful to aquatic life. Additionally, narrowboat dwellers can struggle with solutions to black water and sewage disposal.

The site for River Repair is a 5.68 hectare ex-Thames Water Depot Site which houses an Engineers House and 2 mid-19th Century boiler sheds. Situated where the River Lea splits into the River Lea Navigation, the site's bank exposes 3 large water culverts which deposit surface run-off from the site and surrounding industrial areas directly into the river. Historically the home of mid-1800s filter beds used to supply London's drinking the site is now an expanse of tarmac with a network of gulleys and manholes. River Repair seeks to reignite the notion of water filtration through carefully considered ground treatment and drainage solutions.

To improve the biodiversity and ground water storage, River Repair proposes the extensive rewilding of the ex-depot site with new wildflower meadows and

Top right: Axonometric diagrams for Site Strategy with Rewilding Efforts, Water Storage Pools, Community Buildings and New Drainage Network slowing down drainage by introducing a natural and exposed water harnessing system integrated in the landscaping strategy
Bottom right: New Drainage Systems; Collecting and Redirecting Run-off, Naturally Filtered Swimming Pool, Broken Tarmac with Permeable Surfaces Below
Left: Aerial view of the Site

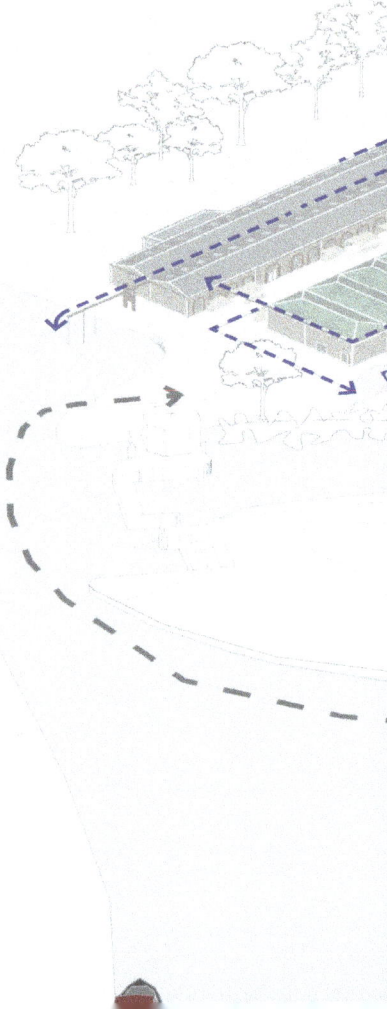

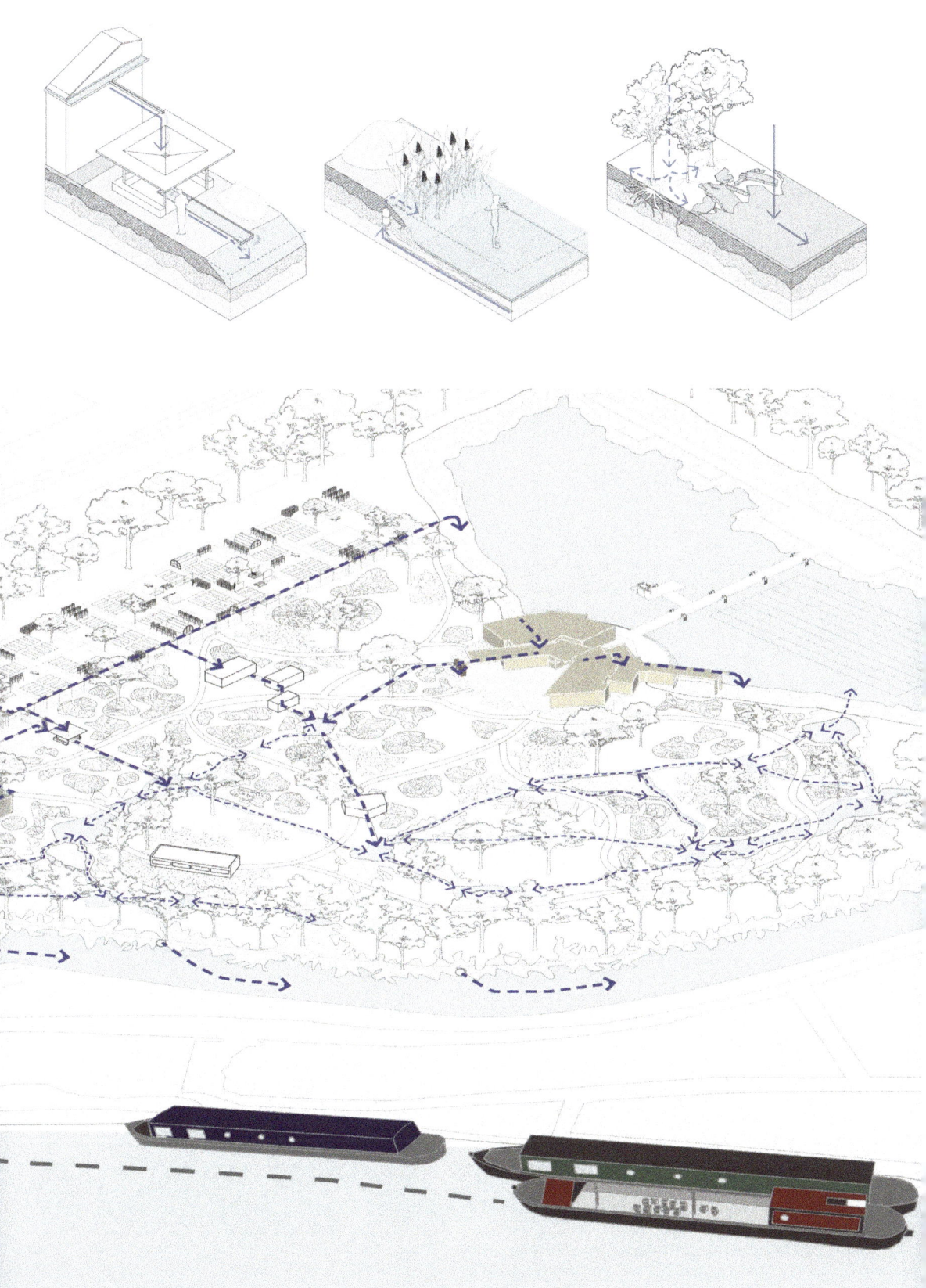

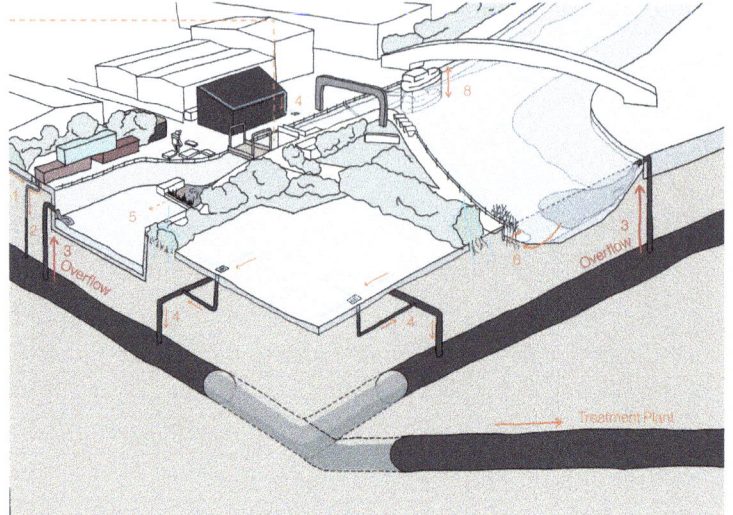
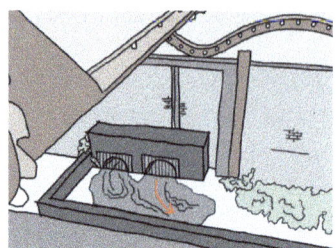

Mains water in
Grey and waste water out
In heavy rainfall, combined waterworks reach capacity and overflow goes back into the river
Rain run off
An existing reedbed barrier in the dock noticeably filters the pollutants
Existing reedbeds naturally clean the river
Pollutants and other illegal toxic substances from surrounding industries are deposited into the dock
Tidal nature of the river

Existing Urban Water Cycle at Cody Dock showing polution build up in the waterways

reedbed-lined pools. The new pools sit on the site of existing manholes and help to store and clean run-off via rhizome filtration before it passes to the river. Networks of gutters, channels and sculptures slow the waters path before redirecting them to one of the pools. The rainwater collection is made visible and celebrated across site making it an architectural feature. Where the tarmac is retained for existing and new accommodation, its edges are cracked and lifted to increase the permeability of the ground.

The accommodation on site offers community spaces for locals, with an emphasis on supporting narrowboat dwellers. The existing boiler houses provide workshops and studios for local creatives and businesses and the site's Eastern riparian has been adapted to provide mooring spaces for narrowboats. One mooring space is allocated to the waste collection boat which passes up and down the Lea collecting sewage disposal from local narrowboats. The second boiler house provides facilities to process this waste into natural fertiliser, used on the adjacent allotments occupied by narrowboat users.

New accommodation includes the network of sculptures and pavilions that redirect and slow rain run-off and a changing and saunas facility for newly proposed natural swimming pools. Located on the original site of the water filter beds, the natural swimming pool is lined with reedbeds and offers storm water collection, alleviating pressure during periods of heavy rain.

Proposed view of the Pavilion Entrance to the Swimming Lake

Proposed Strategic Site Plan

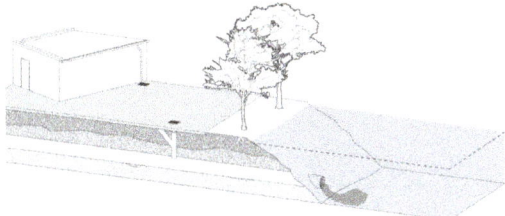

Existing Manhole to Culvert Section

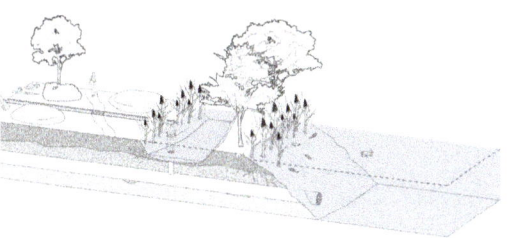

Proposed Manhole to Culvert Section

Artists' Hub and Fertiliser Production

Proposed Filtration and Storage Pool on Site of Existing Manhole

159

KINSHIP AND STAKEHOLDERS
AT THE LOWER RIVER LEA
CORINNA DEAN

In proposing the Lea Valley as a MArch programme site, the intention was to engage students to rethink conceptually how liminal spaces, between land and water, are mediated. The cultural geographer, Matthew Gandy describes the unruliness of water within current etymologies, posing the question, "Can the flow of water unsettle our existing conceptions of space, technology, and landscape?" (Gandy, 2014, p.1).

To engage with the Lea, students were urged to look beyond the river as a singular unit of analysis, beyond the blue/green reductive language of urban planning vocabulary and instead as "an intersecting set of processes, practices, and meanings that cuts across existing disciplinary boundaries", (Gandy, 2014 p.1).

Basing the studio within the Lea Valley we invited students to frame their programmes around conceptualising conditions of care and kinship. The River's misuse over the last centuries is well documented and I will draw on some examples in this short essay.

London's burgeoning urbanism and industry in the 19th century, meant that the rural land surrounding the Lea, often made up of flood plains, witnessed a history of contestation, in which the largely agrarian communities battled against the physical effects of urbanisation.

The encroaching developments seeped into the local inhabitants' relationship with the land and river banks, sites know as 'Lammas' land. The locals were permitted to graze their animals with the annual switch marked by the Celtic midsummer harvest festival of 'Lugnasad', or 'Lammas' Day which signalled the change from planting crops to grazing animals. Later in the year the last day when grass was cut for hay and the hunting season began, was known as the 'Glorious Twelfth'. The continuing legacy of heavy industry, since the industrial revolution, due to the Lower Lea lying downstream, has left the River denuded, and 'forever chemicals' still present in the water alongside accumulated sediments.

Objections to the state of the River back in the 19th century were voiced in the form of strongly worded complaints of its mistreatment questioning its 'wholesomeness'. August 1890, in the general medical journal, The Lancet, under the title 'Pollution of the River Lea' reported 'in some part (the Lea) is inoffensive, in others it was greasy, covered with floating debris and with thick, blackish slimy filth, and pollution by solid material ...while the foreshores were in such a condition to be a nuisance'. The article went on to state the directive against West Ham Corporation to discharge sewage only on the ebb tide ending the article with the damming statement, "the condition of the river is a standing reproach to London". [1] To turn to the Lea's recent history, I want to consider the stewards and stakeholders to understand the complexity of current governance around the Lea. This helps to open discussions around the 'ethical-political' dimensions as to who is engaging with 'urban natures' and challenges current spatial practices. Many sites in the Lower Lea have been occupied by London's back of house services, windowless Amazon sheds, which turn their back on the river, chemical works which leach toxic waste, through Combined Sewage Overflows (CSO), poorly regulated. As industry is moved elsewhere, sites such as the Bromley-by-Bow Gas Holders, decommissioned in 2010, sitting empty for 15 years, are beginning to host ruderal habitats. Labelled successional landscapes, or mosaic habitats due to their ability to host patches of highly site specific responses, these terms are replacing the previous blanket label, Brownfield site. These sites are valued and documented by local grass roots organisations where possible, for their ability to nurture opportunistic flora and fauna, whose growth can withstand polluted soils, aridity and low nutrient levels.

The Lower Lea area around Bow, historically known as the Bow Back rivers, was over laid with the introduction of side channels constructed to provide flood relief, therefore rendering the river a series of engineered canals, and little resemblance to the naturally banked rivers. The artifice of the intervention has led to reduced flow and the deposition and accumulation of silt in these areas (Snook and Whitehead, 2004). Prior to the major infrastructural projects, such as the development of the Olympic Village, Elizabeth line, and Olympic Park to name a few, a landscape strategy and report to assess the valley's landscape characteristics was commissioned by the GLA from the architects, Witherford Watson Mann, 2010. The area was valued for its hybridity of industrial relics, described by the architects as Bastard countryside, because of the hybrid nature of unplanned interventions, and layered evolution. Under current European environmental legislation, the river is no longer considered a River but a Heavily Modified Water Body (HMWB) because of its poor

Photo of the Lower River Lea by Dr. Corrina Dean

ecological status. Attention has now been pulled into focus on the Lea, with pedestrian access recently completed along the whole stretch of the Lea, titled the Leaway by the practice 5th Studio, a 10-year project, save one small area under private ownership. Previous 'no-go' areas, where under worlds thrived of rave venues adjacent to saunas, scrap yards and waste incinerators, feral sites which are now coming under the scrutiny of developers.

Evans who has engaged with the Lea as a teaching site, examines human-nature interactions and set out to list the hierarchies and responsibilities of stakeholders of the Lea. Evans argues that a new type of stewardship and governance is required, citing the rise of the activated citizen responding to socio hydrological configurations. Evans cites the term 'hydrocitizen', a reference to a 3-year study titled, 'Toward hydrocitizenship' [2] which looked at the relationship of communities and stakeholders in the Lea. In order to clarify what responsibilities were undertaken by whom Evans provided a summary of statutory bodies to informally run organisations, starting with the European Union; which manages the Water Framework Directive to large players such as the Environmental Agency; dealing with flood risk, defence, and water quality, to the Canal and Rivers Trust; formerly British Waterways, then the Lea Valley Regional Park Authority; a confusing organisation which is funded by the 33 London Boroughs, to Boat dwellers. Each organisation operates at differing scalar levels to the Lea.

The above references the complexity of stewardship and motives, and perhaps more urgently highlights the need for an opening up of intersectional relationships, previously unexplored, where the ethics of care are at play. Within this practice of care many more expansive methodologies across disciplines have emerged, Tsing calls for 'Patches' as sites for knowing intersectional inequalities among humans (Tsing, 2019). Bolens et al, rallies in addressing the development of New Water Justice Movements united around Riverhood, originally a mid-nineteenth century concept to describe 'the state of being a river' (Oxford Dictionary). New justice platforms define river commons as networked socio-ecological arrangements between the human and non-human, calling for a Riverine practice that shares values and knowledge. (Bolens et al. 2022, p 1132). If one looks beyond the strategic players in the Lea there is a plethora of grass roots organisations such as Surge Cooperative who negotiated a strip of land on the Lower Lea for river restoration activities from Thames Water, or Cody Dock also known as the Gasworks Partnership who negotiated a 999 yr lease from Newham Council, Love the Lea Campaign, as well as the Lea Guardians, a network of organisations monitoring the water quality of the Lea under the umbrella of Thames 21. By engaging with some of these communities with the students, we hope to have encouraged new interactions to create near future visions which inform tangible forms of River kinship.

[1] The Lancet, August, 1890 accessed London Metropolitan Archive, 22 Sept 2023.
[2] The Hydrocitizenship project ran from 2014 to 2017 and investigated ways in which communities live with each other and their environment in relation to water in a range of UK neighbourhoods. The case studies were in Bristol, Lee Valley (London), Borth and Tal-y-bont (Mid Wales), and Shipley (Bradford). Each case study was being conducted by a local team of academics, artists, community activists, and selected community partners ranging from small community groups to larger organisations charged with aspects of regeneration and community resilience.
For references, please see the end of the book.

ECOLOGICALLY LED COMMMUNTY REGENERATION
CODY DOCK

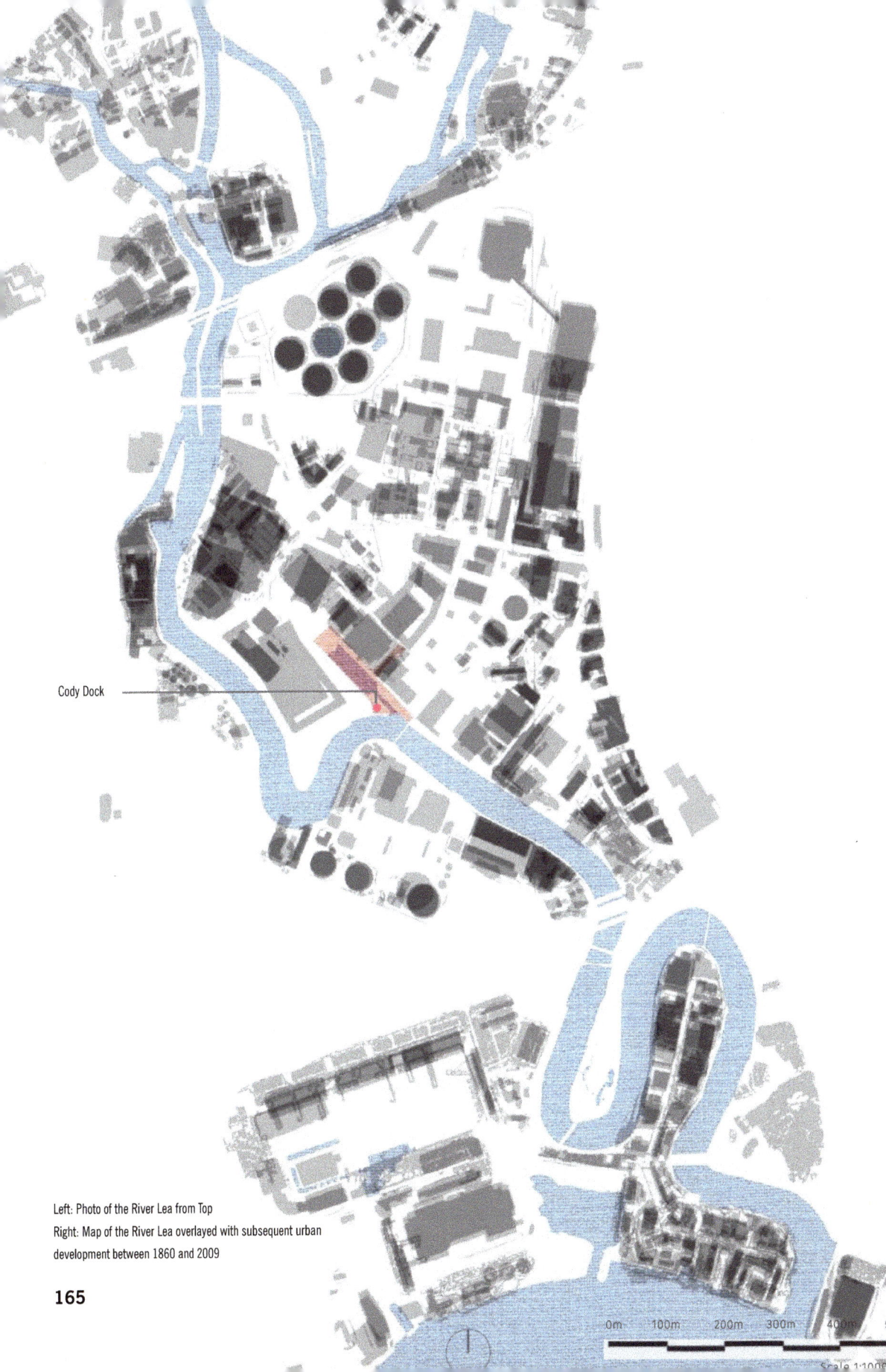

Cody Dock

Left: Photo of the River Lea from Top
Right: Map of the River Lea overlayed with subsequent urban development between 1860 and 2009

THE GROWING SPACE
LIVE PROJECT
2022/23

TUTORS: MARIA KRAMER AND CORINNA DEAN
STUDENTS: RACHEL ARMSTRONG, PRANJAL BAFNA, ARCHIE BROWN, GALINA DIMOVA, ADAM DIN, SEAN HAMILTON, WILLIAM LAMBERT, MANU MOHAN MOHANDAS, AYA NASR, CHRIS PAINTER, MEGAN REES, BLESSING SULAIMAN, FALGUNI THAKKAR, LUCY TURNER, HAMZA KHAN, NICHOLAS KOUSOULOUJULIA WLADYSIAK
FUNDER: UNIVERSITY OF WESTMINSTER QHT FUND PARTNERS: WEBB YATES ENGINEERS, NICHOLAS ALEXANDER, OFCA, GASWORKS DOCK PARTNERSHIPS
SPONSORS: RODECA

David Attenborough's BBC documentary features Cody Dock as an example of community-led urban biodiversity and green space regeneration. It highlights its work in improving habitats, engaging local residents, and using citizen science data to inform local planning. from BBC "Saving Our Wild Isles"

CODY DOCK

Cody Dock is a regenerated historic dock on the tidal River Lea in East London that serves as a model of community-led urban and ecological restoration. Originally constructed in the early 1870s to supply the Bromley-by-Bow gasworks with coal brought from Newcastle via lighters navigating the Lea, it was later acquired by British Gas. After gasworks operations ceased in the mid-1960s, the dock fell into dereliction; part of it was infilled and the site used as a dumping ground until 2009.

In the same year the Gasworks Dock Partnership (GDP) was established as a social enterprise and charity to rehabilitate the former dock into a mixed-use public space. Between 2015 and 2018, GDP welcomed more than 50,000 visitors and engaged over 6,000 volunteers in restoring riverside footpaths and improving the site infrastructure, supported by grants from Thames Water, the Veolia Environmental Trust, Kew Gardens, the Royal Horticultural Society, Newham Council and the Big Lottery Fund.

Cody Dock now operates as a creative industries quarter incorporating public gardens, studio and gallery spaces, a café, community boat initiatives and ecological programmes The site has recorded over 3,000 biological observations documenting more than 250 species of birds, mammals, plants, and invertebrates, highlighting its unexpectedly high level of urban biodiversity in a formerly neglected industrial zone.

Cody Dock received a £1.6 million National Lottery Heritage Fund grant to build a heritage centre using a restored 1913 Thames Ironworks lifeboat-named the Frederick Kitchen-as a glazed pavilion roof. This new facility is also intended as a cultural exhibition space celebrating local social and industrial history alongside ecological interpretation.

How is the practice of architecture responsibly formed in terms of creating new social and cultural relationships with our natural environment?

This is the question DS20 students responded to in the context of the post-industrial landscape around Cody Dock, an abandoned former coke smelting dock that is now a thriving ecological base adjacent to the River.

"When we came to Cody Dock for the first time, I thought, It's a wonderful community, we can learn so much here. It's very multi-layered, along the River Lee, so it has a wonderful ecological environment, which was also in need of cleaning up as it was polluted here. Cody Dock also works with the local community. It has citizen sciences, it has social prescribing, it does community gardening, and also therapeutic gardening. It has a creative community here also, so it's just a very multi-layered, complex place, even though it's relatively small, it has a lot of different stakeholders involved here." M. Kramer

Left: Photo at Cody Dock with The Growing Space Live Project by Edmund Sumner

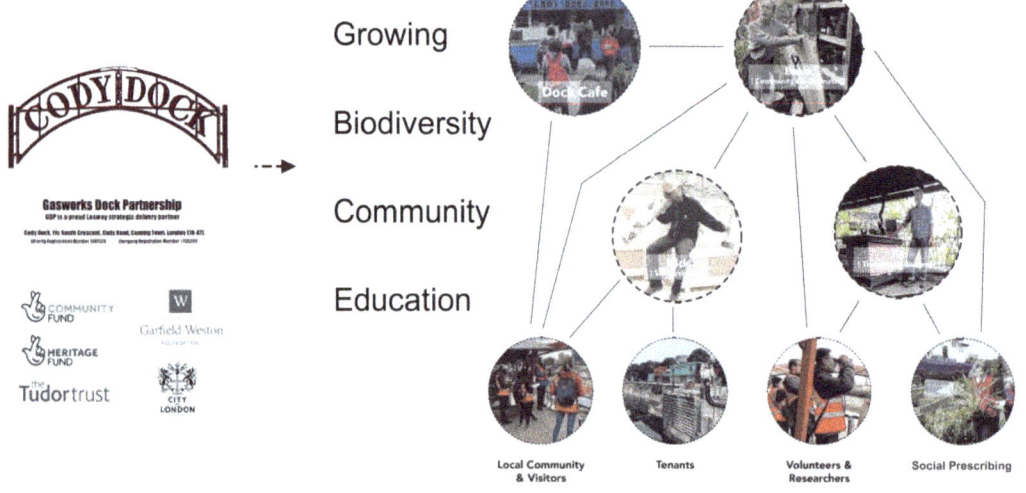

Top: Stakeholder Diagram of Cody Dock/Gaswork Dock Partnership
Right Continuous Stakeholder Engagement throughout different work stages

THE GROWING SPACE

The Growing Space, designed by master's students DS20 and provides space for community horticultural activities. The Growing Space is a 68m2 Douglas fir lightweight timber structure which adds to the existing cluster of buildings making up Cody Dock's community hub. It runs a programme to expand the charity's reach, running gardening and workshops for local schools, as well as space for rent.

Having had the fantastic opportunity to co-design and co-built 'The Growing Space' Live Project we were delighted to further collaborate with Cody Dock and exhibit our student's design proposals along the River Lea. Students were asked to develop visions based on investigative research and live engagement with local stakeholders, which culminated into a group masterplan integrating students multi programmatic radical proposals.

How do we create neighbourhoods which encourage social interactions and place making, whilst promoting ecological awareness and 'civic-ness'?

SIMON MEYER, GASWORKS DOCK PARTNERSHIP

"What led me to start Cody Dock, my wife and I had been living on a boat for a little while on the Lee and we rapidly became aware that there was a shortage of moorings even back 17, 18 years ago, and the number of people living on boats was just growing every year. A lot of people living on boats, unless you're somewhere nice like St Catherine's Dock, are potentially moored up on moorings whose future are not very certain, and it's normally a sort of stopgap until development happens. Then you get pushed out or the price goes up and you can end up paying anywhere between sort of £800 – 2000 a month for mooring your boat. The more I spoke to other boat owners, the more I discovered that people resented paying almost as much as you do when you're renting, even though you own your property or might even be paying the mortgage. And they didn't necessarily want to own their own mooring, but they just wanted to see the money they were paying to improve the area where they lived. And so the idea on the back of the project originally was partly, is there somewhere we could find where a whole group of people could come together and moor their boats?" Simon Meyer, co-founder&CEO of charity&social enterprise Gasworks Dock Partnership

MARIA KRAMER, PROJECT LEAD

"When we came to Cody Dock for the first time, I thought, It's a wonderful community, we can learn so

so it has a wonderful ecological environment, which was also in need of cleaning up as it was polluted here. Cody Dock also works with the local community. It has citizen sciences, it has social prescribing, it does community gardening, and also therapeutic gardening. It has a creative community here also, so it's just a very multi-layered, complex place, even though it's relatively small, it has a lot of different stakeholders involved here."

"With any project, not just live projects, there is quite a gap between RIBA work stage 3, the conceptual design and then actually realising that there is a lot of work involved, and we often squeeze that 'space' of detailing and don't give it much time and attention even though there is a lot of craft required in this project phase. So we're working closely with makers and the structural engineer for this. There were many challenges, like with all life projects. Someone from our group said

"how easy it is to draw a line and how difficult it is to build one".

"The architecture was developed as part of a collaborative process. It has a structure of frames with cross-bracing and dry construction with all elements pre-cut with 3D-printed pegs reducing the construction time to 10 days. The base has six pad foundations with paving slabs, wrapped in polycarbonate, allowing the activities within to permeate out. An inverted roof creates a gutter for rainwater harvesting, irrigating propagated plants."

"The design process was a collaborative effort. Students initially developed individual outline proposals from which we finalised the design in collaboration with our fantastic partners, including structural engineer Steve Webb, promoting knowledge exchange. The funding was obtained from the university's own QHT fund and I have worked with the funders on previous Live Projects, including several 1:1 pavilions, which continue to be used by students and staff both at Marylebone and Harrow Campus. This project is some ways is scaled up version of the pavilion project and is the first time we have built a structure outside the university premises, which was a new challenge. Cody Dock was an enthusiastic partner, with students learning about community-led regeneration and eco-restoration."

A notable architectural feature is the Cody Dock Rolling Bridge, a manually operated pedestrian and cycle crossing over a canal connecting the River Lea to the dock. Designed by Thomas Randall-Page and Tim Lucas of Price & Myers and built by Cake Industries, the bridge rotates on its axis to allow boats to pass and reflects the site's industrial heritage through its use of untreated steel and bent oak, see images on the following pages.

Images above: The Rolling Bridge at Cody Dock
Left: Students paddling on the River Lea with boats from Cody Dock

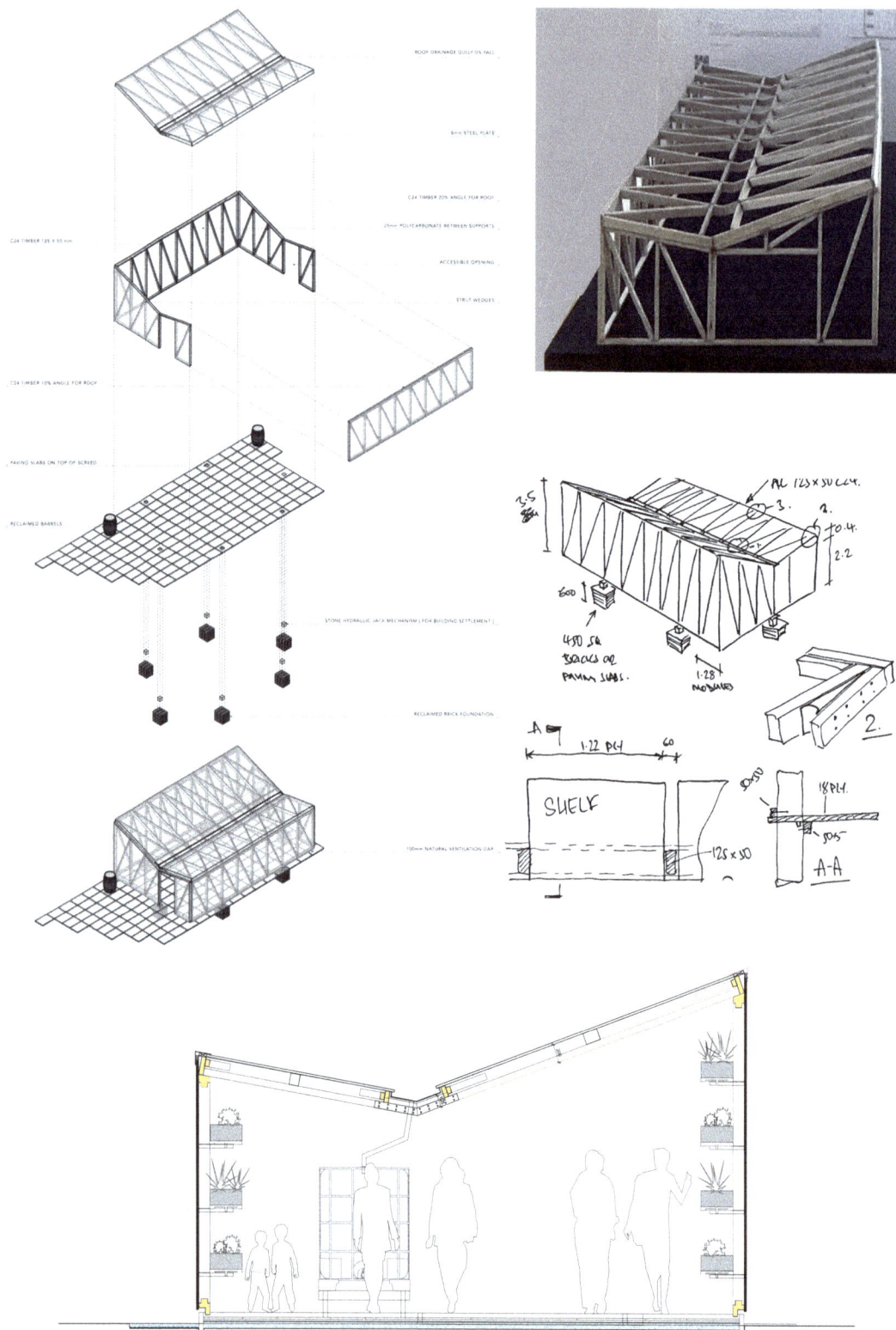

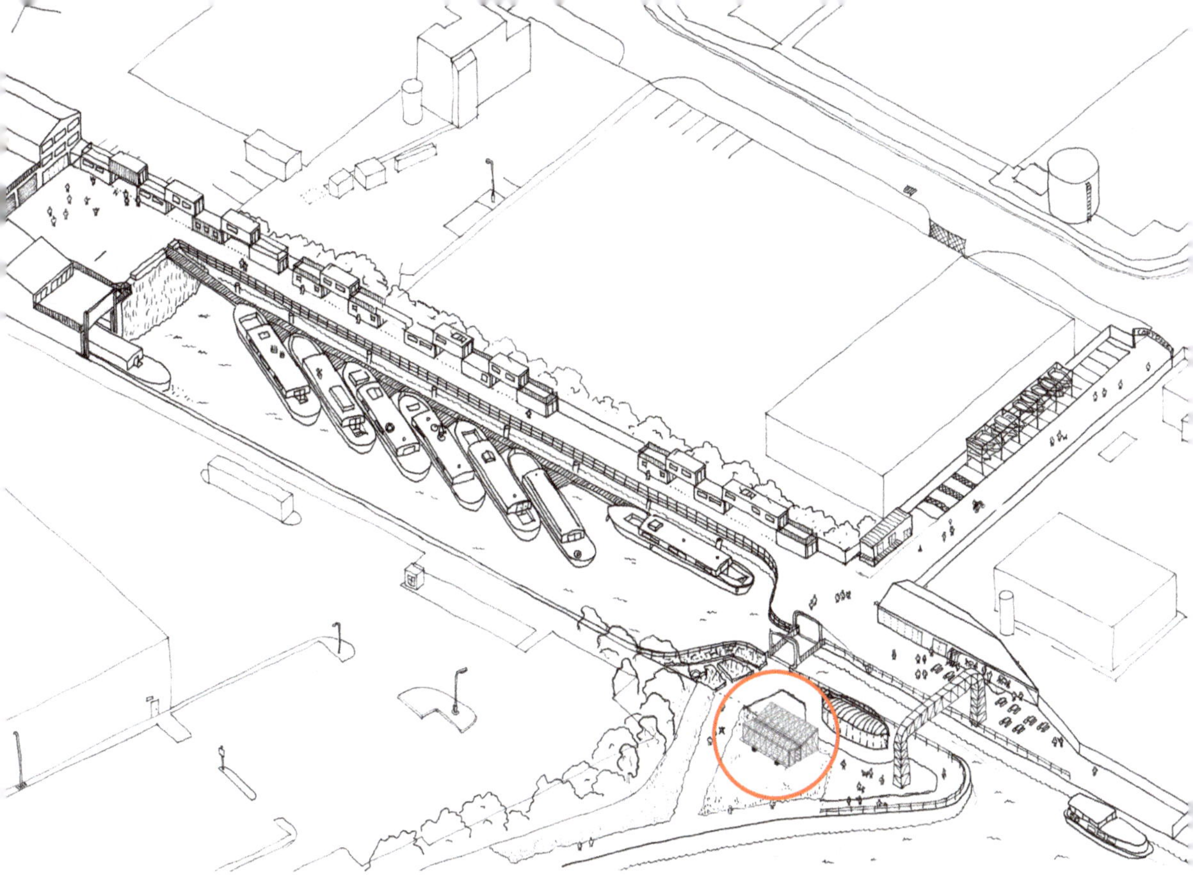

Top: Axonometric strategic plan of Cody Dock highlighting the location of The Growing Space
Bottom: Artist Impression by Will Lambert
Top left: Model by Chris Painter; Left centre: Sketches by Steve Webb
Top far left: Exploded axonometric view by Adam Din; Bottom left: Cross Section

Left: Construction of a prototype of one module at 1:1; group photo by Nic Henninger
Right: Students helping with the construction, all photos by editor

Top: Beam to Column Joint Detail connecting triangulated prefabricated elements
Bottom: Event by The Engineering Club in The Growing Space

Top Image: Translucent polycarbonate facade revealing internal timber structure;
Bottom Image: View from the therapeutic garden

1 year later: Ethnobotanical Workshop led by Julia Briscoe with students of the following year's MArch co-hort at The Growing Space

Top: Night time View of The Growing Space; Bottom: Open Doors at The Growing Space, photos by Edmund Sumner

Top: Exhibition of students work at Cody Dock; Bottom right: OPEN exhibition at UoW; Bottom: DS20 End of Year Open Exhibition at the University of Westminster, photo by author

We had the opportunity to exhibit student work at Cody Dock (see image above). We asked questions such as:

How do interventions have the potential to act as vessels of interaction with social and ecological opportunities, shaping architecture, whilst strengthening local identity and culture?

"I unlock this building every Monday and Tuesday morning and I feel so lucky to come to this beautiful place" Tim Brogden, Therapeutic Gardening Project Manager, Gasworks Dock Partnership

181

STUDENT PROJECTS

The Growing Space
Live Project

This page: Axonometric plan of individual student work and the adjacent Growing Space Live Project
Top right and far right: Ethnobotanical workshop with the following year's student cohort;
Ethnobotany is a multidisciplinary field studying of the relationships between people and plants,
focusing on how different cultures use, perceive, and manage plant species in their environment.
Bottom right: Local community workshop

How do individual student projects relate to Live Projects and visa versa?

Live Projects run in parallel with individual student projects, creating a two-way exchange between academic exploration and real-world engagement. The civic engagement process at the heart of the Live Project offers students a richer, more immediate understanding of the neighbourhood's challenges, opportunities, and aspirations. Through direct dialogue with local stakeholders, students move beyond abstract, hypothetical briefs to grapple with the tangible realities of place-making - including political, social, economic, and cultural dimensions.

This experience feeds directly into their individual projects. Insights gained from the Live Project—such as identified gaps in provision, community aspirations, or site-specific constraints-become embedded in the students' own design thinking. Programmatic choices, spatial strategies, and material considerations in their personal work often reflect a more nuanced response to local needs uncovered during the Live Project process.

The relationship is reciprocal. While the Live Project informs individual projects with grounded knowledge and lived context, the individual projects also contribute speculative ideas, innovative approaches, and experimental design thinking that can inspire or influence the ongoing Live Project. Together, this interplay strengthens both outcomes: the Live Project gains fresh, imaginative propositions, and the students' personal work gains a depth and authenticity rooted in real-world complexity.

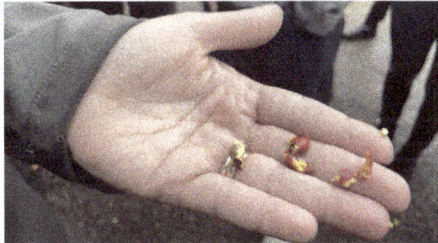

ECO-EXPANSIONISM

CODY DOCK REJUVENATION

BLESSING SULAIMAN

Left: Imagined Eco-Expansionist Society; Above: Artist Impression of the proposed development with view from the River Lea

Every year, millions of people experience the harsh realities of fuel poverty, with thousands tragically losing their lives due to extreme cold in winter and increasingly soaring temperatures in summer. These growing human costs underscore the urgent need to treat the climate emergency with the seriousness it demands. We currently operate within a linear economic system, one shaped by two centuries of capitalist meritocracy, focused on endless extraction and consumption, that is fundamentally unsustainable.

As a self-identified eco-socialist, I believe the mainstream response to the climate crisis is deeply flawed. While movements like Insulate Britain and Extinction Rebellion have brought attention to the issue, their often chaotic and counterproductive tactics have unfortunately reinforced negative stereotypes about eco-socialists - portraying us as unrealistic, disconnected, or even reckless. To drive real change, we must forge a more strategic, inclusive, and practical path forward.

One of capitalism's greatest strengths is its enduring functionality, which has driven growth and development for over two centuries. The term expansionism originally referred to Colonial Europe's efforts to extend its territorial control, under the guise of civilising so-called "barbaric" societies. Eco-expansionism seeks to reclaim this concept, advocating the reappropriation of land once held by the public or local authorities. By combining capitalist efficiency with socialist principles, eco-expansionism offers a bold framework to confront the climate emergency while addressing the deep-rooted social and economic inequalities that define our era. After all, land ownership is not just about territory - it's about power and agency.

Proposed Site Section

Axonometric View of the Proposed Site

Technical Section and Technical Exploded View of Components

Cody Dock is located on the banks of the River Lea in heart of Canning Town, East London, at what was once a former industrial estate. The site has undergone significant transformation, from a once-active gasworks to a neglected area plagued by fly-tipping, before being leased to the Gasworks Dock Partnership by Newham Council for £1 a year over a 999-year term. Historically, this part of London has been overlooked by both investors and researchers, resulting in low economic activity and limited access to nature. Today, Cody Dock has become a vibrant community hub, with ambitious plans for further regeneration.

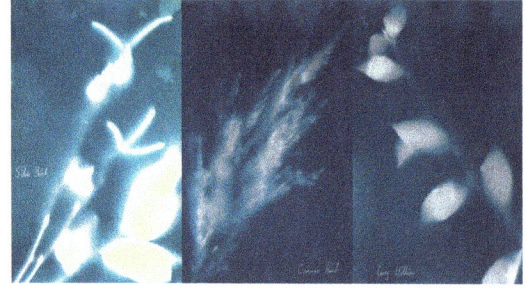

Above: One of the organised canoe trips we took down the River Lea as part of our site analysis.

Below: Cody Dock cyanotypes were created from common plants collected from one of our many forages across the site.

The surrounding area, rich in industrial heritage—from shipbuilding and gasworks to chemical and ironworks—reflects East London's once-proud legacy of industry and labour.

The eco-expansionist vision for Cody Dock begins with the decommissioning of the existing Sainsbury's warehouse on-site. Rather than demolishing it wastefully, the structure will be carefully dismantled, with its components catalogued and added to an on-site material library. These reclaimed materials, in combination with the site's existing ecological assets, will inform a context-driven architectural approach—one that responds to the character of place and promotes low-impact, sustainable construction.

The initial phase of redevelopment will focus on establishing a horticultural hub, serving both ecological and educational purposes. This will act as a catalyst for broader interventions, including community-led housing initiatives and infrastructure that actively contributes to land remediation. Through the reintroduction of native flora and fauna, and the implementation of ecological education programmes, the site will gradually transition into a biodiverse and resilient ecosystem. These nature-based strategies are intended to support the decontamination of both land and water, restoring the ecological vitality of the River Lea and its banks.

Above: Photo of Cody Dock

In essence, the regeneration of Cody Dock encapsulates the ideals of eco-expansionism: the reclamation and restoration of land degraded by decades of capitalist industrial activity, transformed into a model of climate-conscious development. It represents a bold fusion of ecological regeneration, material reuse, and social inclusion—creating a living landscape that is as restorative as it is resilient.

Eco-Expansionism Key Image

TIDAL WALK

LIFE WITHIN THE REEDS

HAMZA KHAN

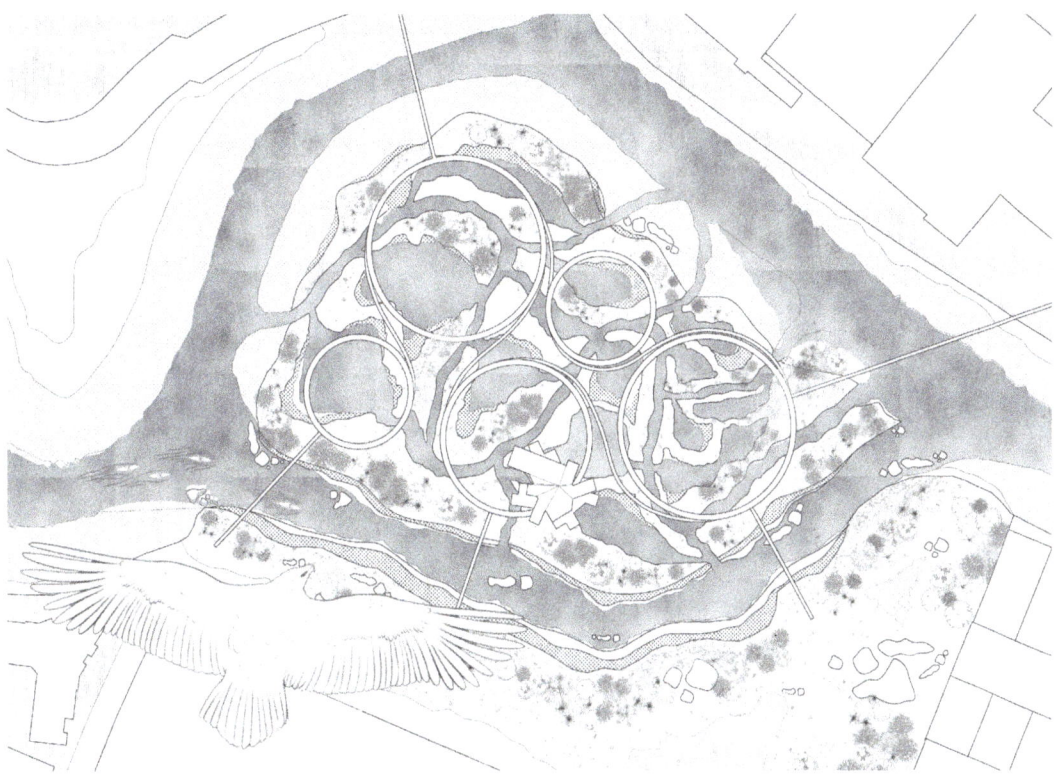

The Predators Descent - Site plan of the proposal expanding the River Lea to provide bird habitats and to increase flooding capacity

In a city shaped by relentless change, it is often the quiet places—and the quiet voices—that vanish first. At Cody Dock, the loss of shared spaces and the steady decline of endangered bird habitats reveal how easily communities and ecologies can be forgotten. By examining the entanglement of urban expansion, social fragmentation, and environmental neglect, Tidal Walk sets out to create a different story.

Tidal Walk emerged as a response to a range of complex and overlapping challenges affecting Cody Dock and the surrounding communities in East London. The area has long struggled with social issues, deep-rooted distrust among residents, fragmented and disconnected communities, antisocial behaviour, and inadequate infrastructure development. Yet alongside these human challenges, there was an equally urgent but often overlooked crisis: the decline of the local ecology. The habitats of endangered bird species—such as Marsh harriers, Peregrine falcons, Swifts, and Kingfishers—have been steadily eroded by relentless infrastructure development, leaving little space for wildlife to survive and thrive. This project was conceived to address both sides of this divide: to heal the social fabric and restore the natural one. By creating a new wetlands sanctuary and an inclusive community centre, Tidal Walk aims to provide spaces where people can learn, reconnect, and take an active role in stewardship of their environment. The project's vision is to weave stronger bonds—uniting communities and restoring the vital ties between people and nature. Creating a shared space of purpose, resilience,

Through the blinds

Silent Lookout

and hope that endures.

One of the key programmes focused on bird watching, but the relationship between people and nature felt fractured. The challenge was clear: how can they coexist without intrusion? Visits to Walthamstow Wetlands and Cody Dock revealed a flaw in traditional bird hides—they confine the observer and distance them from the natural world.

This led to the idea of a bird blind—not a barrier, but a skin that blends with the landscape. Built from reclaimed timber, with transparent openings and subtle apertures, it invites quiet observation without disturbance. A space for stillness and reconnection, where the boundary between human and habitat softly fades.

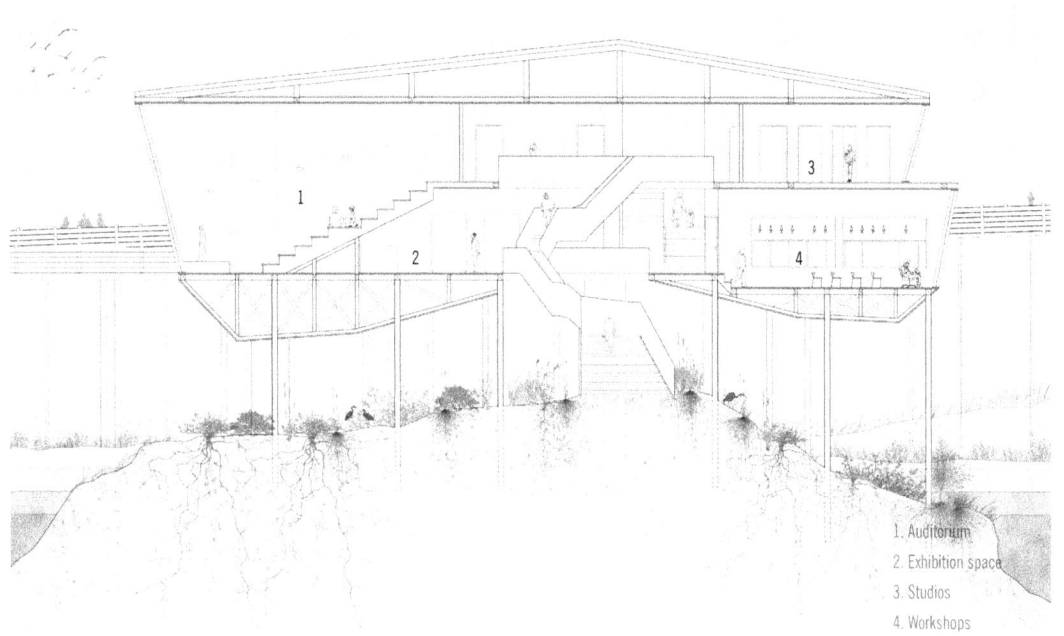

1. Auditorium
2. Exhibition space
3. Studios
4. Workshops

The community centre offers a versatile space for learning, connection, and shared purpose. The auditorium invites schools and residents to discover and learn about the rich history. Exhibition spaces celebrating artwork and cultural identities.

Rewilding workshops encourage people to care for the landscape together, fostering pride and belonging. Studio spaces support local start-ups and small businesses, helping skills and ideas take root close to home.

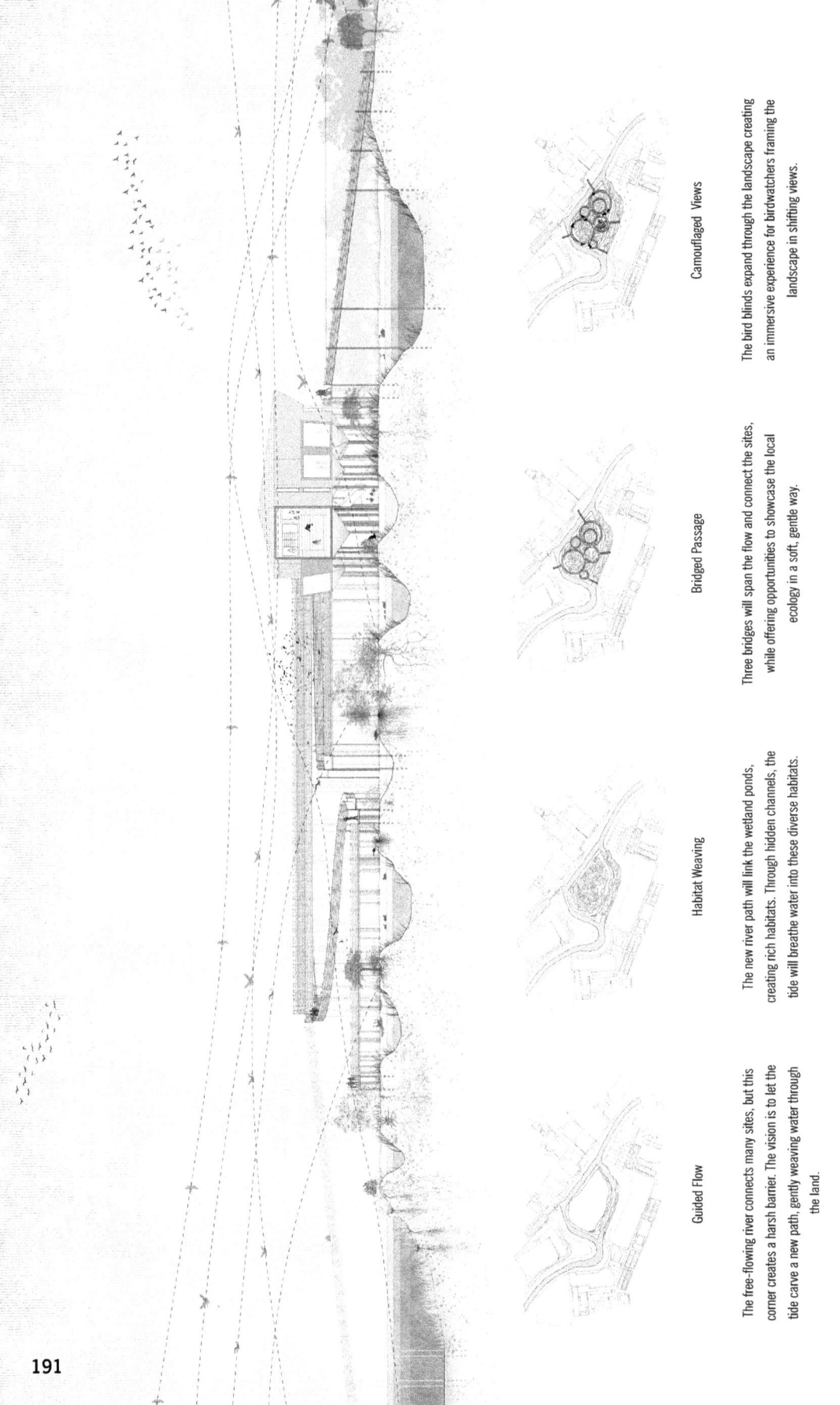

Guided Flow

The free-flowing river connects many sites, but this corner creates a harsh barrier. The vision is to let the tide carve a new path, gently weaving water through the land.

Habitat Weaving

The new river path will link the wetland ponds, creating rich habitats. Through hidden channels, the tide will breathe water into these diverse habitats.

Bridged Passage

Three bridges will span the flow and connect the sites, while offering opportunities to showcase the local ecology in a soft, gentle way.

Camouflaged Views

The bird blinds expand through the landscape creating an immersive experience for birdwatchers framing the landscape in shifting views.

Construction Sequence

Artist Impression - Rewilding the city edge

192

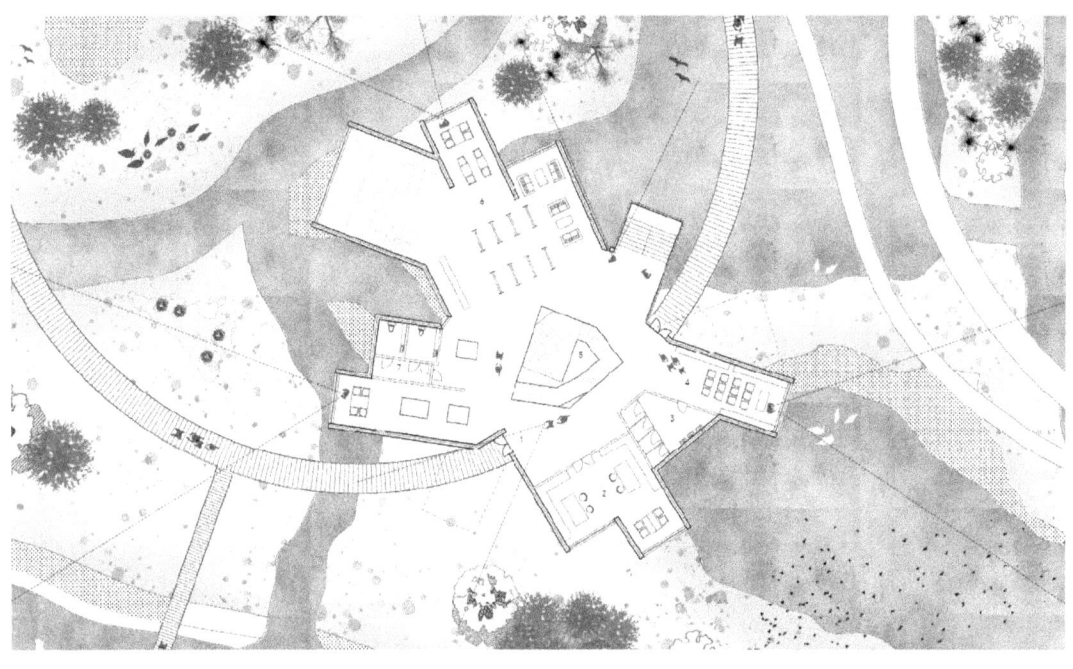

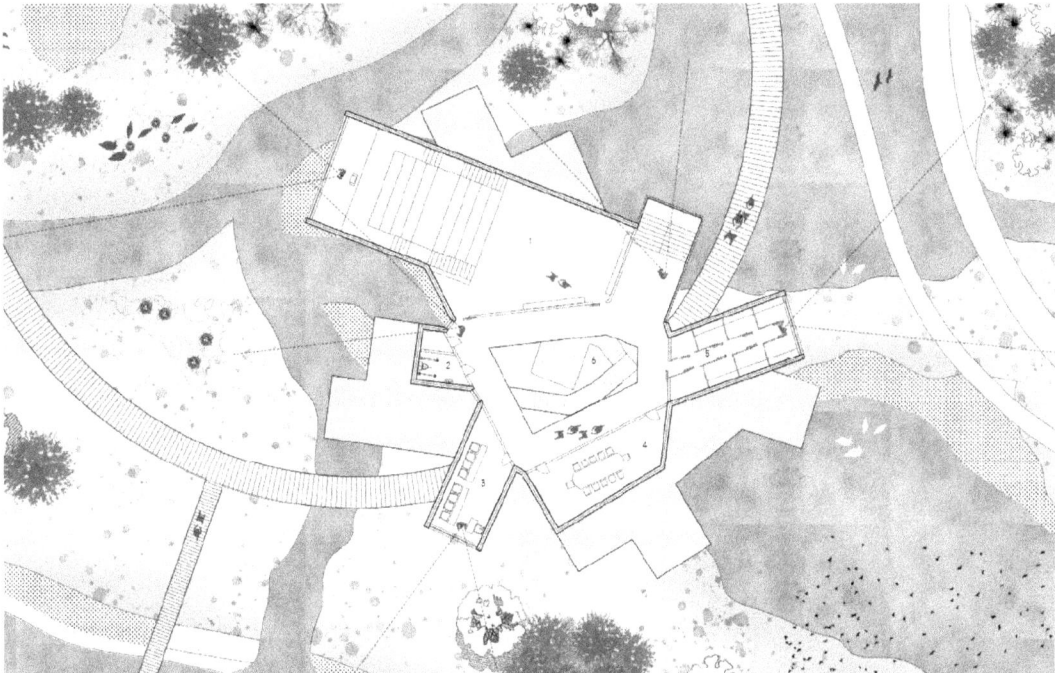

Celebrating the landscape - Ground and First Floor Plans

The structure was conceived with an open-plan design, fostering social interaction among community members through expansive exhibition spaces and dynamic workshops. The two floors distinguish public and private realms: open, fluid areas invite connection, while enclosed spaces nurture focused classes and mentorship. Generous openings and the building's careful orientation frame key views that celebrate the surrounding landscape. Subtle voids draw gentle traces of the outdoors within, uniting and enlivening the structure as a harmonious whole. Conceived as a bridge between two once-disconnected worlds humans and birds, it invites both to dwell in balance, united by a shared reverence for the landscape.

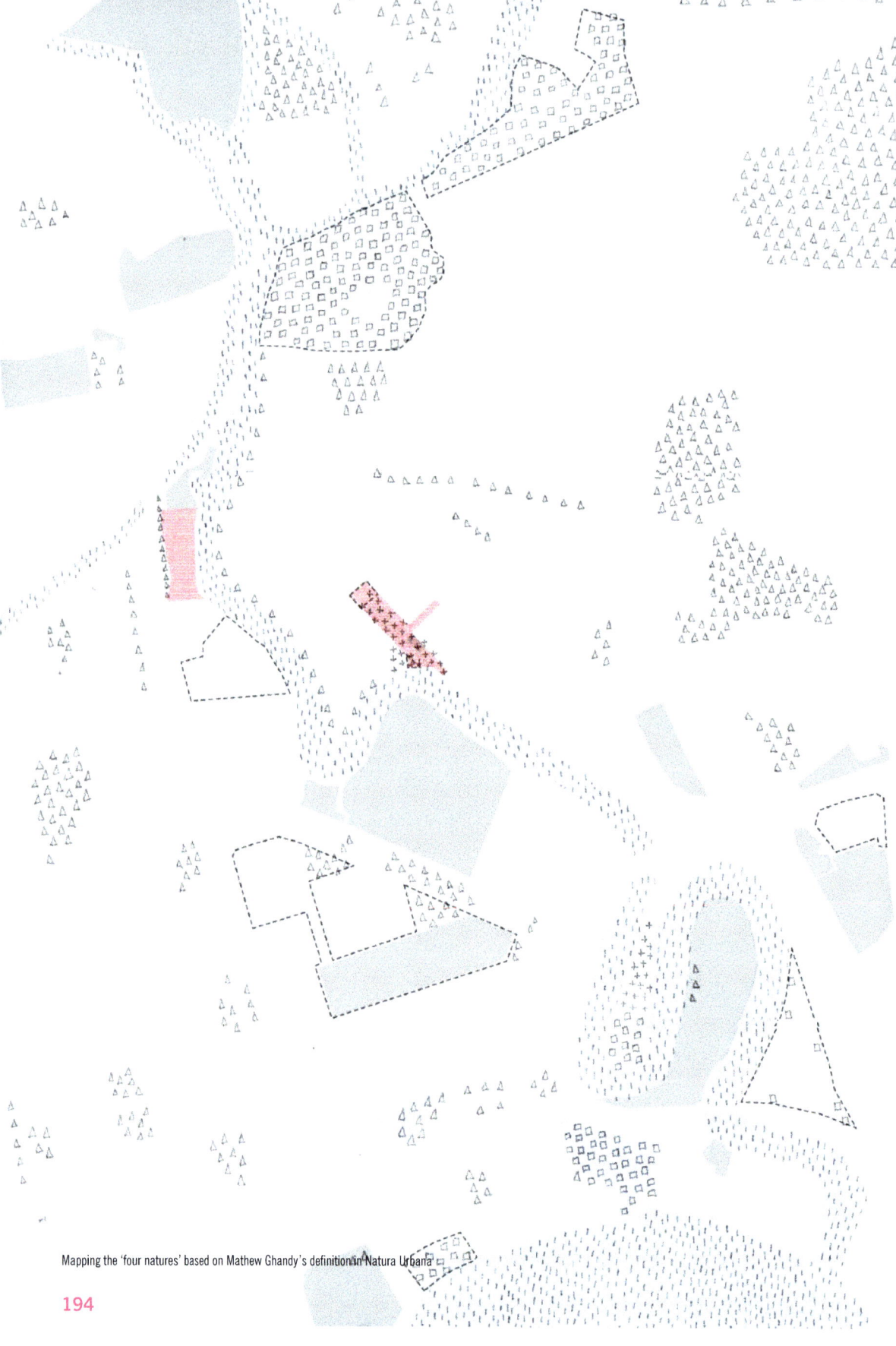

Mapping the 'four natures' based on Mathew Ghandy's definition in Natura Urbana

RUDERAL AUTOPOESIS

EMBRACING FOURTH NATURE

WILLIAM LAMBERT

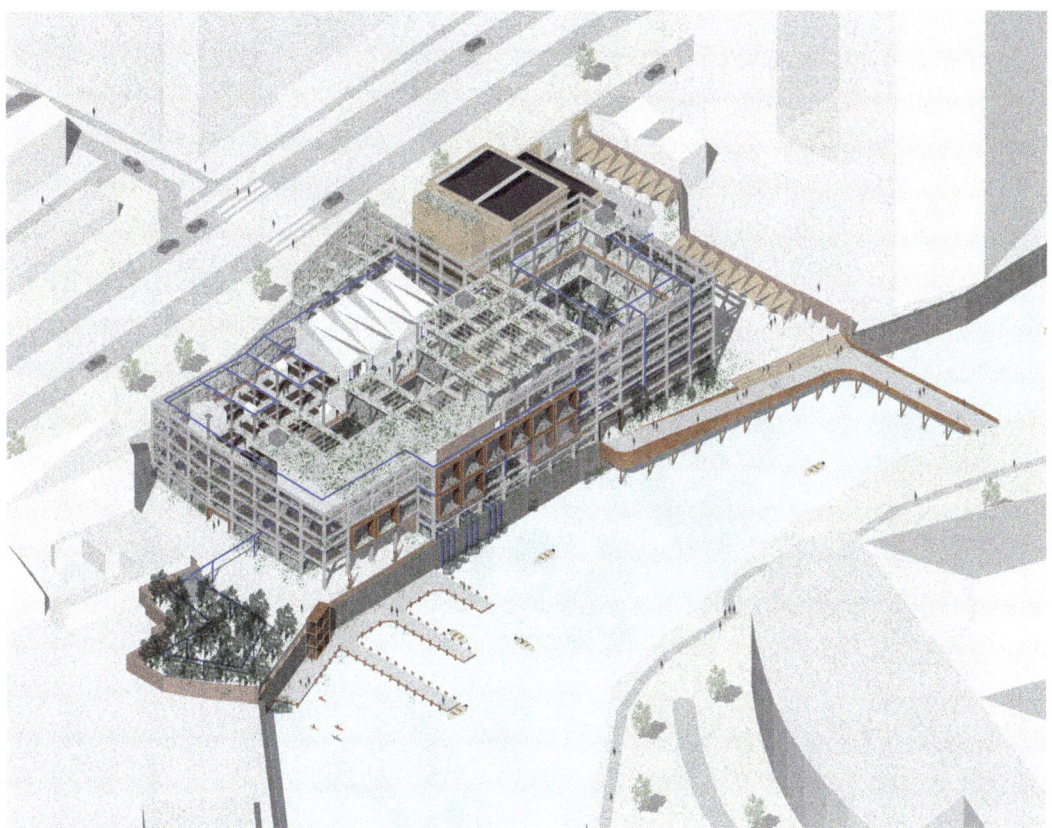

Artist Impression of the Ruderal Autopoiesis Proposal

The River Lea originates in Bedfordshire, running along the Essex border and between Tower Hamlets and Newham in East London before meeting the River Thames. Around this area of the lower Lea Valley is an expanse of large-scale housing developments that fail to create identity or support the rich ecology of the river, with the average stay of residents being less than 4 years. This project seeks to integrate ecological and socio-economic systems with a proposal for the adaptive reuse of 23-26 Gillender St, a series of warehouses on the bank of the Lea, into a multi-use community centre.

Urban Ecology

According to Matthew Gandy's 'Natura Urbana', industrial metabolism (a field within urban ecology) suggests there are flows of energy and material to connect 'socioeconomic' systems with ecosystems. Within this, Gandy also refers to ecologist Ingo Kowarik's fourfold typology of urban nature as a means of definition. Each of the first, second, third and fourth natures interlink ecological metabolisms with socio-economical metabolisms to varying degrees due to their characteristics.

An ecology report produced by the Gasworks Partnership at Cody Dock, a community gardens and creative quarter situated 500m down the Lea, suggests that disused sites and no-go areas have created great opportunities for post-industrial habitat succession (fourth nature) and host rich urban biodiversity as a result compared to second or third nature alternatives that tend to be more controlled. In order to preserve rich urban ecology, this project considers the preservation of fourth nature as a key strategy within the multi-programmatic scheme, unlike current neighbouring residential developments.

Interlinking Metabolisms

In response to the research undergone on the surrounding context of the site, the programme looks to provide a programme that bring together existing 'ruderal' community centres/activities, allowing them to expand and further build communities on this site. Residents highlighted several centres for activity that are reasonably successful such as the R-Urban community growing and the Teviot community centre which host a multitude of activities such as Arabic classes and martial arts.

Spatially the project integrates what are typically controlled interior spaces in amongst programmatic elements designed to support second, third and fourth nature, in attempts to break the cultural standards of controlling nature at a distance.

Ruderal Zones

As previously identified, a key requirement for ruderal species to flourish is disturbed surfaces. This project takes a radical approach in which existing elements of the warehouses undergo a controlled demolition to break through areas of the concrete slab floors and walls, leaving rubble that can be scattered to form disturbed ground. Different sizes of rubble are arranged in different locations to provide a range of surfaces left to be taken over by fourth

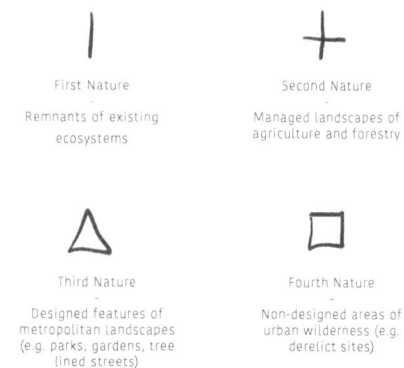

First Nature
Remnants of existing ecosystems

Second Nature
Managed landscapes of agriculture and forestry

Third Nature
Designed features of metropolitan landscapes (e.g. parks, gardens, tree lined streets)

Fourth Nature
Non-designed areas of urban wilderness (e.g. derelict sites)

nature. This not only generates and reuses waste materials, but opens up the building to the elements whilst retaining the key structural grid of columns and concrete members of the façade.

The rubble can be placed in different arrangements over a layer of soil, stacking large pieces around columns, finer towards the edges and some arranged flat to form a path. These subtle changes in surface treatment allow for a range of growing and human activity.

Polycarbonate panels can be opened allowing a subtler threshold to form between the 'interior' spaces such as the research centre, soil treatment plant and distillery located along the ruderal zones border. Access to these zones is denied from the public by infilling the frame with wire mesh, limiting human impact on the developing fourth nature. However, the thresholds are still permeable allowing for pollination across thresholds and stays visually permeable for people.

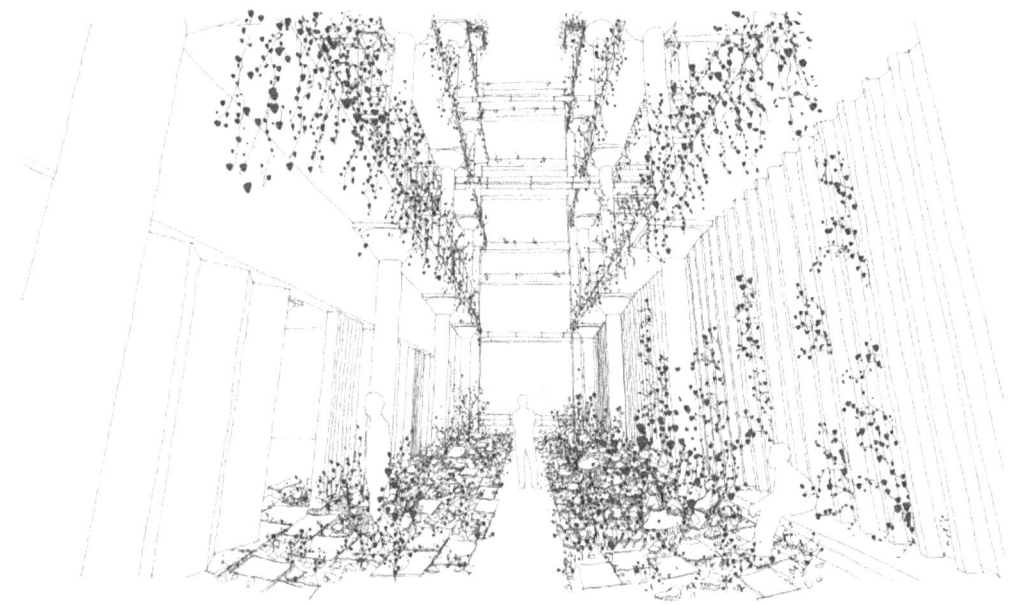

The proposed warehouse cut through route - 5 years later

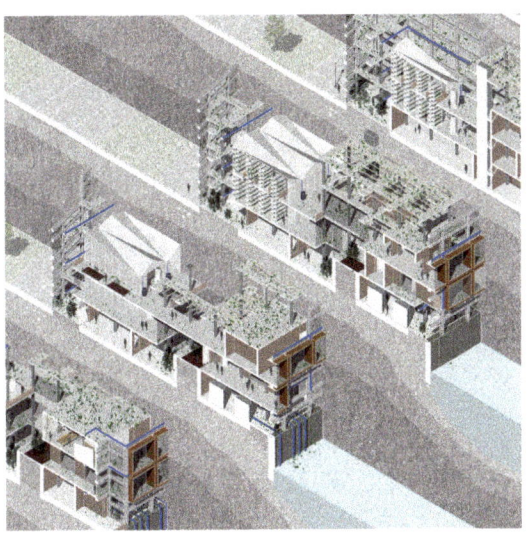

Sliced isometric sections through the proposal

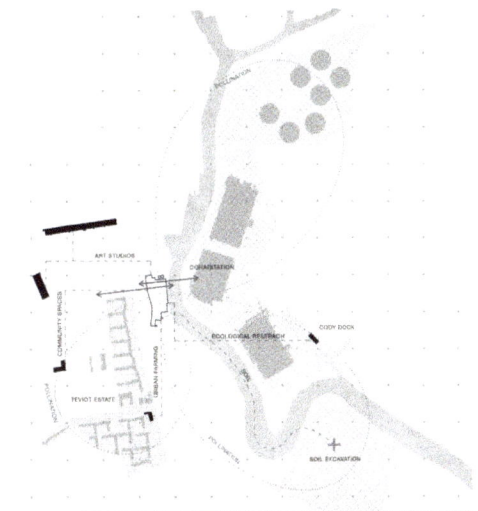

Top: Diagram illustrating ways of interlinking the proposal into its programmatic context and masterplan; Above: Collage render of community meeting space

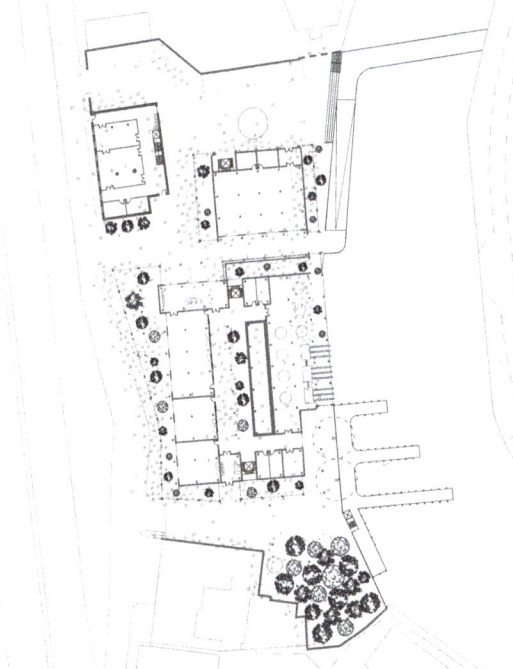

0m 100m

Bottom left: Proposed Site plan
Bottom right: Section through existing and proposed with internal green courtyard, existing cast concrete columns and areas of the floor rebars remain, whilst brick infills and roof removed

univerCITY

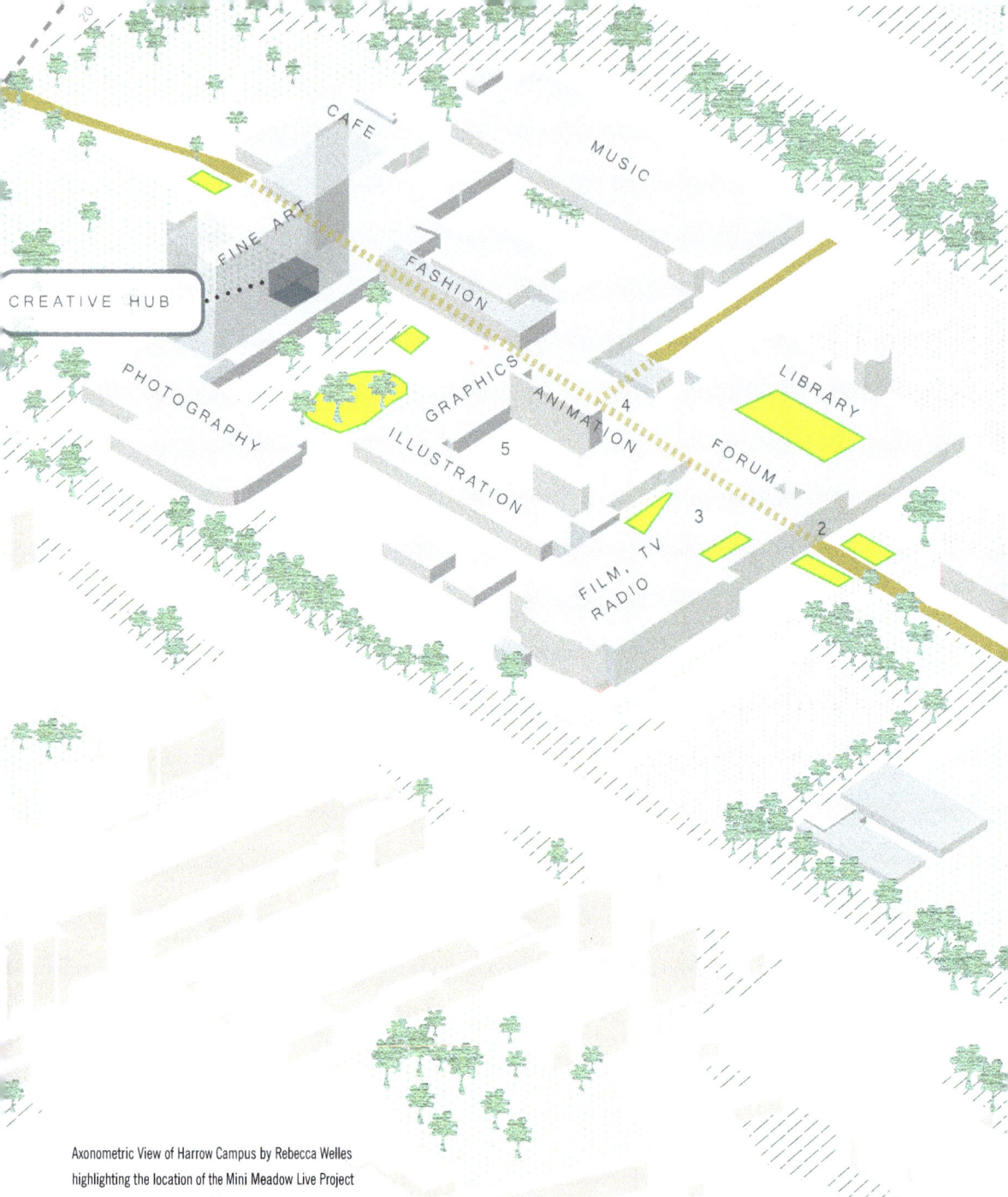

Axonometric View of Harrow Campus by Rebecca Welles
highlighting the location of the Mini Meadow Live Project

What will the campus of the future look like? We investigated and developed visions of what a campus of the future could be, in the context of our very own Campus at Harrow. New developments will be taking place in the short and long-term at this site and this Live Project was part of the Vice Chancellor's vision to create Botanical Gardens at the campus, including exhibiting students work, which ended up becoming the Mini Meadow Live Project. Initially we focused on landscape concepts for the campus, including ideas for a pavilion which forms the Pavilion Prototype pavilion, which was later constructed at the rear podium at Marylebone Campus, see end of this chapter. These initial proposals followed larger architectural ideas with a programmes focusing on student living with enhanced communal offerings, developing approaches with spatially ambitious

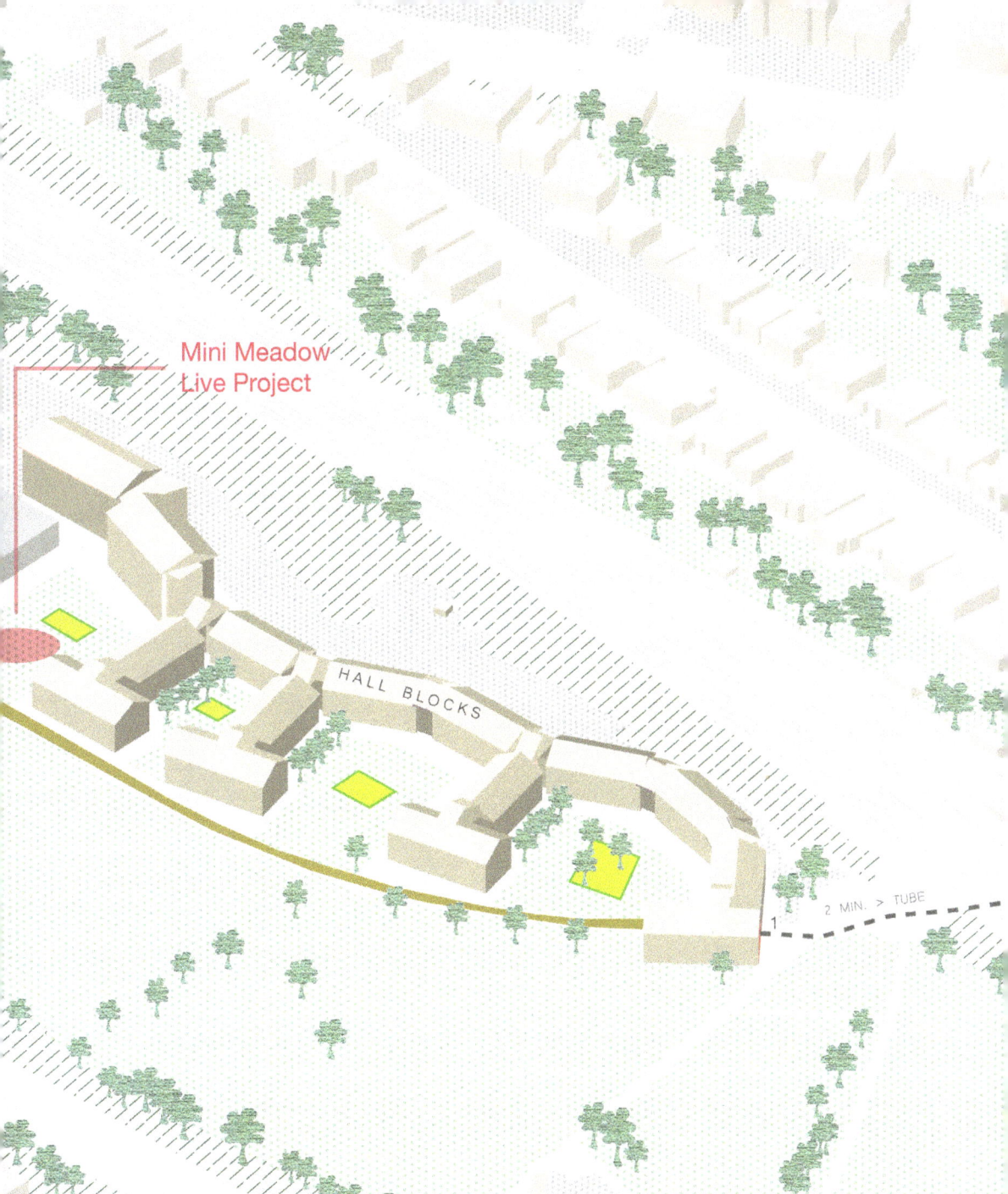

concepts as integral part of the landscape ideas. How can campus ideas challenge the status quo, and what would the ideal university be like? The work is based on values, such as inclusivity, celebrating equality and diversity. We promote well-being through design with the aim to improve physical and mental health, as well as expanding social interactions. Relationships between culture and nature, between architecture and ecology were explored whilst celebrating the wonders of biodiversity with a one-planet and climate-action approach. We focused on sensory, experiential designs with dynamic, inventive, visionary material and spatial outcomes. We aspire to an architecture with a phenomenological approach, that is conveying an intense spatial quality, which is contextual, intuitive, 'bottom-up', where facets of light, views, materiality, and access to green spaces are implicitly considered.

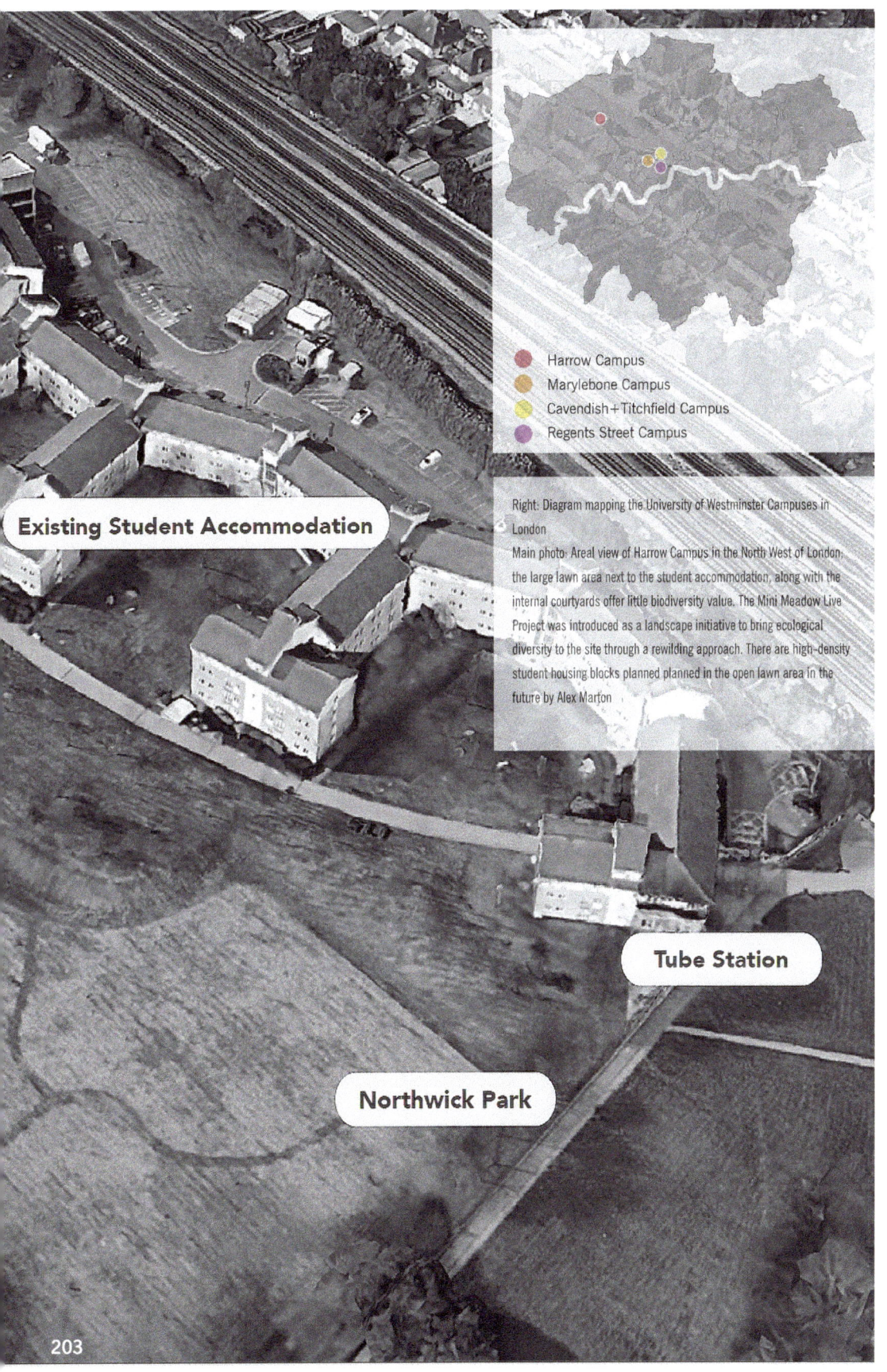

- Harrow Campus
- Marylebone Campus
- Cavendish+Titchfield Campus
- Regents Street Campus

Existing Student Accommodation

Tube Station

Northwick Park

Right: Diagram mapping the University of Westminster Campuses in London

Main photo: Areal view of Harrow Campus in the North West of London, the large lawn area next to the student accommodation, along with the internal courtyards offer little biodiversity value. The Mini Meadow Live Project was introduced as a landscape initiative to bring ecological diversity to the site through a rewilding approach. There are high-density student housing blocks planned planned in the open lawn area in the future by Alex Marton

The Mini Meadows Live Project, photo by the author

MINI MEADOW
LIVE LANDSCAPE PROJECT
2022-2023

TUTORS: MARIA KRAMER AND BRUCE IRWIN
STUDENTS: OMAR ABU WISHAH, FATIMA AL-GERSANI, ARJUN BANSAL, JULIA BRODZISKA, EVANGELOS CHRISTOU, MERYEM GELDIYEVA, VALENTINA GONZALEZ-CASTANEDA, RALUCA HAMZA, CHRISTY PROTHERO, ALEX MARTON, JESSICA MORRISON, ANDREA-LAURA PETRESCU, GEORGE SORAPURE, SOFIJA STUPAR, BERLIN TAS, HASNIHA THANGANATHAN, LAURA VASILE, REBECCA WELLER, HAMZA KHAN
PARTNERS: ALESSANDRA FODERARO, UNIVERSITY ESTATES TEAM, ADP ARCHITECTURE

The Mini Meadow Live Landscape Project was co-designed with BA Architecture students and staff from the School of Architecture and Cities to promote biodiversity and well-being within the campus. This was part of a project, where we looked at Harrow Campus holistically and students interviewed local staff and students to find out their needs and aspirations.

The planting has been designed to prolong the flowering species of the seasons, to create a space where there is food available for insects all year round. A super pollinator meadow mix has replaced most of the single species lawn to create the 'Mini Meadows', which is low maintenance and provides further food source.

Below: Landscape plan below by Rebecca Welles; Right: Photo of the Mini Meadow

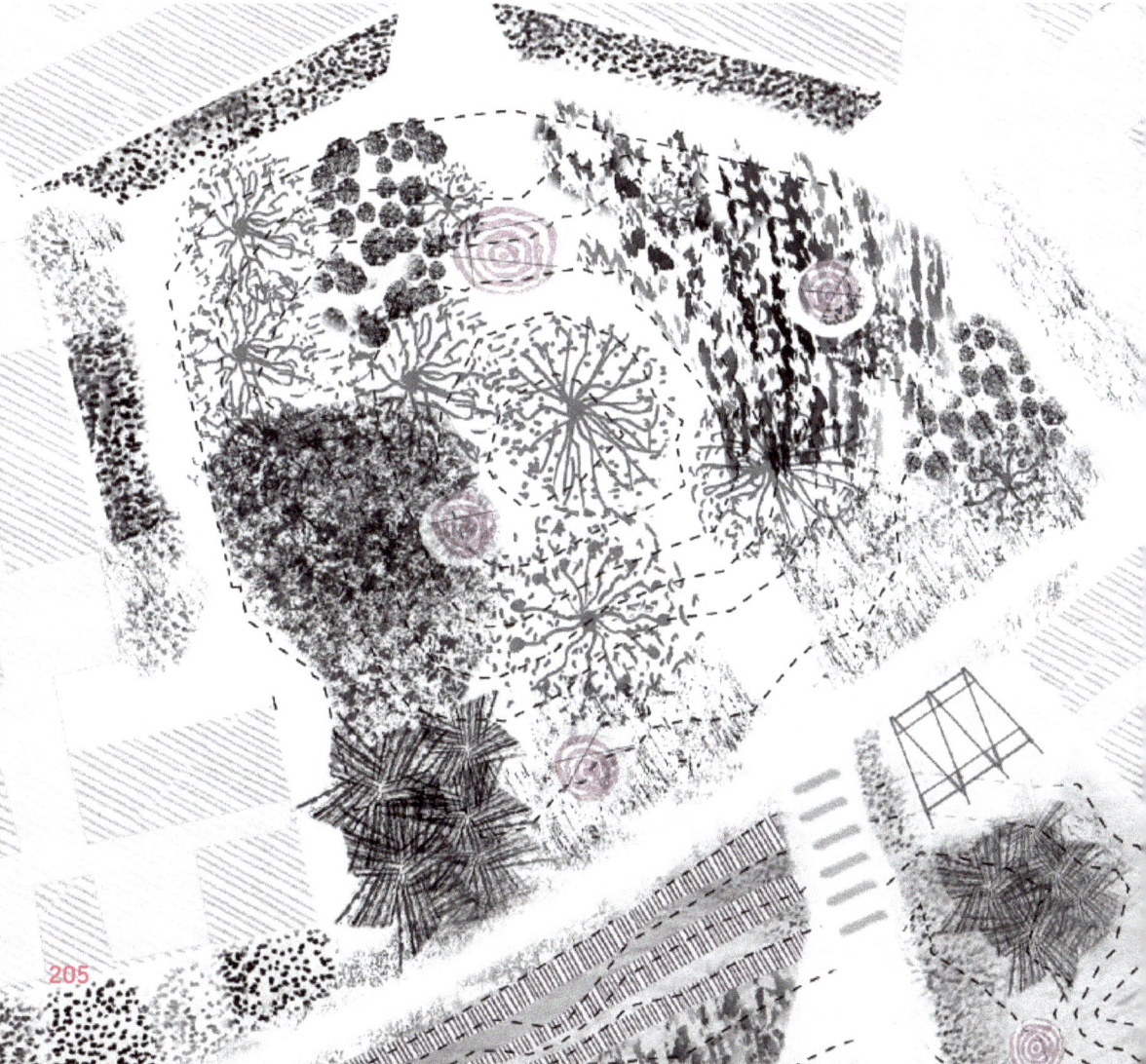

Wild Flower Meadow in Summer by Jessica Morrison

Wild Flower Meadow in Winter by Jessica Morrison

Top: Engagement by student from Marylebone Campus with students from Harrow Campus finding out what they are missing and what they enjoy
Centre: Mapping of sounds of the site at Harrow Campus by Jessica Morrison
Bottom: Artist Impression of pavilion proposal within landscape strategy by Rebecca Wells

Top right: Engagement by student from Marylebone Campus with students from Harrow Campus finding out what they are missing and what they enjoy

Centre right: Strategic landscape Plan by Laura Vasile indicating how the Mini Meadow could grow to the other student accommodation courtyards

Right bottom: Artist Impression of seating zone within biodiverse planting ideas by Christy Prothero

Top: Landscape proposal for the large lawn area of the Harrow Campus by Berfin Tas

Photo of the monotonous biodiversity-poor lawn at Harrow Campus, photo by the author

We worked closely with the Estate Team who engaged a landscape architect (ADP) to help specify the plants and organised the tender. This is the only Live Project where students were not at all involved in the implementation of the design. There were charrettes with the landscape architects where we showed the students designs which informed the final proposal.

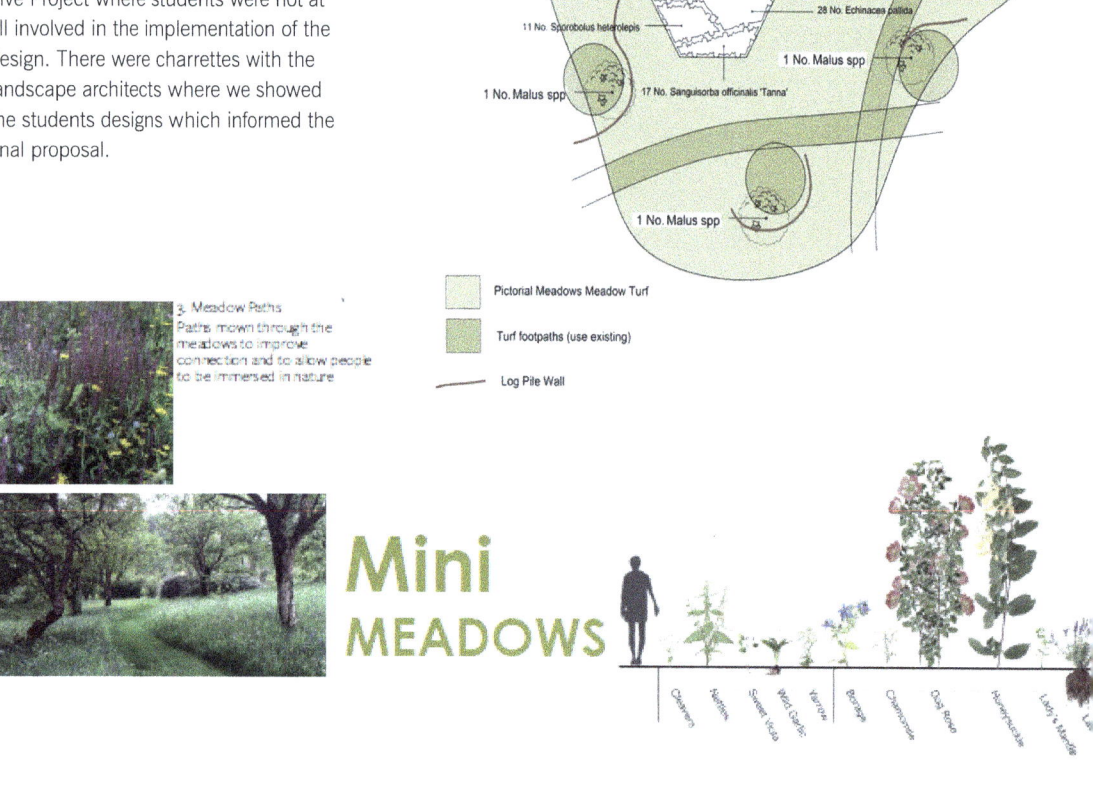

Mini MEADOWS

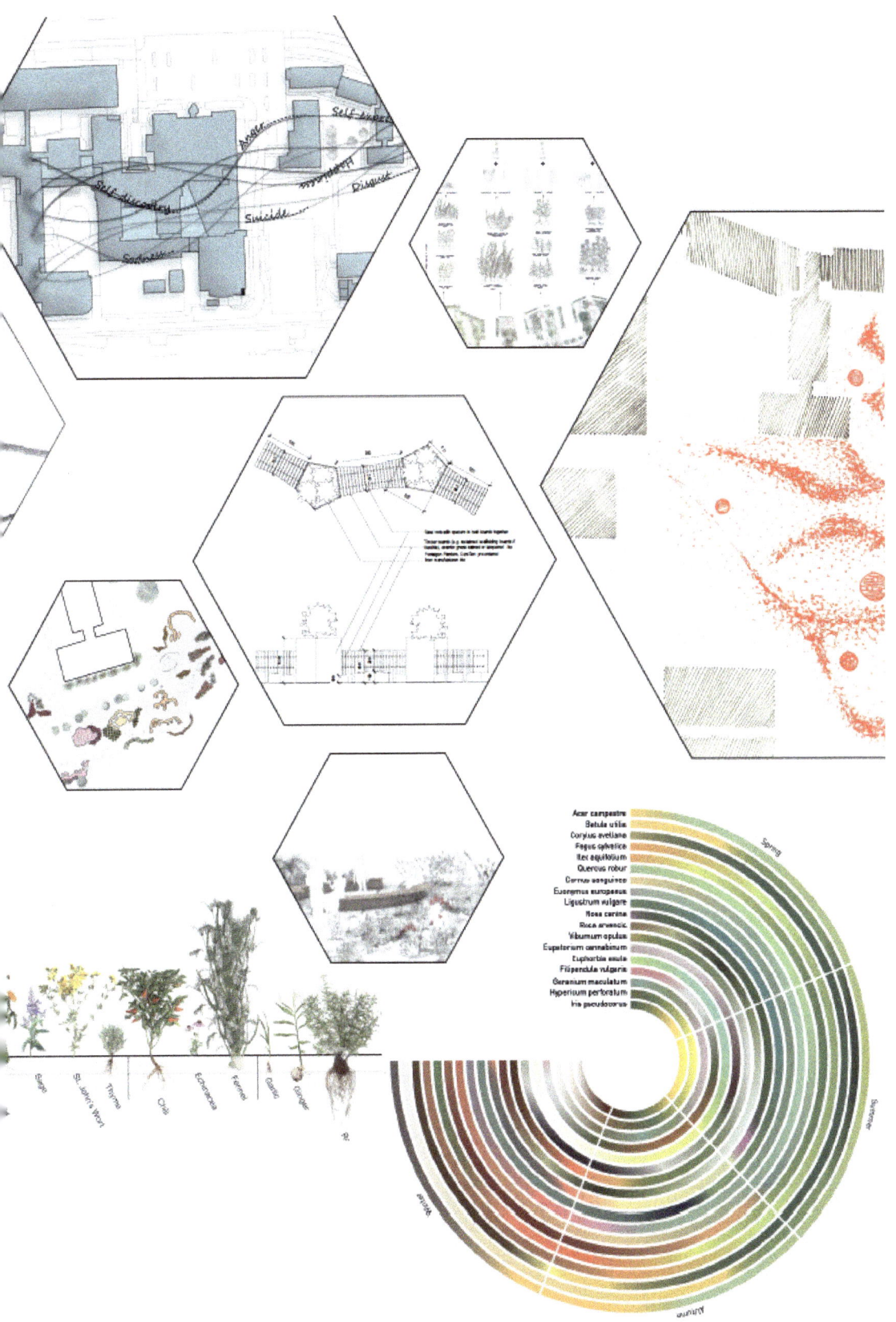

Top: The Mini Meadows Live Project during the College Summer Party, photo by author

Top: The Mini Meadows Live Project with blossoming biodiverse flowers, photo by author

MINI MEADOW LIVE PROJECT — ALEX MARTON

STUDENT PROJECTS

GEORGE SORAPURE

BECKY WELLES

NORTHWICK CRAFT COLLECTIVE
STUDENT LIVING & COMMUNITY CERAMIC STUDIO
REBECCA WELLER

Top: Proposed Strategic Landscape Plan at Harrow Campus; Left: Making slip tiles

This project is developed based on the visions of what a University campus of the future could be. Interviewing a wide range of local students and staff about their needs and aspiration was the basis for concept and programmatic development. The core concept was to provide the opportunity for students and the local community to participate in crafting architectural elements on the site, allowing for a sense of ownership. Aiming to strengthen rather than displacing existing community networks.

This project is developed based on the visions of what a campus of the future could be, in the context of the Westminster University's campus at Harrow. New developments will be taking place at the site and the semester 1 brief was to support the Vice Chancellor's vision to create a Botanical Garden at Harrow. In semester 2 the brief was for a hybrid programme including student living, incorporating the local community and the potential for outdoor learning.

Stakeholder engagement, interviewing and surveying a wide range of local students, staff and the local community about their needs and aspiration was the basis for the concept and programmatic development. These participatory activities promote a deeper understanding of on-site needs creating an awareness of the complex relationships of stakeholders. Following the stakeholder engagement, core brief developments were promoting well-being, improving physical and mental health, as well as expanding social interactions and inclusivity.

Harrow Campus is situated in the North West of London, a direct 25min tube ride from the Marylebone Campus. The campus has generous open spaces and situated adjacent to Northwick Park Hospital and relatively separated from the diverse, local community. It is home to courses, such as fashion, music, journalism and the arts. There is existing student housing for ~600 students on site.

Northwick Craft Collective aims to encourage students to engage with the local community, improve student sleep cycles and to create a sociable and vibrant place for local residents in Harrow. The proposal provides 40 sleep pods for students, as well as flexible study spaces, community ceramic studio, community kitchen, student kitchen & play zone for local children to use. The community spaces are organised around outdoor circulation spaces to provide maximum potential for social interaction. The bedrooms are developed based on providing an acoustic sanctuary focused on sleep and relaxation, without the distractions of work and technology.

The design development process was enacted through sketches, model making at various scales, and research through visiting garden precedents including the masterplan of the Olympic park. This iterative approach allowed for continuous refinement of both spatial relationships and material choices, ensuring that each design decision directly responded to the community's expressed needs and aspirations.

1:1 ceramic tiled cladding system

The outdoor circulation strategy underwent significant development throughout the design process. Initial concepts explored traditional corridor systems, but stakeholder feedback emphasised the desire for more informal, garden-like pathways that would encourage spontaneous encounters. This led to the creation of meandering routes that connect different programmatic zones while providing opportunities for pause and

Artist Impression of the ceramic studio.

Top: Rebecca carrying out stakeholder engagement on the Westminster University Campus at Harrow. Above: a studio group visit with the Vice Chancellor to the Olympic park as research for the project.

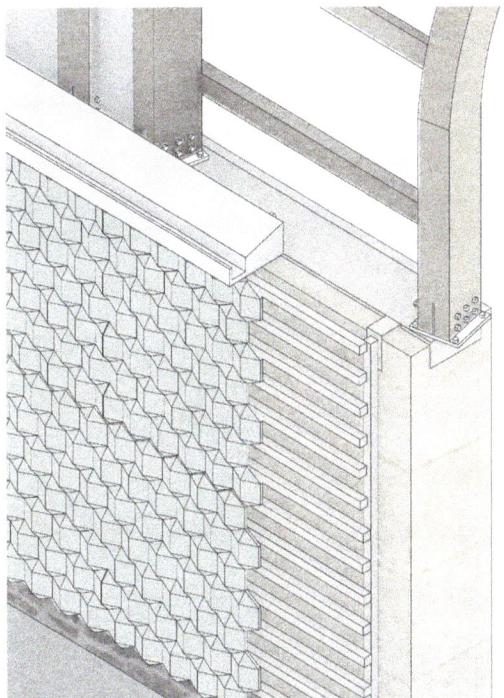

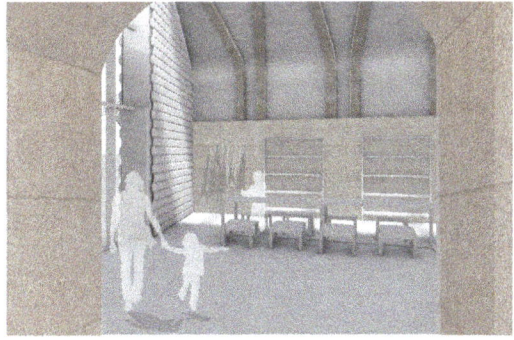

Entrance of the ceramic studio.

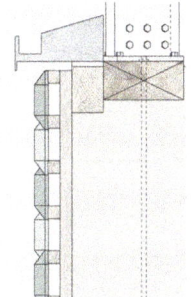

Axonometric detail drawing of the low carbon structure.　　Section Detail of low carbon wall.　Glazed ceramic tiles exhibited at exhibition.

reflection. These circulation spaces were designed to blur the boundaries between interior and exterior, with covered walkways that extend the usable space throughout various weather conditions.

The project also explored a low embodied energy approach. Where possible low embodied carbon materials were chosen including cork, glulaminated timber, ferrock foundations & cob structural walls. Some materials fabricated on site, including the tiled cladding and cob walls, reducing emissions from transportation of materials, other materials sourced from less than 4km from the site.

The proposal uses a combination of timber structural elements (glue-lam & CLT) and low embodied energy construction methods, including cob and expanded cork structural walls. The cladding is made out of a combination of polycarbonate panels and terracotta tiles made on site by students and the local community.

The Northwick Craft Collective offers a model for campus development that strengthens rather than displaces existing community networks. Ultimately, this project represents a vision of campus life that extends beyond the boundaries of institutional walls, creating a living laboratory

Above: Section through the ceramic studio.

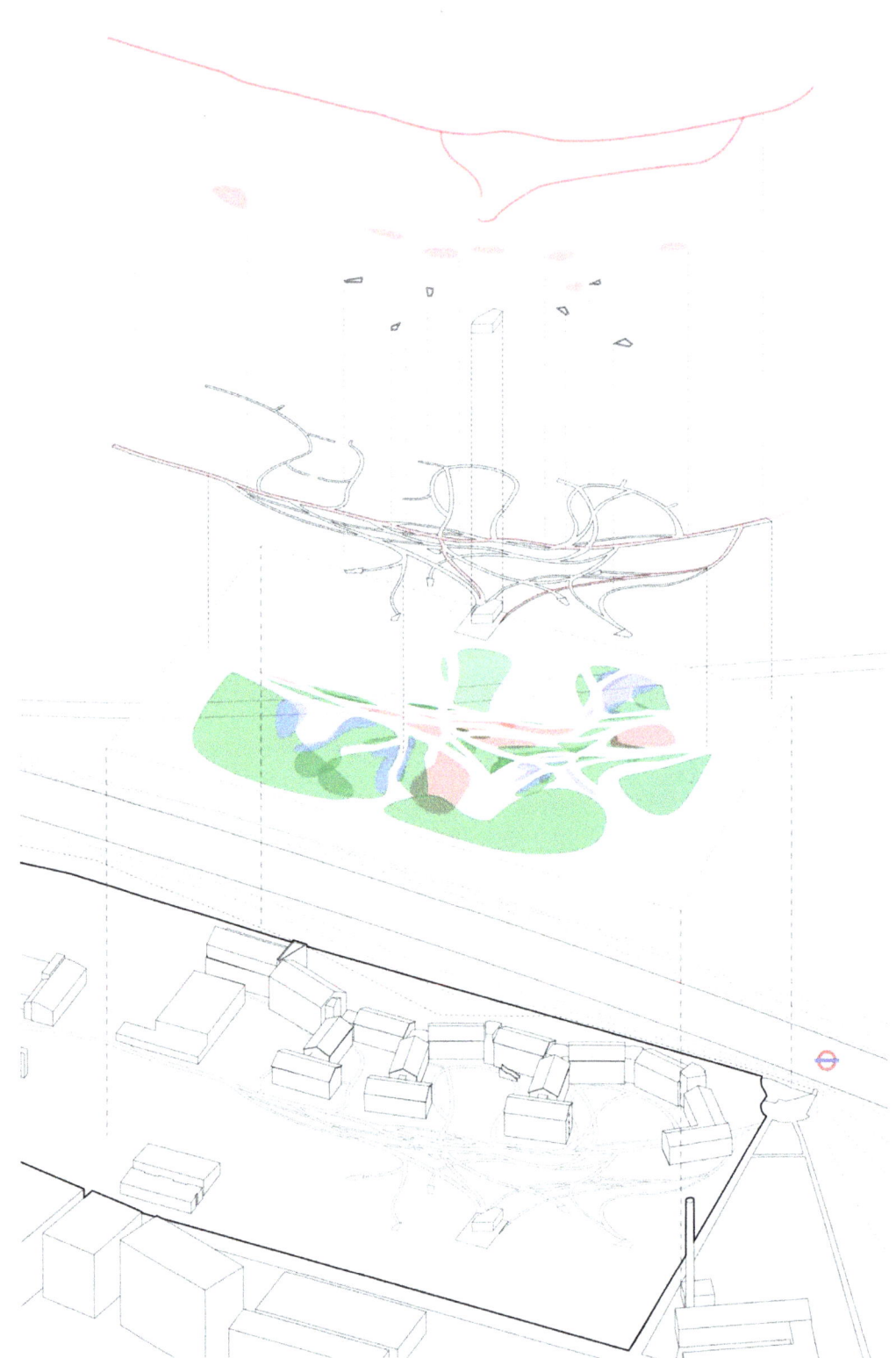

Explosive axonometric view of proposed landscape strategy with new path network, pavilions and a proposed social hub

CONNECTING THE CAMPUS

FROM ISOLATION TO INCLUSION: DESIGN INTERVENTIONS FOR SOCIAL WELLBEING

GEORGE SORAPURE

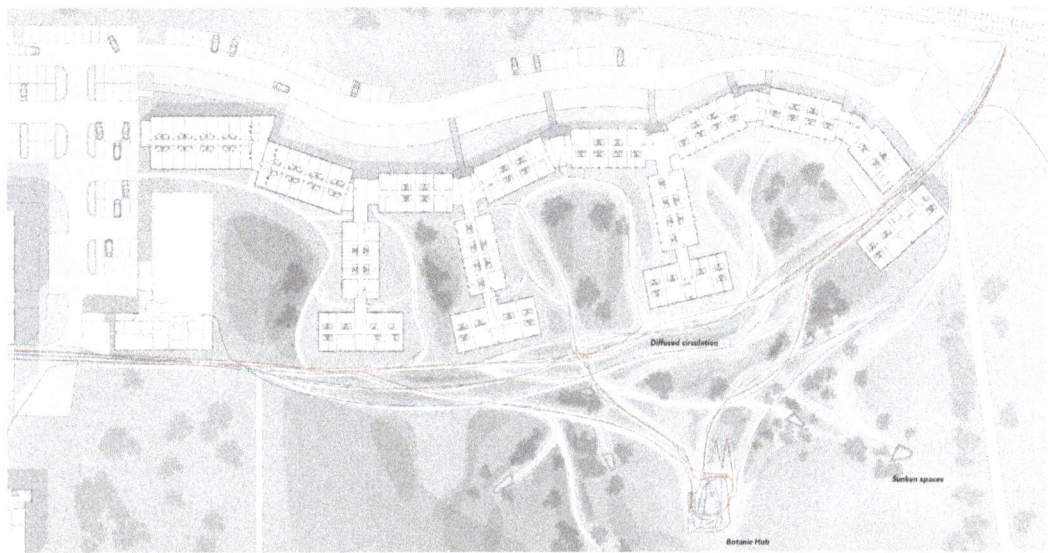

Top: Strategic Landscape Plan with new connecting routes, pavilions and social hubs

The current UoW Harrow campus accommodation amplifies social anxiety through poorly planned spaces that create exposure and limited escape routes, harming students' well-being and academic growth. A re-imagined landscape strategy using diverse planting, varied topography and private sunken areas with multi-programmatic opportunities, provides safe, calming environments that reduce stress, encourage choice in social engagement, and reconnect students with nature. The architectural proposal is seamlessly integrated within this academic garden with layered thresholds.

In social anxiety disorder, also called social phobia, everyday interactions cause significant anxiety, self-consciousness and embarrassment because students fear being scrutinized or judged negatively by others.
Triggers of social anxiety:
- Fear of negative judgment, embarrassment, or humiliation
- Anxiety about visible signs of nervousness that may cause embarrassment (e.g., blushing, trembling, sweating)
- Avoidance of social interactions, attention, unfamiliar people or of situations where you might be the centre of attention
- Anticipatory anxiety before events and intense distress during them
- Post-event self-criticism, expectation of worst outcomes

The existing UoW Harrow campus student accommodation achieves its goal to maximise profit margins, while disregarding the intense social environments that emerge from the architecture. Students are packed into small indistinguishable units that exist in environments made up of harsh inaccessible boundaries, blind spots, unwanted view pathways, open private spaces and claustrophobic single route access spaces. These environments, both inside the accommodation and outside in the courtyards, creates a nightmare for those who suffer from social anxiety. This will drastically effect students emotional and physical well-being, as well as their education and growth as a young adult. Attempting to identify nodes of social anxiety triggers of the site allows an opportunity to adapt these spaces to improve the mental and physical health of the students.

The everyday exposure to nature, the ritualistic process of tending to crop and the anti-anxiety properties of the botanicals combined should provide a natural lifestyle through the campus landscape that effectively reduces stress and anxiety. Providing safe and quiet farming spaces for ritualistic reflection would provide opportunities for individuals to remove themselves from everyday stresses and triggers.

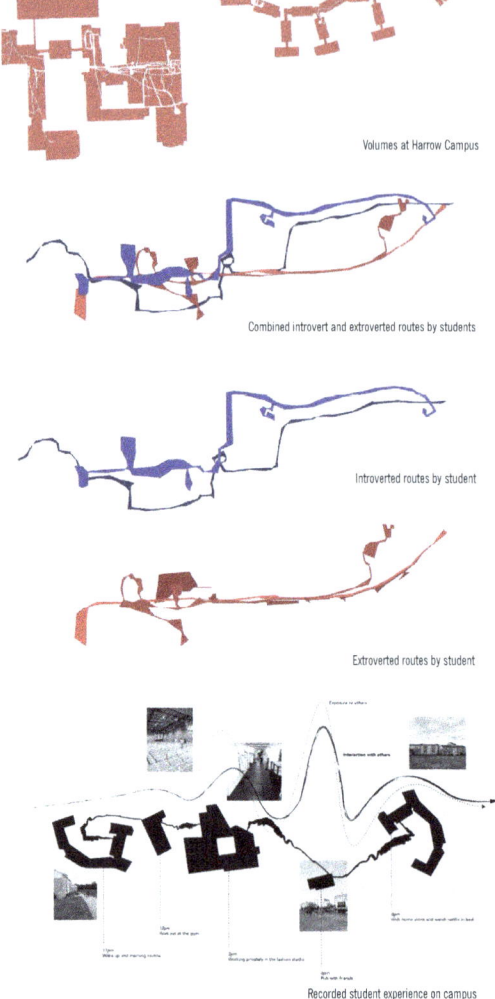

Diagrams of various routes taken by students at the campus

Sketch testing open and enclosed, solid and transparent spaces

Artist Impressions of exposed and enclosed spaces within the proposed landscape

The University of Westminster campus has a unique relationship with the surrounding architectural, cultural and spatial environment of Harrow. The campus's built environment, as well as its students, stand out from the surroundings, creating a microcosm of young creative students in an enclosed bubble that has little relationships to the community beyond its gates. The site is expansive, boasting a multitude of creative facilities such as photography light rooms, Fine art studios, fashion catwalks, events spaces and music studios. From the space analysis, it can easily be deduced that the university campus exists within a large quantity of green space. These vast greens are rarely accessed by students or staff and are left largely ignored, only to be see as a buffer space between the accommodation and the learning facilities. The green exists as a monoculture of short cut grass without any diversification of flora and fauna. This opens up expansive opportunities for architectural intervention.

The landscaping strategy consists of points of open communal experience and private areas for reflection and relaxation. Both the topography and the density of the planting creates moments of exposure and enclosure within the grounds. The arrangement of these spaces lets students choose how they want to engage with others while on the campus without isolating anybody.

The open landscape: The open environment carves into a multi level landscaping space, allowing the flora and fauna to develop at varying heights to enclose and submerge wanderers.

Sunken spaces: Through exploration, students looking for private spaces can find sunken levels where they can relax, reflect or momentarily remove themselves from the busy lifestyle of a student.

Artist Impression of the proposed student accommodation with flexible social spaces and as integral part of the landscape

Diagrams demonstrating how the flexible architecture encourages social interaction

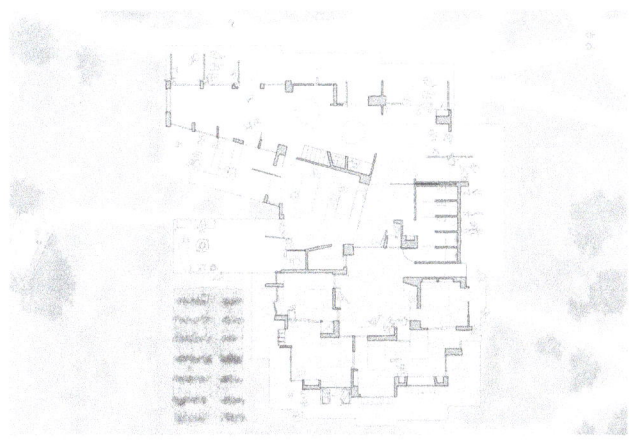

Proposed plan of flexible student living accommodation

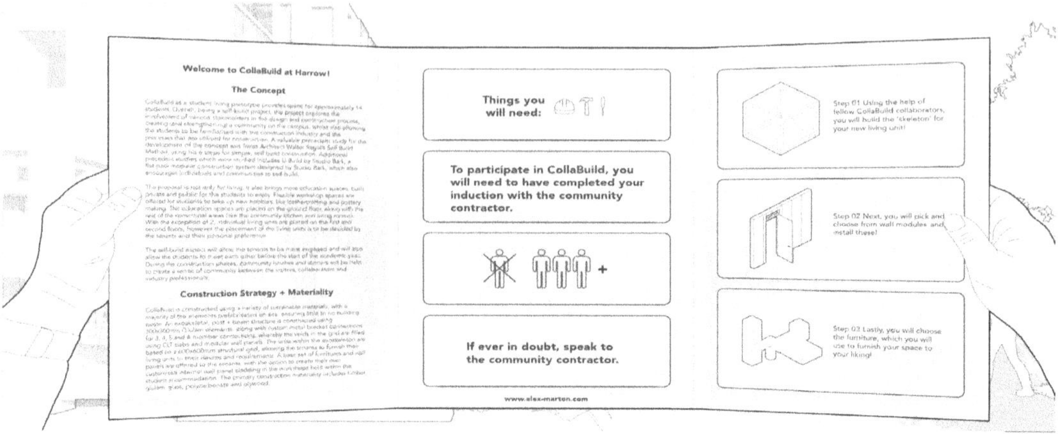

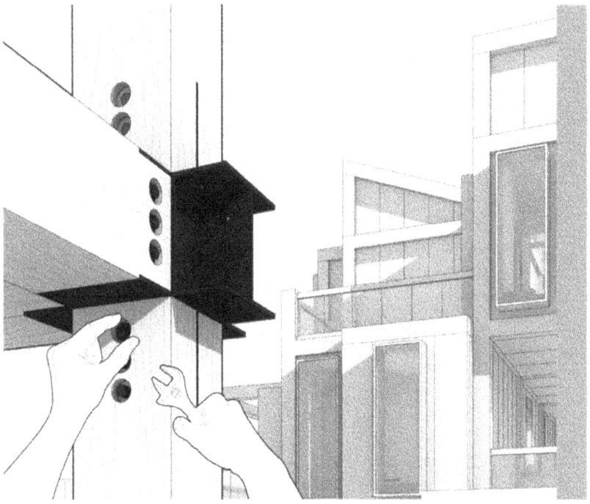

Top: Assembling, filling and transporting the prefabricated wall panels; Top: Introduction and induction Leaflet for the CollaBuild project

COLLABUILD

A COLLABORATIVE PROTOTYPE FOR STUDENT LIVING
ALEX MARTON

Exterior perspective view showing prototype living units being inhabited and being constructed by students

Collabuild is a self-built, modular student housing prototype designed to empower students to construct and customise their own living spaces. Using a prefabricated Glulam grid and off-the-shelf materials, the project promotes hands-on learning, sustainability and community. Stakeholder input shapes flexible layouts and shared workshop spaces, encouraging social connection and skill-building. With its scalable design and environmental focus, Collabuild rethinks student accommodation as a collaborative and educational experience.

Collabuild is a student accommodation prototype that explores the intersection of self-build, prefabrication, and community-led design. Situated on the Harrow Campus of the University of Westminster, the project reimagines how students might live, learn and build together. Rather than offering a conventional top-down housing solution, Collabuild invites students to participate directly in the construction and customisation of their living spaces, turning the housing process into a formative experience of collective making.

At the heart of the proposal is a belief that students, as future designers, builders and citizens, should be engaged with how the spaces they inhabit are made. The project employs a modular, glulam-framed construction system set on reversible concrete stilts. This structure is built on a 600x600mm grid, allowing for efficient prefabrication using off-the-shelf materials, minimal waste and high adaptability. Each unit is customisable, with interchangeable wall panels and layouts chosen by the students during the design process.

The construction is divided into two main phases: campus-based prefabrication followed by an on-site self-build process. Students, with guidance from a community contractor, collaborate to build their own rooms, gaining hands-on experience and building relationships before the academic year even begins. This process also includes shared meals and workshops, encouraging a strong social foundation and sense of belonging within the community.

Environmental considerations play a key role throughout. The use of glulam significantly reduces the carbon footprint compared to steel or concrete, while hay-filled wall panels and polycarbonate elements provide thermal insulation and allow for daylighting and ventilation. The buildings are designed to work with passive heating and cooling strategies, including cross ventilation, solar gain, and shading through polycarbonate folding panels

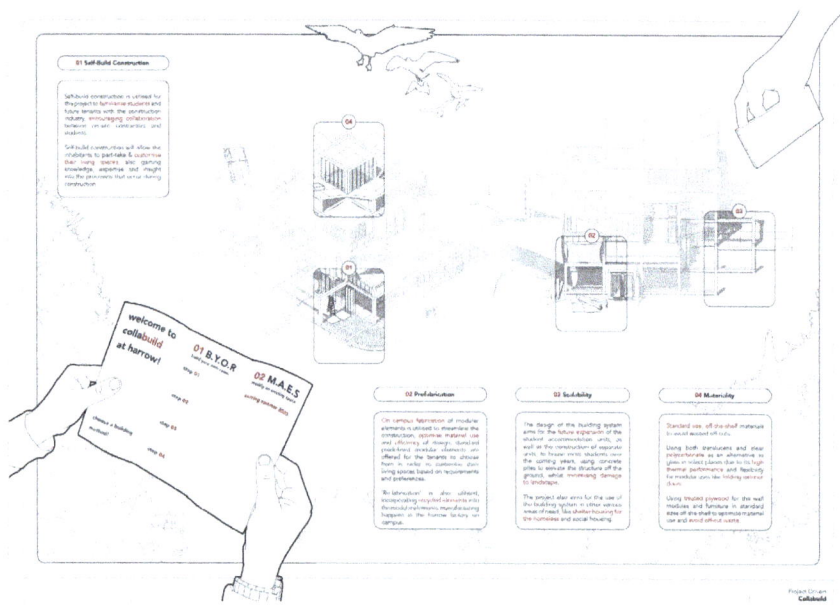

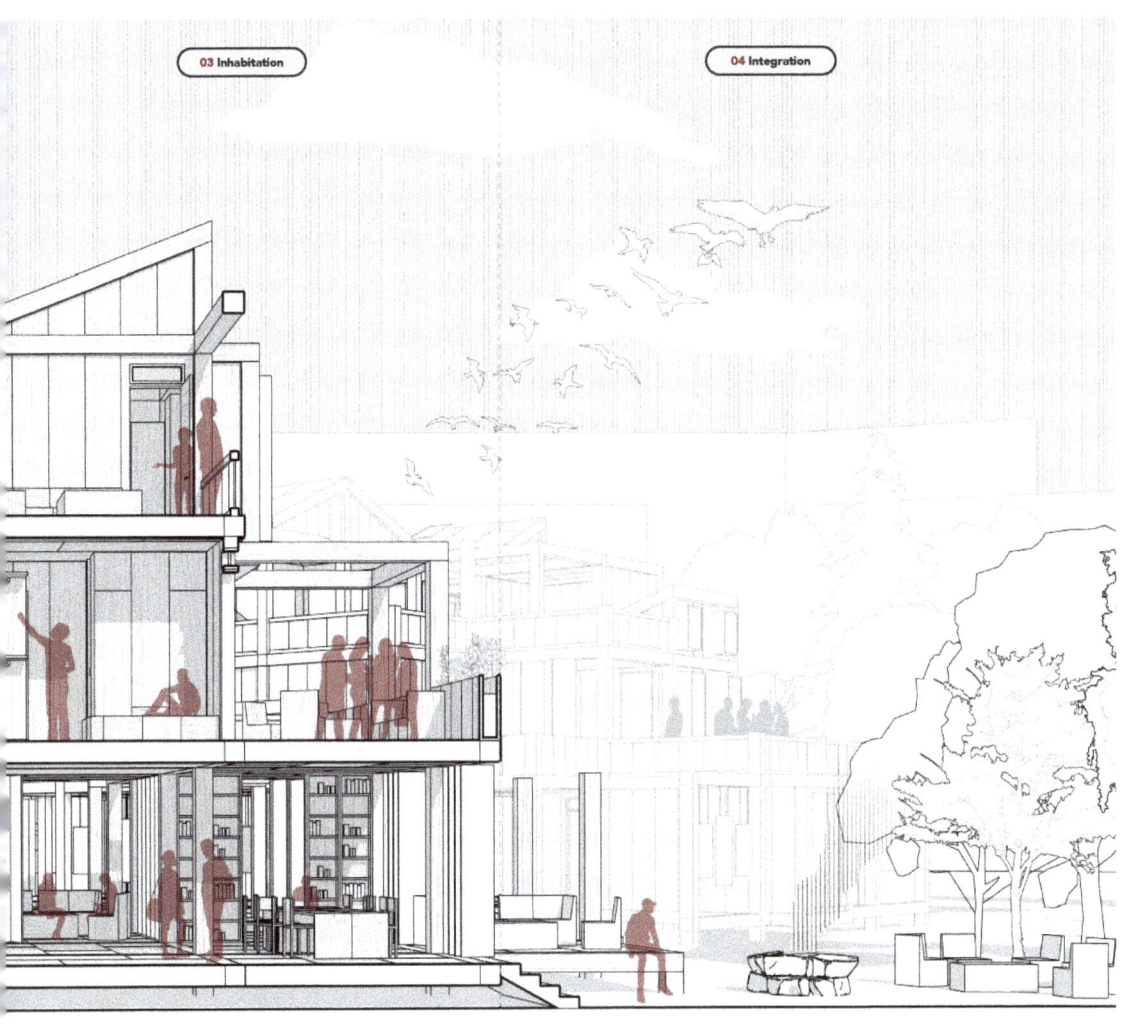

03 Inhabitation 04 Integration

Top: Cross Section with students helping construct and redevelop their homes
Bottom left: Axonometric view of the proposal with different project stages and instructions

and operable skylights. Landscape integration, such as surrounding planting and biodiverse gardens, is also used to enhance microclimates and ecological value on campus.

A 1:1 prototype was developed to test the buildability and feel of the proposed construction system. This included a mixed-material wall panel with polycarbonate on one side and plywood on the other, revealing hay insulation within, a gesture toward transparency in construction and material choices.

Stakeholder engagement shaped the design at every stage. Conversations with students revealed a need for greater privacy, modular storage, improved ventilation, natural light and better shared activity spaces. These insights informed both the layout of individual units and the inclusion of communal hubs for skill-building workshops, such as pottery, leathercrafting, and model-making, fostering both practical learning and personal expression.

The project is designed to be scalable and flexible. While developed as a student housing solution, the modular system has the potential to be adapted for emergency housing or social living projects, responding to broader housing needs with the same ethos of agency, affordability, and sustainability.

Collabuild is more than a housing proposal, it's a framework for learning through doing, for designing with empathy and for living with a deeper connection to materials, people and place. It envisions a future where architecture is not only something we move into, but something we participate in building together.

The Pavilion Prototype at the rear podium of Marylebone Campus

PAVILION PROTOTYPE

LIVE PROJECT

2022-2023

TUTORS: MARIA KRAMER AND BRUCE IRWIN
STUDENTS: OMAR ABU WISHAH, FATIMA AL-GERSANI, ARJUN BANSAL, JULIA BRODZISKA, EVANGELOS CHRISTOU, MERYEM GELDIYEVA, VALENTINA GONZALEZ-CASTANEDA, RALUCA HAMZA, CHRISTY PROTHERO, ALEX MARTON, JESSICA MORRISON, ANDREA-LAURA PETRESCU, GEORGE SORAPURE, SOFIJA STUPAR, BERLIN TAS, HASNIHA THANGANATHAN, LAURA VASILE, REBECCA WELLER, HAMZA KHAN
PARTNERS: RODRIGUES ASSOCIATES, JAN KATTEIN ARCHITECTS, BLOQS

Staff and students developed a pavilion prototype at the rear podium of the Marylebone Campus as part of the three-year QHT funded Community Centre Live Project gaining direct, hands-on experience of the making, planning and construction process, enhancing and broadening their range of skills.

Initially students developed ideas for pavilions as integral part of the Landscape Strategy for the UniverCity brief. The pavilion would then be tested as a prototype at the rear podium at Marylebone Campus. We organised model making workshops, where students developed marquettes at scale 1:5 exploring various structural frames. These were originally based on parallel grids which requires cross bracing. To overcome this, we tried to introduce a more 'diagonal approach' where the primary structure is arranged in a way to provide inherent cross bracing due to its composition, see some examples on the following page.

The 1:1 prototype developed out of a combination of students work, is based on a triangulated modular system and two alternating modules have been built with students' help in collaboration BloQs. The prototype includes a lightweight translucent polycarbonate roof to protect from rain. It is also used and still has the base grid to experiment with innovative cladding solutions including ideas for upcycling and developing co-creation methodologies with the local community.

This Project derives from the previous 1:1 pavilions students built, that now have a permanent home at our Harrow Campus. The Pavilion Prototype is permanently housed at the rear podium of Marylebone Campus, where it is continuously used by staff and students.

After the Mini Meadow Project we learned to include external consultants further to help with the 'gap' between concept design and technical design, in this case we had the fortune to collaborate with Jan Kattein, who has a great track record of Live Projects.

Above: Building the prototype at BloQs

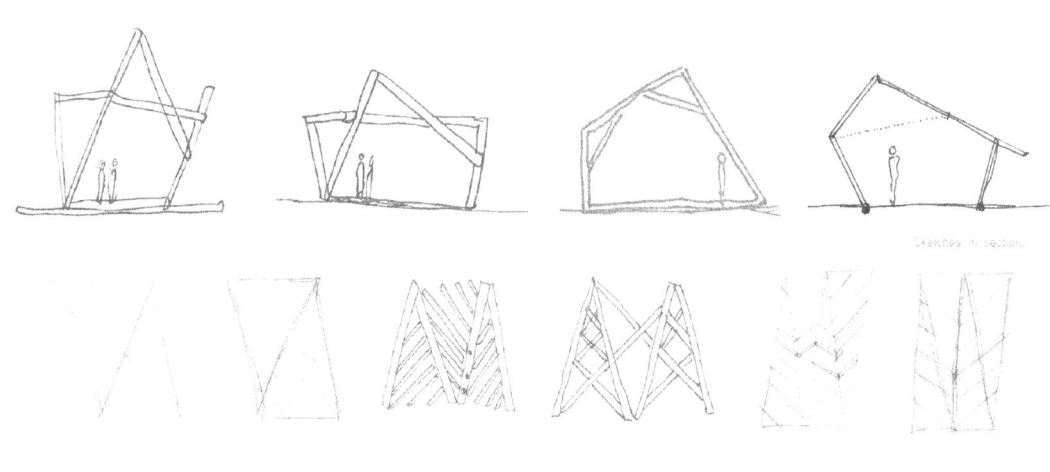
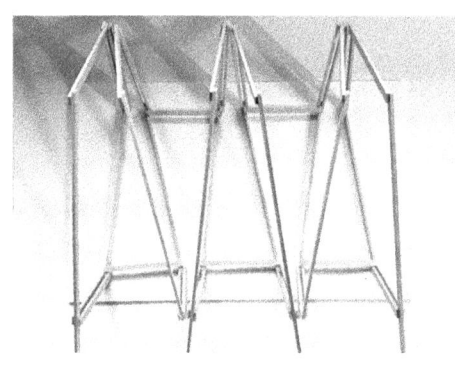
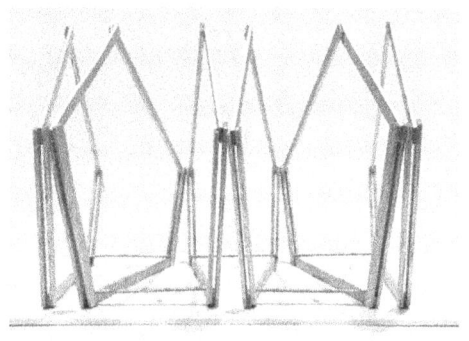

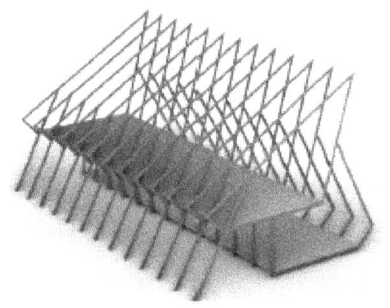

Student sketches and models developing prototype ideas

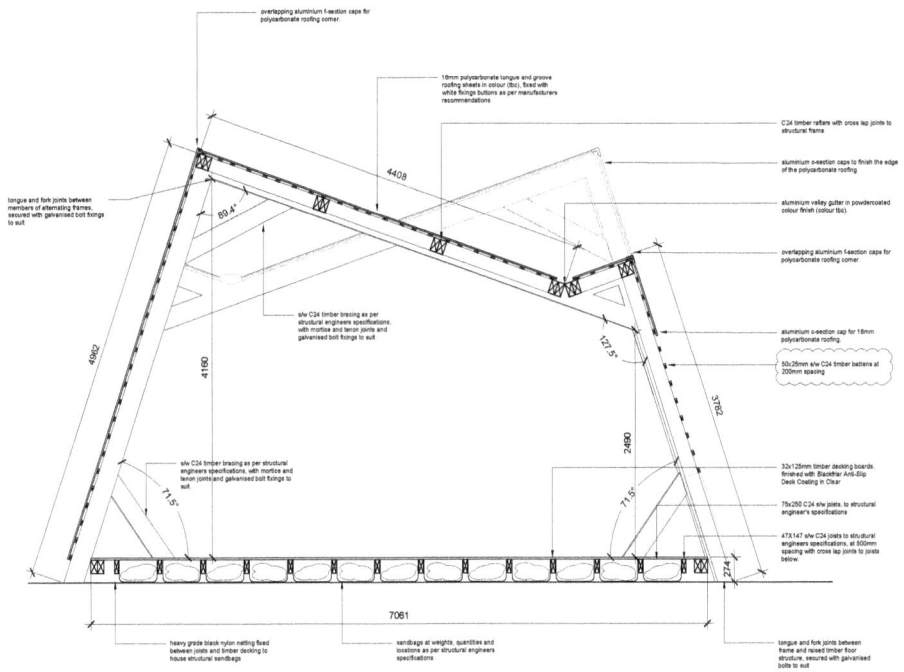

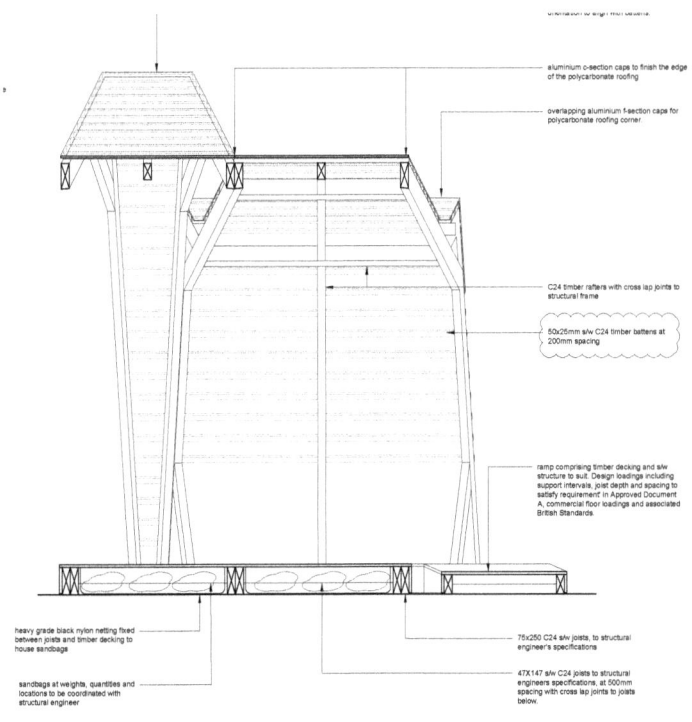

Cross Sections Detailed Drawings by Jan Kattein Architects

Installation of hand-made slip bricks cladding elements on the Pavilion Prototype

Top: Group photo with students of DS3.2 showcasing individual cladding ideas on the Pavilion Prototype at BloQs
Left: Students developing different cladding ideas for the prototype;

Top left: Digital model of the Pavilion Prototype
Top bottom: Construction of the Pavilion Prototype at the rear podium
Top right: Final Pavilion Prototype

CAMPUS LIVE PROJECTS

TATLIN TOWER
AT MARYLEBONE CAMPUS

~1972

The Taitlin Tower was designed in 1919 with a scale model presented in Moskow, which was reconstructed in the 70s and then erected at the rear patio of the University of Westminster. It had a great impact on modern architecture and became a famous symbol of utopian thought.

The Tatlin Tower, formally titled the Monument to the Third International, endures in architectural discourse as a symbol of radical imagination, utopian ambition and the complicated legacy of modernism. Conceived in 1919–1920 by Vladimir Tatlin, a central figure in the Russian Constructivist movement, the tower was intended to celebrate the triumph of the Bolshevik Revolution and serve as the headquarters for the Communist International. Although never built, the structure's spiraling steel geometry and visionary program have made it one of the most iconic unbuilt projects of the 20th century. Its enduring influence lies not in its physical presence, but in its capacity to provoke, challenge and inspire new generations of architects, theorists and artists who engage with the role of architecture in shaping society. In the contemporary architectural landscape-marked by crises of climate, capital, and meaning-Tatlin's Tower continues to resonate as a provocative symbol of what architecture might aspire to be.

At the heart of the tower's lasting significance is its bold rejection of classical forms and its embrace of industrial modernity. Tatlin's design proposed a massive, tilted, spiraling steel structure that would dwarf the Eiffel Tower, symbolizing a decisive break from bourgeois aesthetics and capitalist symbolism. Its internal program was even more radical: rotating glass volumes housing governmental and informational functions-the legislature, the executive, press operations, and radio communications-each moving at different temporal rhythms. These dynamic elements reflected an unprecedented fusion of architecture with time, function, and political ideology. While the project was technologically unfeasible at the time, its ambition marked a critical shift in architectural thinking-from the static monument to the kinetic machine, from the object to the system.

Tatlin's Tower occupies a unique position in the realm of unbuilt architecture, or what has been called "paper architecture." Its failure to materialise is not a mark of irrelevance but of mythic potential.

The tower exists in the imagination, in drawings, models, and endless reinterpretations—freed from the constraints of budget, material, and political compromise. This freedom allows it to operate as a kind of architectural manifesto, perpetually open to new readings. In today's discourse, where speculative and theoretical projects continue to thrive as critiques of contemporary practice, the tower exemplifies architecture as a mode of cultural production, not merely construction. It reminds us that unbuilt works can have profound impacts on the built environment, shaping how we think about space, function, and ideology.

Top and right: Tatlin Tower at the rear podium at the University of Westminster's Marylebone Campus

The Tatlin Tower

Monster Devouring Architecture Dept.

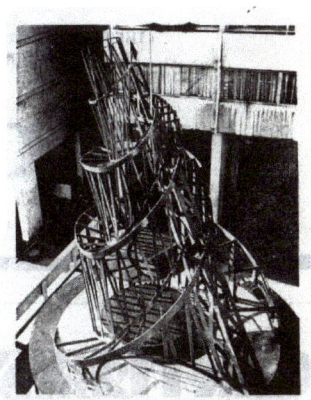

As those who frequent Luxborough Lodge will have realised, the Poly now possesses its first internationally famous 'Work of Art'; the Tatlin Tower, which was until recently attempting to dominate the South Bank from its position high on the Hayward Gallery, was dismantled during the vacation and reconstructed in a corner of the podium.

This model of Vladimir Tatlin's design for a monument to the Third International in 1920 was built early this year from two drawings and many photos of the original model - the original scheme, which was to be 1500 feet high, was never realised. Tatlin intended to have three suspended volumes within the structure rotating at different speeds, these were to be used as an assembly hall, legislative and administrative offices. As an avant-garde structural design, the project had considerable impact and influence on contemporary artistic thought; it epitomised a new consciousness, first represented through the constructivist movement, which was soon to prevade European art and technology.

It was the idea of one of the architectural tutors, Alan Diprose, to try to get the tower after the "Art in Revolution" exhibition had ended. The Arts Council were asking £5000 for it, and several bodies were interested in it, including the New York Museum of Modern Art; the Poly eventually agreed to pay £2000 and we got it. A number of students believe that this monument has no place in the Poly; but there are several factors in its favour: the Luxborough podium is crying out for a large mass of colour to relieve the monotony of the white concrete, this red, thirty-five foot structure is a start; it could be claimed that the tower is a symbol as relative to the Poly today as it was to Russia in 1920 - it represents a fusion of the two fields of art and technology; the publicity that this place has gained from owning such a monument can only help us on our way towards recognition as a forward-looking establishment (PCL could even be called TTP).

It was first hoped that 'our' Tatlin Tower could be placed on the library roof of the CAABT building, but there was not enough room for it; the next most obvious position was the podium in front of Reception, the most outstanding dis**advantage** here was that it would be sandwiched between the buildings. It is unfortunate that the location is now the podium behind the Reception, and although it is in full view from Luxborough Street, it cannot be properly seen from the Marylebone entrance.

This work was acquired through the efforts of one individual who by determination and persistence (and many donations) managed to realise his objective. If you admire the sculpture in its context, then it is worth having in our Poly; if you deplore the acquisition, you must still realise that there is great potential for many more such schemes, by no means limited to the field of arts.

Top: Monument to the Allure of the might-have been - a drawing of the side of Tatlin's monument.
Photograph: N. Punin Archive, St Petersburg
Left: The Tatlin Tower at the rear podium of the Marylebone Campus of the University of Westminster
All images from University of Westminster Records and Archives at Titchfield Campus

Tatlin's Tower continues to ask fundamental questions about the role of architecture in shaping futures. In an era marked by aesthetic excess and political uncertainty, the tower's unfulfilled promise lingers as an open invitation to imagine alternative futures.

The tower invites a deeper reflection on the entanglement of architecture with politics.

In its original conception, it was not merely a monument but an operational center for revolutionary communication-a space for producing and disseminating ideology through the new technologies of its time. As such, it represents one of the most explicit attempts to use architecture as an instrument of political transformation. In contemporary debates, where the neutrality of architecture is increasingly questioned, Tatlin's Tower offers a potent example of architecture as active agent-capable of shaping public consciousness, aligning with or resisting power, and expressing collective will.

Tatlin's Tower asks architects to consider not only what is possible to build, but what is worth building, and for whom. Tatlin's Tower remains a symbol for architectural discourse as it sits at the intersection of form, function, theory, and political discourse.

Construction of the Tension Pavilion, photo by H. Charrington

TENSION PAVILION
LIGHTWEIGHT TENSEGRITY STRUCTURE

2016
STRUCTURE MODE, WEBER INDUSTRIES, BASE STRUCTURE, WILL MCLEAN
STUDENTS

The Tension Pavilion, designed by StructureMode, is a lightweight structure featuring a tensegrity ring and a tensile fabric membrane. It was initially created for the Vision exposition in London and later exhibited at HOK's London office.

StructureMode: Tension is a lightweight pavilion with a tensegrity ring and a tensile fabric membrane. Tensegrity is a structural system that was developed by Kenneth Snelson and Buckminster Fuller in the 1960's. It is characterised by compression elements that do not touch, but are suspended in a 'sea' of tension cables, as well as being a self-stable system that does not rely on external structures for its stability, such as compression rings or guy ropes. Pioneering research into the system by Fuller and Snelson led to a series of sculptural experiments, but pure tensegrity has rarely been utilised for a building structure.

The sinuous geometry used for Tension provides a minimal base on three points, formed of three arches and three valleys to support an anticlastic fabric surface. There are 24 tensegrity modules that together form a torus, each having varying geometry to generate the smooth curvature. All coordinates were generated using Grasshopper, parametric modelling software, and the pavilion was analysed using Oasys GSA.

StructureMode undertook meticulous form-finding to derive a stable tensegrity geometry, rigorous non-linear analysis to optimise the size of all elements and physical testing to prove the system was accurately modeled.

StructureMode, Weber Industries and Base Structures worked closely together to refine the connections to maintain legibility of the structure while keeping it simple to fabricate and easy to erect.

We have gained detailed knowledge of methods required to adapt and safely design tensegrity structures. We can now develop a tensegrity system that follows any geometry and scale it up for large scale structures. We are very excited by the structural potential and future applications of the system.

Left and right: Construction of the Tension Pavilion, all photos by H. Charrington
Bottom right: Render by StructureMode

Internal View of the Oculus Pavilion

THE OCULUS PAVILION

LIVE PROJECT

2017-2018

TUTORS: MARIA KRAMER AND ERIC GUIBERT
STUDENTS: GAIA BUSCEMI, SIMON MCLANAGHAN, YOUJONG WON, NIKOLA BABIC, GENTRIT BUNJAKU, AHMED ELMASRI, ALOYS HEITZ, DOMINYKA KYBARTAITE, ANDREAS MAKRIS, AESHA MEHTA, ALEXANDER ONUFRIEV, CHRISTINA PETRIDOU, MATTHEW REA, VITTORIA REGA, LINA NOUERI, PATRICIA BOB
FUNDER: UNIVERSITY OF WESTMINSTER QHT FUND
PARTNERS: WEBER INDUSTRIES, STRUCTURE MODE, FABLAB

The Oculus Pavilion was QHT funded and designed and built by third year students from the School of Architecture+Cities at the University of Westminster at the rear podium of the Marylebone Campus.

Innovative design and production methods were used with all the structural elements CNC cut and the design and construction was algorithmically supported with Grasshopper software.

The circular structure with a view into the sky was inspired by Architect Vladimir Tatlin's 1919 design for the Tatlin Tower, a design not realised until a sculpture was built in 1971 as part of the 'Art in Revolution' Exhibition at the Hayward Gallery, see further information on the following page. The 1971 sculpture was reconstructed at the rear patio of the University of Westminster's Marylebone Campus, the same location where the students' Oculus pavilion was initially exhibited. Tatlin's Tower was an 'avant-garde structural design' which had a considerable impact on contemporary artistic thinking.

"In the squares and in the streets we are placing our work... Art should attend us everywhere that life flows and acts."
Vladimir Tatlin

An oculus, orientated to the South, catches sunlight, and provides framed views of the sky. The Oculus Pavilion showcases innovative design and construction methods: Its horizontal and vertical members form a shell-like structure. "This is an exciting opportunity for students to experience the detail design and building process first hand, understanding the complex development of translating a cutting-edge proposal into a build structure. We used innovative CNC technology manufacturing more than 300 component pieces at the university's own Fabrication Laboratory. With the help of the structural engineers StructureMode and Weber Industries we managed the construction process promoting knowledge exchange and applied research. " Maria Kramer

After the initial design workshop, the detail design of the Oculus Pavilion, which is a circular structure with specific view into the sky, was finalised and manufacturied. in December.

Models have been laser cut at scale 1:20 and 1:10, helping to develop the design process. A 1:1 prototype of three ribs of the structure was built from which it becam apparent that the tolerances between the horizontal components were too tight and needed to be adjusted. The design has been developed via Grasshopper software and all structural elements were be CNC cut in the Fablab of Westminster University.

The site is on the rear podium of University of Westminster. It is an outdoor terrace, where students can go to socialize, have lunch...etc. The podium is also the link between the public Luxborough Street and the communal Hall of Residence for students. It is the buffer zone between the University of Westminster podium level, the Hall of Residence and the down-going services stairs to Ambika P3 and the delivery bay. The double-character of the place allows people to walk through as well as to sit and relax or mingle. The site is really rich in potential but was lacking in fluidity. Indeed the seating/eating area was delimited by potted trees and flower pots and consisted of several tables flanked by chairs. There was no true gradients of privacy and the eating space was clearly demarcated from the passage area.

Commencing with individual concept ideas based on an initial outline brief, a design was chosen through peer and panel voting and further developed, closely mirroring a competition set-up in the professional environment. While this approach generates heightened engagement in the initial stages and individual empowerment, there may be some disengagement once a design has been chosen, as students might feel detached. However, it's crucial to recognise that significant design input is still necessary throughout the detailed phases, achieved through regular group explorations and discussions - architectural interventions are inherently collaborative efforts. We chose the following year with the Woven Pavilion to have a more communal approach even for the intial design stages to maintain broader engagement and feelings of ownership.

A strong feature of the design was the occulus. The idea of aiming to create an opening towards a single point that would frame the sky which provide the interior with a focal point. We collectively decided to experiment with a 1:1 version of the occulus, which we cut out of cardboard. We tested views from specific angles as well the potential to catch the sun. We decided to try and avoid framing the student halls to the right (West) to create a separate world, to capture the sun, whilst opening the view to the sky above.

In the early stages we realised that we had to many ideas on how the shape could work. We managed to fine tune the form, but were divided between two basic forms for the structure to grow from; these forms were a Spiral transitioning into the space or a circle/oval maximising the internal space.

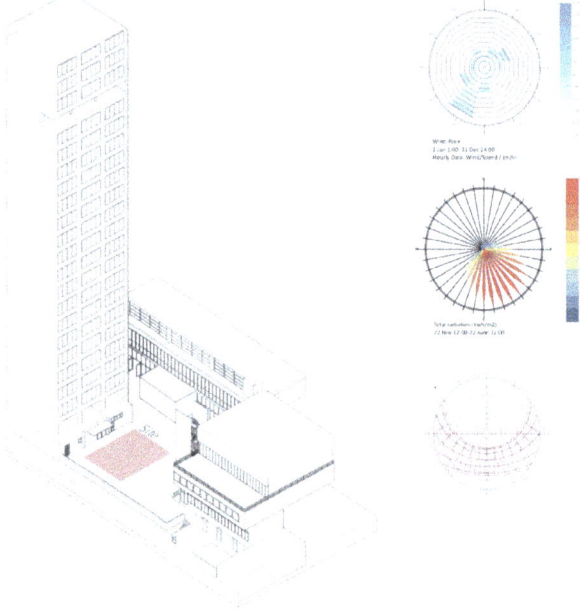

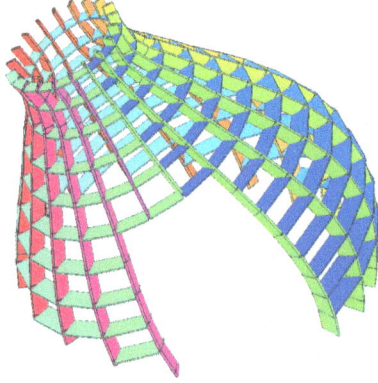

Centre: Environmental study of the site by Simon McLanaghan
Bottom right: Determining the location of the Oculus on site
Bottom left: Digital model showing tension and pressure of shell structure, StructureMode

246

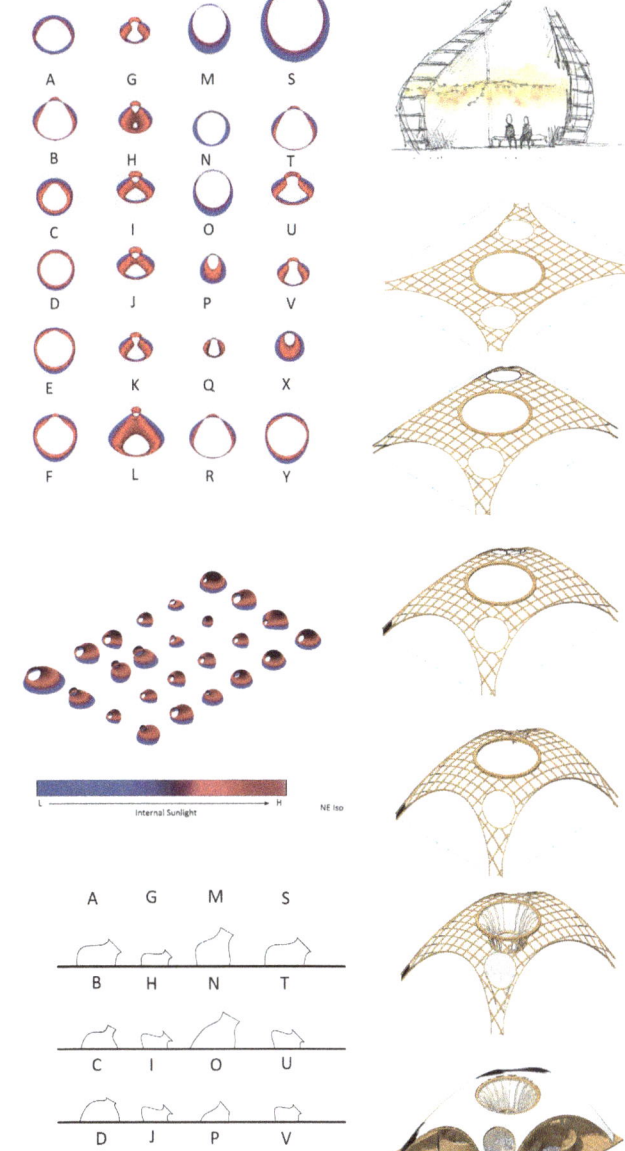

Top right: Sketch by Sasha Onufriev
Centre abd rught: Simon McLanaghan analysing different shapes
Photos left from top: the initial rear podium, exploring the site and siting potential interventions regarding size and location; Group discussions of pavilion design development in the studio
Bottom: Models at different scale testing different angles of the onion

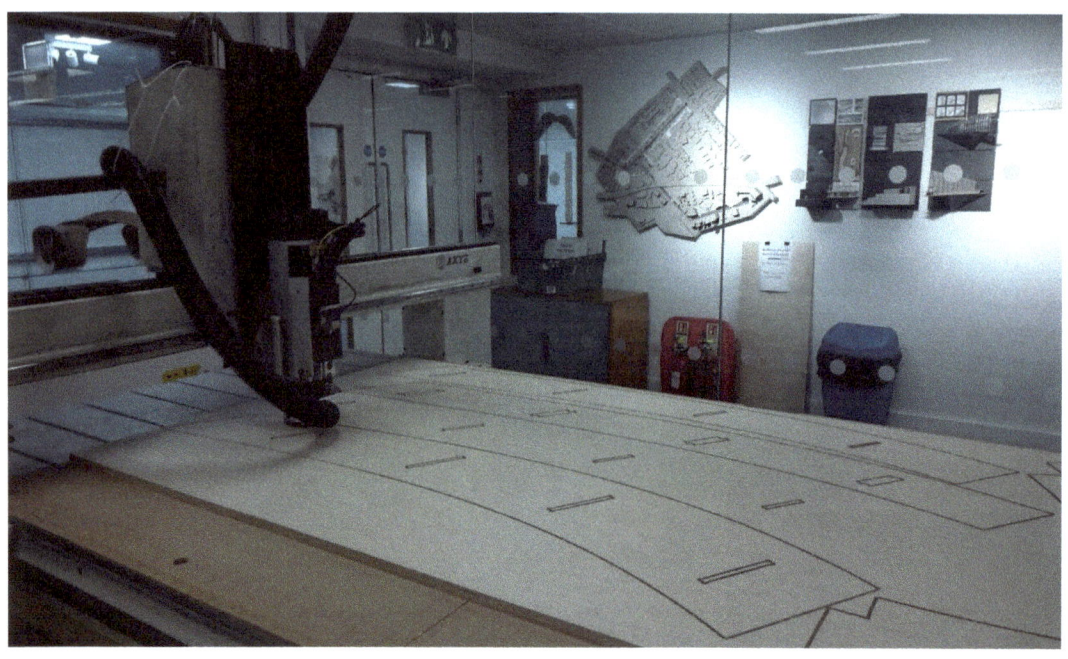

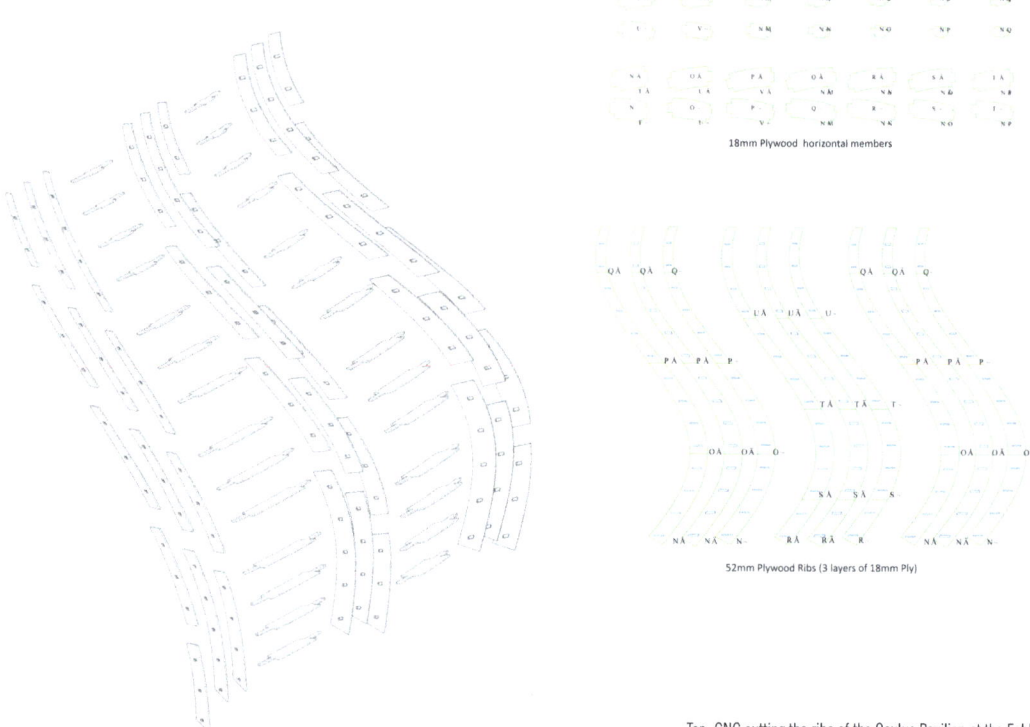

Top: CNC cutting the ribs of the Oculus Pavilion at the FabLab
Centre: Digital Model with CNC cutting patters by Sasha Onufriev and Simon McLanaghan
Bottom right: Axonometric View of the Oculus Pavilion including separating vertical and spiral elements, by Sasha Onufriev and Simon McLanaghan

1:1 PROTOTYPING

Once the CNC files had finished we began to physically construct the three sections of Ribs; breaking down the system into a series of steps:

1. drilling a series of wholes into each singular component of the ribs, and applying glue to the inner faces of each piece, the piece would then be attached to its member, with a spliced connection and screws would be placed into the wholes either side of the splice, re-inforcing the connection, speeding up construction time and compressing the glue between the layers of Ply.

2. begin identifying and slotting the horizontal members into their respective slots, this process began by laying the ribs flat on the floor allowing multiple people to work on placing the members at once. In order to make sure the connections would align each rib have every mem-ber glued and attached whilst on the ground, until all slots were filled and dried.

3. This involved a lot more physical labour and patience, as each rib needed lifting into place and aligning with all horizontal members of its sister rib. This process involved several people balancing the weight of each rib, whilst one or two people would walk along aligning each member, after several adjustments and a lot of resistance the members finally came together with tight but slightly moveable connections.

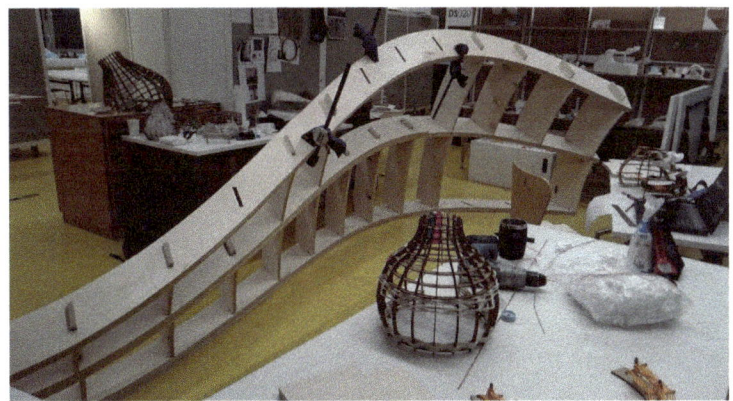

 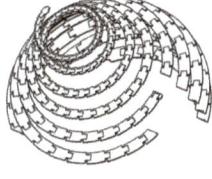 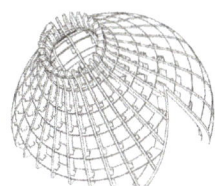

Centre left: The first stage of the Glulam process was setting up a jig to protect and secure all the control points of the curve being created. Once all pieces were cut, each would be coated with liquid adhesive and then be placed all together inside the jig. To compress each control point, a series of G clamps were put in place to help the curve set. After several hours of drying time the G clamps were removed leaving only the glue laminated wood and the excess glue, that had been forced out of the gaps, which was sanded down.
Left: Construction of the pavilion

Bottom: Relocation of the Oculus Pavilion to Harrow Campus,
Left: Construction of the Pavilion at Marylebone Campus
Photos following pages: Constance McGuire

Left: The Oculus Pavilion at Maryebone Campus; Top: Looking out through the oculus from withinw; Top: DS3.2 students with structural engineer Geoff Morrow and Maria Kramer

The Woven Pavilion Live Project at Marylebone Campus

WOVEN PAVILION

LIVE PROJECT

2018-2019

TUTORS: MARIA KRAMER AND ROBERTO BOTTAZZI
STUDENTS: HAFSA ADAN, SADEN ALABBASI, LARISSA ANGONESE, SINA BAHJAT, SMIT BARADIYA, SODUEARI GRAHAM-DOUGLAS, NESLIHAN GULHAN, BEATRIZ CECILIA JIMENEZ, OMAR KHAN, DARIA KUSHNIR, BIBIANA MALAWAKULA, ILLIA MARYNIN, HILONI SHETH, MIHRIBAN USTUN, MARTIN VASILEV, ADRIANNA WALESZCZAK, ZHANGELDY KAUPYNBAYEV, MILES GIRALDEZ
FUNDERS: UNIVERSITY OF WESTMINSTER QHT FUND
PARTNERS: WEBER INDUSTRIES, STRUCTURE MODE, FABLAB

The Woven Pavilion was QHT funded and designed and built by third year students. The project was part of the London Festival of Architecture. The structure was developed with the help of the structural engineers StructureMode and Weber Industries promoting applied research and knowledge exchange. The pavilion uses digital fabrication tools for construction and development in collaboration with the in-house Fabrication Laboratory.

Each pavilion is constructed from two catenary-shaped arches, fabricated from 18 mm laminated plywood panels. These arches are linked by 6 mm plywood sheets, which are slotted to create ribbon-like strips, producing a delicate, feathered appearance. The arches are built in modular segments that can be bolted together on site. This assembly method allows all work to be done safely at ground level - one end of the lightweight arch is lifted while the next section is secured in place.

The outer cladding is not only decorative but also serves a crucial structural role, adding stiffness to resist side-to-side wind forces. While initial calculations based on standard building codes were overly conservative due to the complex geometry and pre-buckled form, physical load testing was carried out. The structure was tested to failure, compared to the estimated wind loads.

The geometry of the arch is based on the catenary curve, which is the curve that an idealised hanging chain or cable assumes under its own weight when supported only at its ends resulting in optimum structural form. Because catenary arches exert a horizontal outward force, stability is achieved through ballast at the base of each arch rather than ground anchors or tie rods. The ballast, which also prevents sliding under wind pressure. These foundation were designed as informal benches attached to each side of the arch and filled with 12x25kg sandbags to hold the structures in place, avoiding any ground fixings or ties between the arches. The arches were later reinstalled at Harrow Campus.

Bottom: Exploratory DS3.2 student models using plywood in tension

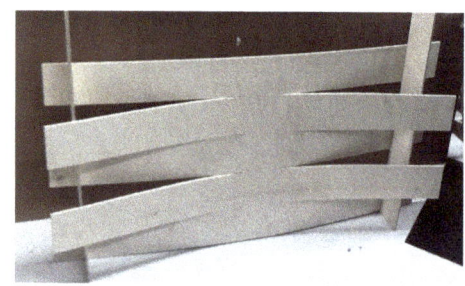

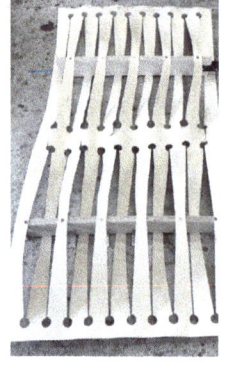

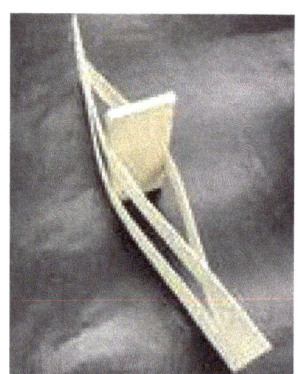

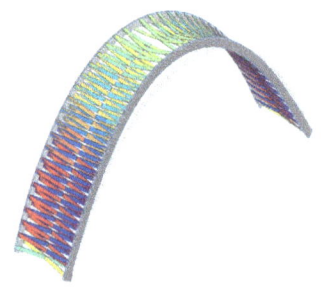

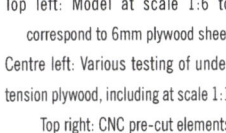
Top left: Model at scale 1:6 to correspond to 6mm plywood sheet
Centre left: Various testing of under tension plywood, including at scale 1:1
Top right: CNC pre-cut elements

Far left: Due to the complex, pre-buckled shape of the structural cladding, load tests were carried out and taken to the point of failure, to prove that the structural capacity is above any predicted wind loading

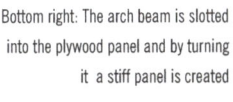

Bottom right: The arch beam is slotted into the plywood panel and by turning it a stiff panel is created

Bottom: Re-installation of the Woven Pavilion arches at Harrow Campus

Top: The panel elements are stored under the first arch
Bottom far left: Digital model of the three woven arches
Bottom right: It was a rainy day when we installed the arches, which did not dampen our enthusiasm.
Left:: Re-installation of the arches at Harrow Campus

Top: The three arches at Marylebone Campus, photo by Clare Hamman
OPEN exhibition where we integrated a bed as part of the structure and won 'Best in Show'

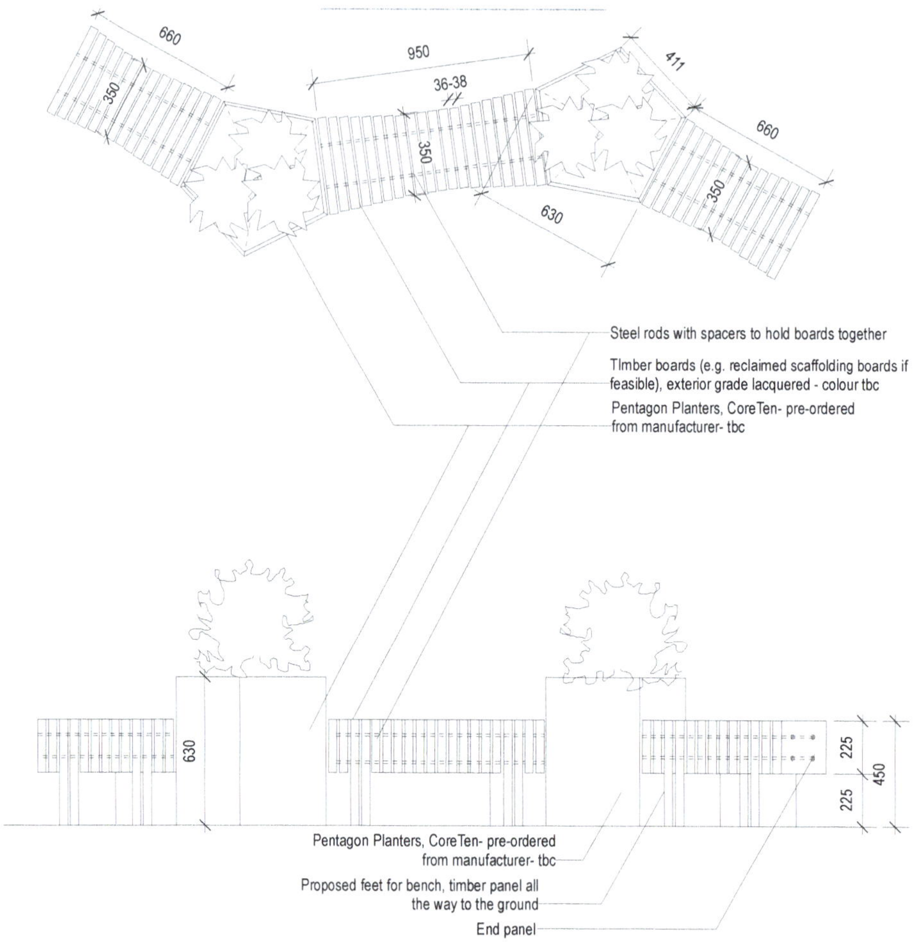

Steel rods with spacers to hold boards together

Timber boards (e.g. reclaimed scaffolding boards if feasible), exterior grade lacquered - colour tbc

Pentagon Planters, CoreTen- pre-ordered from manufacturer- tbc

Pentagon Planters, CoreTen- pre-ordered from manufacturer- tbc

Proposed feet for bench, timber panel all the way to the ground

End panel

SENSORY BENCH

GREEN FUND

2022-2023

CHRISTY PROTHERO, REBECCA WELLER

The Sensory bench project was part of the Green Fund initiative by Dain Son Robinson and Andrew Pitchford. Students Rebecca Weller and Christy Prothero developed this exciting project as part of the Live Design Practice.

The idea is to re-green the rear podium of the Marylebone campus, with the modular pentagonal design, made out of scaffolding boards. "Students learned about the entire design and construction process, we had meetings with makers to discuss detailing and feasibility and students took the lead on the construction, learning so much from the complexity of managing the different aspects of building, including health and safety procedures."

Through the design, our team aims to improve the experience for students, staff, and visitors to Westminster University campus. The seating encourages social connection on campus, which enriches the experience of students, staff, and visitors. The seating offers a place for people to connect with nature, and escape from hectic city centre, therefore improving well-being at the University. Furthermore, the seating offers the potential for learning, by providing a place for informal tutorial sessions within a natural setting and enriching students' learning experience.

This project exists to further develop the knowledge for live-build projects and to enhance student's employability and green credentials. Students were able to experience first-hand the entire design and construction process, which is often difficult to obtain in an academic, as well as in a professional environment. Students be able experienced the complex, non-linear process, engaging with stakeholders early on in their career and learn about plant life and biodiversity and led on this project.

"This project is important to us and other students because we want to make effective changes to improve biodiversity and well-being at Westminster. We are extremely excited about the prospect of the Green Fund project and the chance to promote and include green issues within the built environment. The project will offer a chance to have a creative impact in the real world and to use all the knowledge and skills imparted through our architecture degrees to have a positive impact and legacy at our University.

This project is important to gain real life practical experience, experiencing the entire design and construction. During the process we will gain important technical knowledge of materials and design systems. We will also learn about costing and budgeting, which will be invaluable going forward in our careers into the professional world. We are enthused by the rewarding opportunity for teamwork and bonding, collaborating across disciplines, with staff and students. The project will also be fantastic for improving our time management and organisation skills. Live Build projects of this type are a great vehicle for developing students' confidence in demonstrating the impact their skills can offer, and developing their organisational, management and creative capacities in a practical context promoting green issues early on in their careers. "

Top: The Sensory Bench Live Project in the foreground with the Woven Pavilion and Pavilion Prototype Live Projects in the background; Left: The closeness of plants when seated

This project was driven by the students, who took the lead in the tendering process and details independently. The finished bench was crafted entirely from new scaffolding boards, An early plan to repurpose used scaffolding boards was abandoned when it became clear that embedded screws and nails would damage cutting tools. Students selected and planted a variety of hardy, low-maintenance plants, ensuring the installation would remain vibrant and resilient throughout the seasons. Their involvement at every stage gave the project a strong sense of ownership and craftsmanship.

MATERIAL EXPLORATION

APPLIED MAKING

MARIA KRAMER

Embodied knowledge challenges the traditional view of knowledge as purely mental and abstract. It highlights the inseparable connection between the body, the mind, and the environment in shaping how we learn, perceive, and understand the world.

"If you are ever stuck for inspiration, ask your materials for advice." Louis Khan

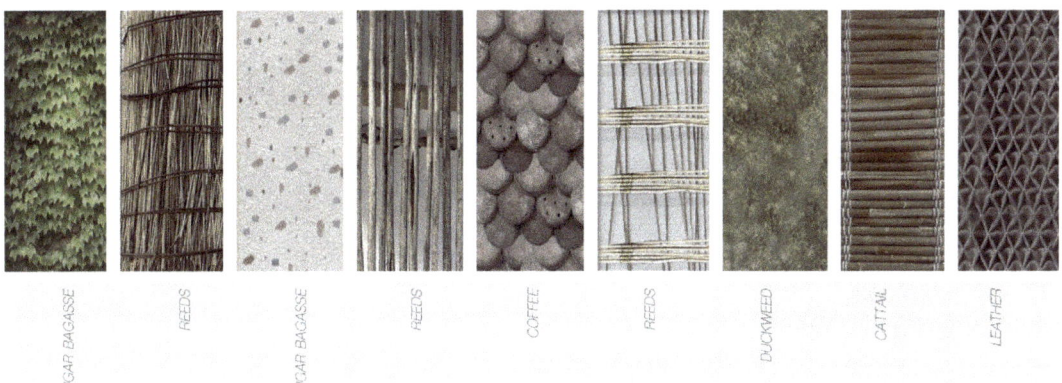

SUGAR BAGASSE | REEDS | SUGAR BAGASSE | REEDS | COFFEE | REEDS | DUCKWEED | CATTAIL | LEATHER

MATERIAL RESEARCH AS DESIGN

In a regenerative approach to architecture, materials are not generic. Each material has a story: it is grown, mined, processed, transported, assembled. Studying clay, reed, straw, timber, or waste plastics means exploring their ecology, culture, and performance. Embodied carbon - the CO_2 emitted in the production and transport of materials - has become one of the most urgent environmental concerns in architecture, making material choice a critical climate decision. Questions emerge: How does this material weather? How does it perform thermally or acoustically? How can it be joined? Can it be reused or returned to the earth? How can regenerative materials be promoted and applied further despite the many regulatory and economic hurdles?

Making prototypes, testing joints, failing and adjusting - this is design as process. And like in Live Projects, multiple variables influence outcomes: team structure, collaboration, stakeholder input, context analysis.

LEARNING THROUGH THE HAND

We often say we "think with our hands." Cognition is deeply embodied and there is an intelligence embedded in physical making. There is an "automatic meaningfulness" in the act of fabrication. When working with wood, metal, clay, or fabric, one must confront real constraints: joint strength, bending, shrinkage, structural logic. This parallels the 'Live Project' in architectural education, where working with real clients introduces stakes, negotiations and situated decision-making.

MUSCLE MEMORY

Architectural education provides a unique window for hands-on experimentation - a space where students can test, break, rework and understand materials through physical engagement. Model making is more than representation: it builds muscle memory - a tacit knowledge of proportion, joint logic, structural and material behaviour that remains in the architect's body long after graduation. This embodied familiarity is difficult to develop through drawings or digital models alone.

In practice, architects often face constraints of budget, time and liability that limit testing and playful trial-and-error. The studio becomes a crucial period where this bodily intelligence is cultivated. Cutting timber, casting plaster, weaving reed and prototyping forms neurological pathways - a kind of physical literacy - which later underpins intuition in professional decision-making.

When students explore materials through making, they begin to understand space and structure from the inside out rather than relying on abstraction. Such tactile engagement encourages confidence in detail thinking and fosters a form of internalised craft knowledge that can guide effective collaboration with engineers, builders and fabricators in the future.

Left: Cutting an opening into the hanging hessian fabric for the Floating Forum Project

TOWARDS A NEW VERNACULAR

In a largely digitalised profession, architects risk losing contact with material immediacy. The virtual workspace cannot replicate the feel, smell, sound, or resistance of true materials. A phenomenological and situated approach celebrates physicality with all the senses.

Applied making suggests the possibility of a new vernacular - one not based on stylistic mimicry, but on responsive, local, process-led design. It aligns with system thinking: understanding site ecologies, histories, and material flows. It embraces vertical integration not as top-down control but as a bottom-up collaboration with craftspeople, fabricators, and communities. Making thus becomes both rational and poetic - an iterative dialogue between vision and matter. It links architecture back to the body, to experience and to the world.

Top: Ethnobotanical workshop at the Growing Space, where students wove with reeds and bindweed;
Bottom + right: Students testing materials in relation to the River Lea and as part of individual project explorations

Left: Experimenting with bagasse, a waste product from sugar cane as soil supplement; the waste could be used for more productive and environmental solutions rather than just burning it for electricity, as is usually the case by Jonathan Hubert Raffay

Right: The alluvium rich soil of the lower Lea provides the perfect mix for daub. The extraction of this would create wetlands along the river; experiments with making daub from different ratios of clay, soil, sand, and straw. The mix that contained equal

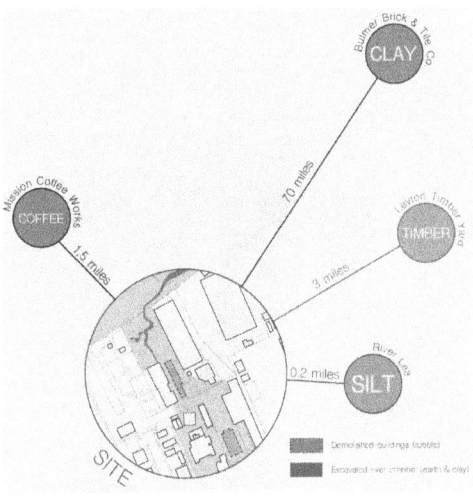

Experiments with coffee waste; demolition material is graded and forms 60% of aggregate and the gabion plinth. River Lea silt makes up remaining 40% aggregate (less due to its smoothness); higher clay content to prevents use of cement or lime in earth mix; timber for formwork sourced from timber yard in Leyton nearby; clay and earth mix from excavated river channel on site and Bulmer Brick Works. Coffee is added to earth mix to neutralise polluting odours from adjacent waste depot and substation and provide base for smelling wall.

Top: Diagram showing origins of the materials used; Coffee tiles arranged as facade cladding, by Lottie Greenwood
Bottom and centre: Model of a 'rammed coffee wall'; all image this page by Lottie Greenwood

PLANTS

An integrated supporting frame creates a planting form of varying conditions, allowing for a wide range of species to thrive. Areas differ in terms of sunlight, shading, wind, aspect and exposure.

BIRDS

Designed nesting niches offer shelter for birds and other animals. These are carefully positioned further from human interaction and to maintain the structural integrity of the earth wall.

POLLUTANTS

The concentration of coffee in the rammed earth increases and the wall thickens when in proximity to building vents to reduce air pollution. The coffee acts as a neutraliser and plants cleanse the air further.

SMELLS

Niches in the walls are filled with scents for people to engage with as they pass by. The smells are maintained and constantly evolve, much like a garden.

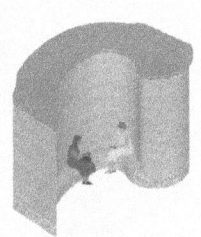

PEOPLE

The wall provides moments for sitting, sheltering and observing, whilst encouraging interaction with the rammed earth and an external community space for social activities.

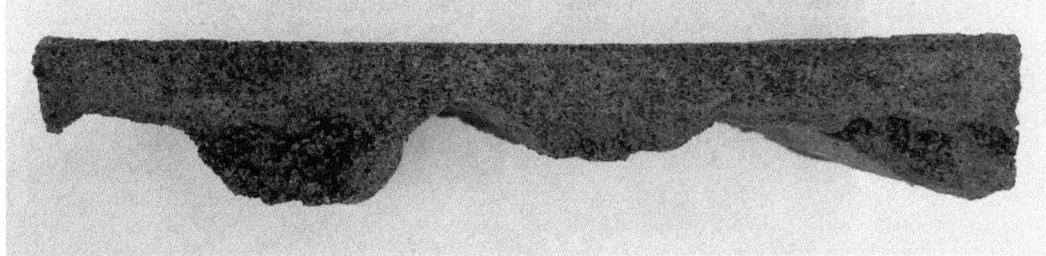

Tile made out of beeswax and coffee chaff tested for weathering at the Pavilion Prototype at the rear podium

Samples made out of coffee chaff and eco resin by Elina Defries

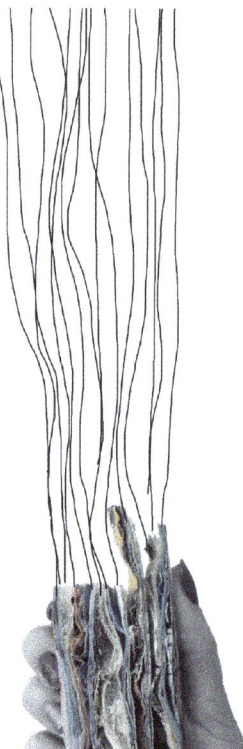

Top: Duckweed from the River Lea combined with resin, biodegradable plastic and plaster to create tile composites by Elina Gleed
Right: Diagram how weaving plastic bags into insulating panels by Natalia Petrova

Cattail harvested adjacent to the River Lea and testing material possibilities by Alistair Search

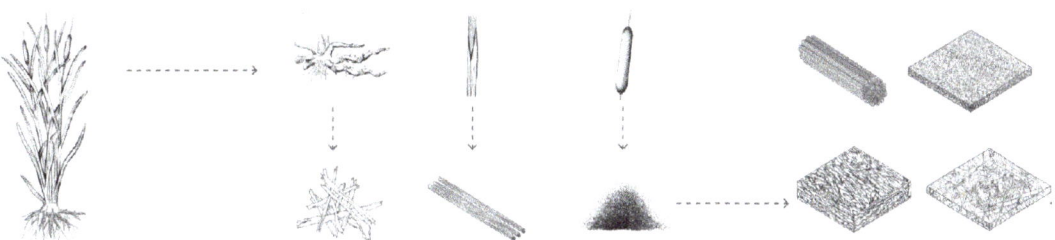

Process of making cattail panels by Alistair Search

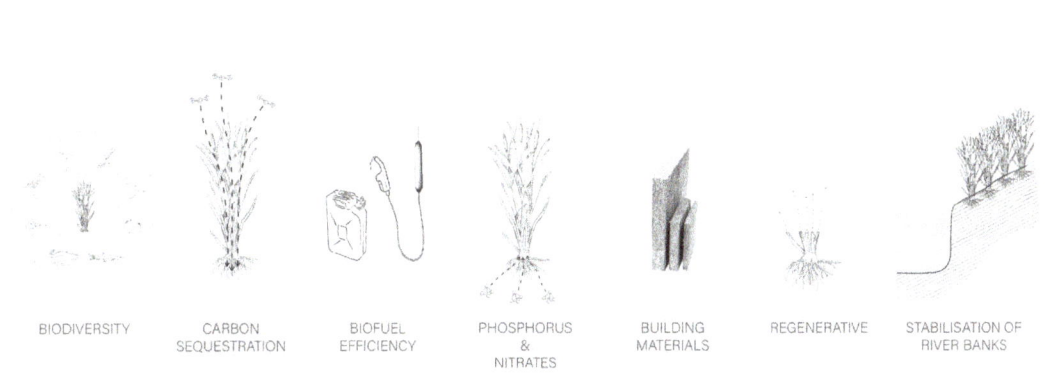

BIODIVERSITY — Cattail provide essential habitat, resources and nest sites for numerous animal species, including various birds, amphibians and fish.

CARBON SEQUESTRATION — Compared to trees which store most their captured carbon within the woody mass and leaves, reeds and Cattail sequester most of their carbon underground and are extremely efficient at it.

BIOFUEL EFFICIENCY — Cattail is 300% more efficient than corn on a land area to fuel produced basis, and has great potential to be used to produce green fuel. Cattail Fuel Pellets, enormous potential to be a viable and commercial source of clean energy.

PHOSPHORUS & NITRATES — Although, phosphorus and nitrates are great fertilisers, this in turn also fuels the growth of algal blooms, penny wort and duckweed along the Lee. Cattail is a great absorber of these nutrients and will help prevent the invasive growth of river weeds in this proposed natural swimming pools South of the site.

BUILDING MATERIALS — Cattail has the potential to produce robust, strong and environmentally friendly building materials. Typhaboard and other developments in the construction world are progressing to get Cattail construction materials certified.

REGENERATIVE — To be harvested for biofuel production and some building materials (not those that require the root), Cattails can be cut at the bottom of the stem and will grow back. Construction timber is harvested every 20 years, whereas Cattail can be harvested annually.

STABILISATION OF RIVER BANKS — Due to their strong roots, Cattails can be planted and used to stabilise river banks and help reduce the risk of river bank erosion and landslides.

Why Cattail? by Alistair Search

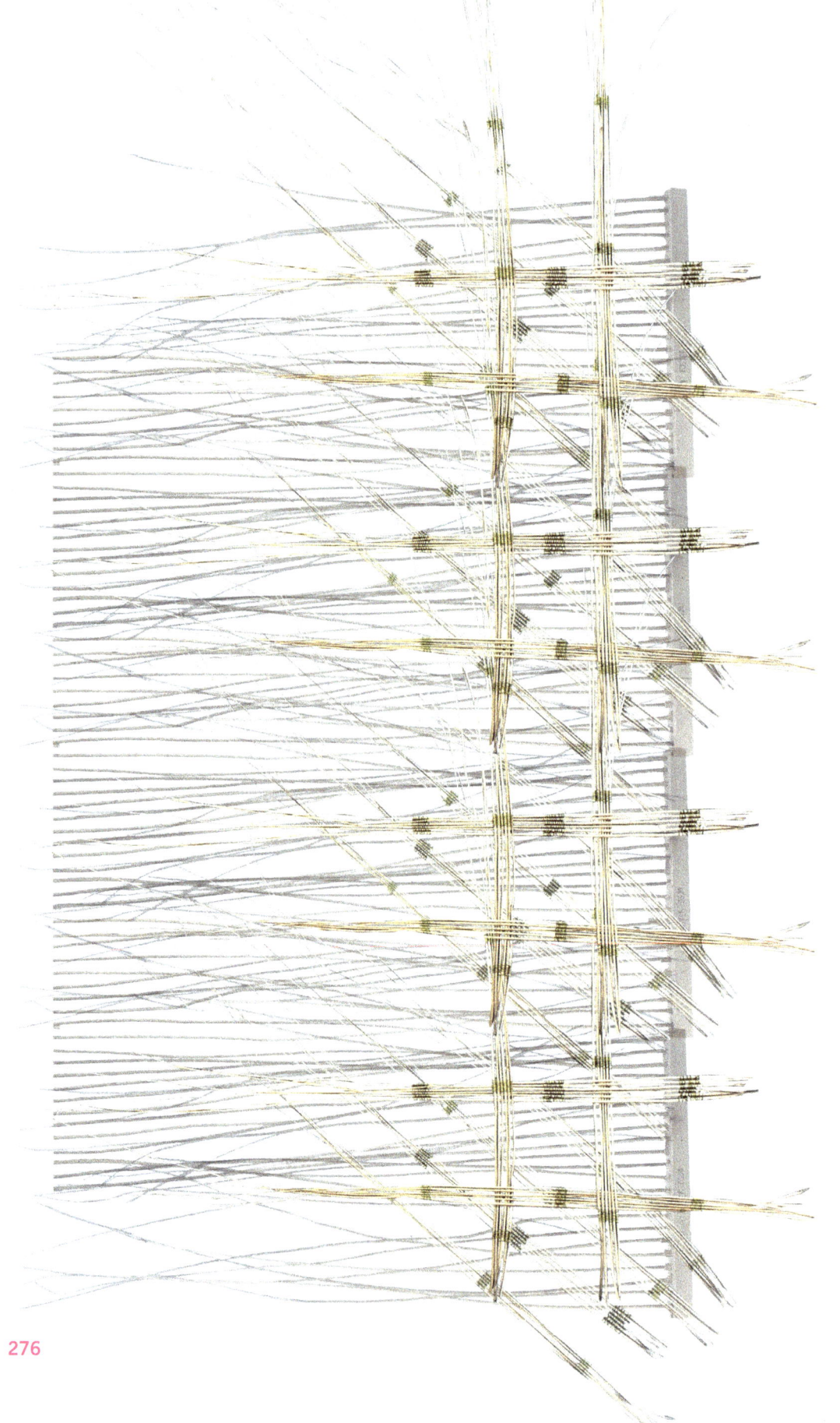

REPAIRING THE RIVER

ETHNOBOTANY ON THE RIVER LEA

JENNY FOSTER

Top: Weaving with reeds and bindweed
Bottom: Drying bindweed to weave with reed

Top: Read beds along the River Lea - both natural and man made.

  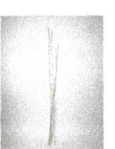 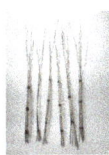

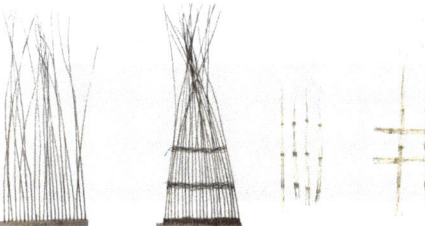

Prior to the Olympic Park development, there was no data on the environmental credentials of the whole of the River Lea. After funding of £1 million was received for an ongoing environmental audit, at least 88 species of birds and 6 species of bat have been identified. New biodiversity targets were set in place for future developers. Reed beds provide good habitats for high density biodiversity and also have little to no impact on proposed developments. River reed or phragmites is an invasive and persistent plant that is prominent along the River Lea. In 2016 Thames21 spearheaded 'Project Reedbed', encouraging volunteers to maintain existing and plant new reedbeds along the river. Reedbeds can oxygenate the water benefiting aquatic life and removing pollutants.

In addition to their ecological importance, reeds also provide a valuable local material resource. Phragmites australis (common reed) has long been used for construction, weaving, and insulation - historically applied in thatching and more recently explored in contemporary biodesign. Reed can be harvested and woven into panels, mats, and modular components for lightweight structures, shelters or interior installations. When dried, the material becomes remarkably strong yet flexible, making it excellent for basketry, cladding and fabrication workshops. Using River Lea reed as a building or craft material not only reduces waste from maintenance cutting, but also creates opportunities for community-making projects, circular-economy design and live-build teaching. Integrating reed harvesting and weaving connects ecological stewardship with hands-on making and material experimentation.

Left: Combining the reeds with a weaving technique allows them to lie flat adjacent to one another. After stacking lots of these formations, models began to look like passive shading devices. Combined in varying configurations, horizontally and vertically, the reeds have the potential to provide effective shading. The reeds also create an architectural interest and make reference to some of the most important plants surrounding the local area.

REEDS MAKING

BIO MATERIAL SYSTEMS

MARIA SARAGURO

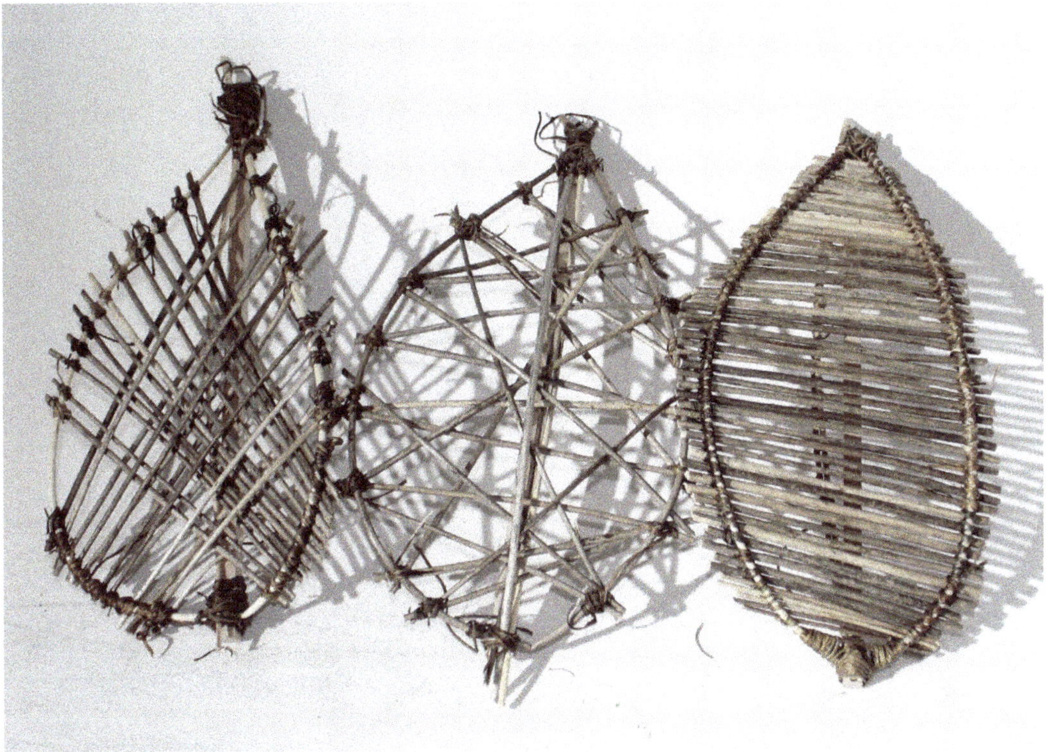

Material exploration models crafted from common reeds, investigating structural techniques and aesthetic possibilities for eco-friendly architectural applications.

In this reed material exploration, the material was employed in two distinct ways. On one hand, reeds were utilised in their original fibrous state, retaining their inherent structural strength. When soaked for 24 hours, they became flexible, allowing them to be shaped into shading panels with varying degrees of opacity. On the other hand, the fibrous material was broken down and processed to create tiles with a range of properties, including insulation, waterproofing, and even transparency. This material exploration was directly applied in the development of the individual project 'Weaving Gender', within the Applied Making chapter.

SHADING FACADE SYSTEM PANELS

Exploration of various patterns, transitioning from more densely arranged to more open configurations to create shading panels. By varying the spacing and arrangements of the reeds, not only serves an aesthetics purpose but, also contributes to the functionality of the shading panels, allowing for nuanced control of light and shade. During the making process of the panels various weaving techniques were used to allow different grades of light through the reeds.

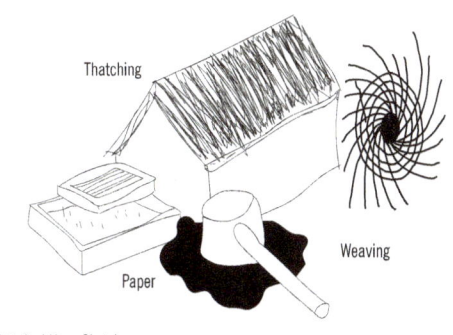

Historical Uses Sketch

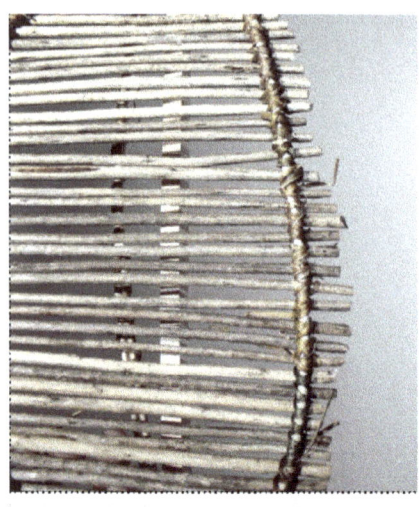

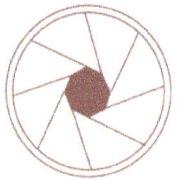

90% Aperture

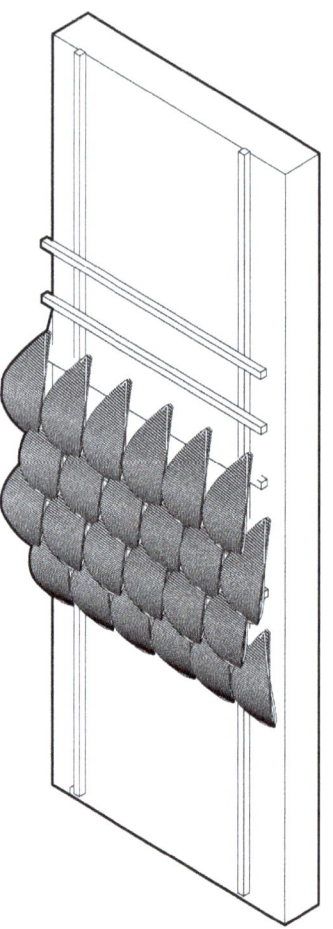

Shading Facade Panel System

60% Aperture

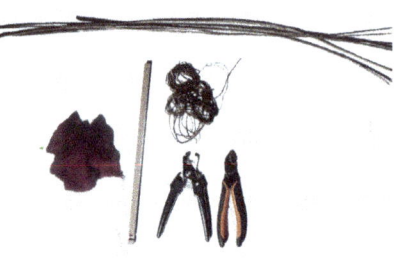

30% Aperture

Various weaving techniques were used to allow different grades of light through the reeds.

Tools for making panels; making the frame to start weaving the reeds; using bindweed for joining reeds

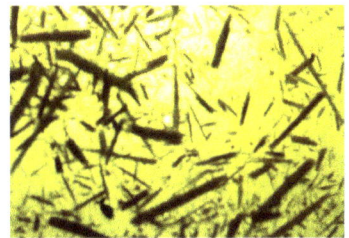 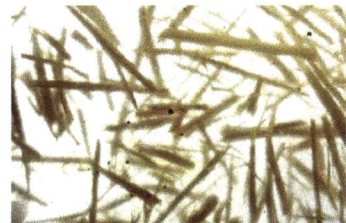 

REED TILES

A series of explorations involves the use of shredded reeds in crafting tiles and insulation boards. The use of natural adhesives and binding agents during the making process fosters an eco-friendly approach, facilitating the seamless reintegration of products back into earth.

The following material exploration uses different cuts of reeds to create translucent and tactile tiles allowing different degrees of translucency based on the quantity of material offering a spectrum of visual effects.

REED FIBRE INSULATION

The smaller fibres particles can trap more air within the insulation material, providing better thermal resistance. Fibres can be more uniformly distributed in an insulation panel ensuring consistent insulation performance throughout the area where they are applied. This uniform distribution helps eliminate cold spots that can occur with larger, uneven materials.

REEDS PANELS

Exploration of various patterns, transitioning from more densely arranged to more open configurations to create shading panels. By varying the spacing and arrangements of the reeds, not only serves an aesthetics purpose but, also contributes to the functionality of the shading panels, allowing for nuanced control of light and shade.

TRANSPARENT REED TILES

As previous experiments, shredded reeds were used to make boards of varying thickness. Ingredients like Matcha powder were incorporated to achieve a natural green hue, with the aim of simulating organic patterns found in nature. Natural binding agents, including corn starch, Agar Agar, and water, were used as the primary components in the process The following material exploration uses different cuts of reeds to create translucent and tactile tiles allowing different degrees of translucency based on the quantity of material offering a spectrum of visual effects.

Blending reeds into pieces using a house blender; Making a paste to mix the shredded reeds; moulds to make the shape of the fibre boards

Top: Shredded reeds with binding solution to make reed fibre boards: water, agar agar, glycerol, matcha powder; Bottom right: Binding solution water, corn starch

A continuation of experiment 3: Hexagon panels made from fibres and bio-resin

SLOWING FAST FASHION DOWN

SUSTAINABILITY FUND 2025

ANNA LONG AND TUGCE YIGIT

	Experiment 1	Experiment 2	Experiment 3	Experiment 4	Experiment 5
	Fibres	Fibres	Fibres	Fibres	Fibres
	Glycerin	Baking Soda	Epoxy Bio Resin	Cement	Cement
	White Vinegar	Corn Flour		Water	Sharp Sand
	Tapioca Starch	Water			Water
	Water	Heat			
	Heat				

Fast fashion waste has been a global issue for many years, severely impacting our climate and environment. Our relentless drive for consumption has spiralled into an excessive cycle: clothing brands produce cheap, low-quality clothes, sell them at inflated prices, and discard them as trends shift, and social media influencers intensify this. Our project explores how fashion waste can be reimagined as a material resource in architecture, raising awareness of sustainable design practices.

As Master of Architecture students studying in the same design studio at the University of Westminster, we came together to apply for the Sustainability Fund. We were given a £1,500 grant for our project to investigate how textile waste from the fast fashion industry could be reimagined as a material resource for architecture. We produced and tested a series of material prototypes, each varying in density, texture, and structural integrity. We aim to advance the conversation around circular material practices, environmental responsibility, and the potential for textile waste to contribute to a more sustainable urban future.

Historically, the Industrial Revolution made textile production more efficient, enabling fashion styles to spread across different social classes. The rise of synthetic dyes and the emergence of ready-to-wear clothing in the late 19th century introduced a fashion culture. A move towards more practical and comfortable clothing forced the rise of department stores, whilst fashion magazines further democratised trends. Between 2000 and 2010, fast fashion rapidly increased, transforming the industry by producing inexpensive, trend-driven clothing. Globalisation of digital technologies, especially social media, accelerated the spread of trends, making fashion more fluid and diverse.

Today, we face the consequences of what fast fashion has created. Sustainability and ethical fashion have become significant concerns as the industry faces environmental and social critiques. Discarded clothing is often exported to developing countries, where it is either dumped or incinerated. Due to the widespread use of synthetic fibres, much of this waste is non-biodegradable and extremely difficult to recycle; therefore, it is burnt. Incineration releases harmful greenhouse gases that contribute to the depletion of the ozone layer, affecting our climate. Despite these realities, the fast fashion industry continues to grow.

Before starting the experiments, we categorised the fabrics into three groups: denim, natural, and synthetic fibres as these are the most common fibres used in the fashion industry. We aimed to see which binders would hold the fibres together the best. For the first two experiments, we tested using different natural binders which are biodegradable. Experiment 1 used glycerin mix, which produced a spongey and malleable texture. The colours of the fibres remained strong, as they had 'melted' with the mixture on the stove. Experiment 2 used a baking soda mix, which produced harder bricks, however, were more crumbly and therefore less strong. The colours had faded as the mixture had overpowered them. Both experiments required heat to activate the binding process, making the process energy-intensive and thus not environmentally friendly. Additionally, the resulting prototypes from both experiments were not structurally strong enough to be used in the architecture industry. Experiment 3 used bio-resin, which produced stronger prototypes and allowed the fibres to remain visible. The chemical process of the bio-resin produces its own heat,

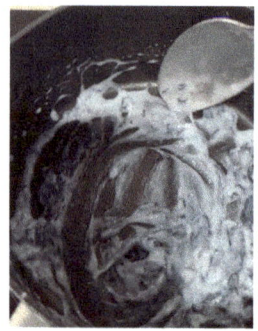

Experiment 1 (top left), Experiment 2 (top right), Experiment 3 (bottom)

Experiment 5: Mixing the concrete and synthetic fibres (left), removing the prototypes from the moulds (centre), crumbly texture of the prototype after compression testing (right)

For experiment 4, we used cement, water, and fibres, with the fibres acting as the aggregates. The visibility of the fibres were lost, however, the prototypes had a hard form and smoother consistency outcome. As concrete usually has aggregates, we used sharp sand in experiment 5, however, these prototypes were weaker and more crumbly, perhaps due to the size of the shredded fibres making the concrete lose its strength properties. We were on a tight timeframe and therefore could only allow the prototypes to cure for 7 days before testing, which would reach 65% of its strength potential (28 days of curing would be most ideal for testing, reaching 99% of its strength potential).

The small compression testing machine had a maximum applied compressive force of 45kN, which was not high enough to properly test the cement prototypes, as they were quite strong and hard. The concrete prototypes exceeded the 45kN, however, they were crumbly upon touch as the materials weren't binded together enough, due to the fibre sizes. They had a spongey texture when crushed, providing resistance against the machine, which meant the machine didn't know at what point the test had truly failed. We moved testing to the large compression machine, which unfortunately broke after testing the plain concrete, and the denim 4g concrete prototype. The plain concrete is likely to be the strongest out of the sample as it contains no added fibres and had a strength of 10.7MPa on day 7 of curing (a full strength of 16.5Mpa). Different aggregates and cement:water ratios would create different concrete mixes and strengths.

Presenting at the Sustainability Fund 2025 Final Presentations

Our material library

Exhibiting our work at the OPEN Exhibition 2025

thus not requiring additional heat. Bio-resin is expensive and the sustainability of the resin depends on the source of the renewable material and the energy used in production.

We believe that our intentions of reusing fast fashion textiles in architectural materials cover four of the United Nation's Sustainability Goals which are:
- No. 9, Industry, Innovation and Infrastructure
- No.11, Sustainable Cities and Communities
- No.12, Responsible Consumption and Production
- No.14, Life Below Waters

The short-term impact of our journey was to produce a material library for our Architecture department at the University of Westminster. We hope our research and intentions will inspire other students to rethink about fast fashion consumerism and methods of how to reinterpret waste material into different forms in the architecture field.

We presented our project in June, at the Sustainability Fund Final Presentations, to the panel, which included Professor Peter Bonfield (University of Westminster's Vice Chancellor), Graham Hobson (entrepreneur and founder of Photobox), as well as the Fund team, Andy Pitchford and Morgan Lirette. Questions and comments from the panel and the audience provoked interesting discussion surrounding our project and its future possibilities, including from an entrepreneurial point of view, and real-life testing and applications in the industry. Additionally, we exhibited our project and the prototypes at the OPEN Exhibition 2025 at the University of Westminster. This was an opportunity for us to network with those in the industry and to share our project's future ambitions.

Our future ambitions are to reapply for the Fund again next year, to be able to continue advancing our project further with collaborators and inspiring students, and the wider community, to think more consciously about their fast fashion consumption habits. We hope to make more connections in the industry and in general, reaching to a widespread network, as the fast fashion crisis currently remains, and will continue to be, a huge problem.

Tutor: Maria Kramer; Instagram: @slowingfastfashiondown

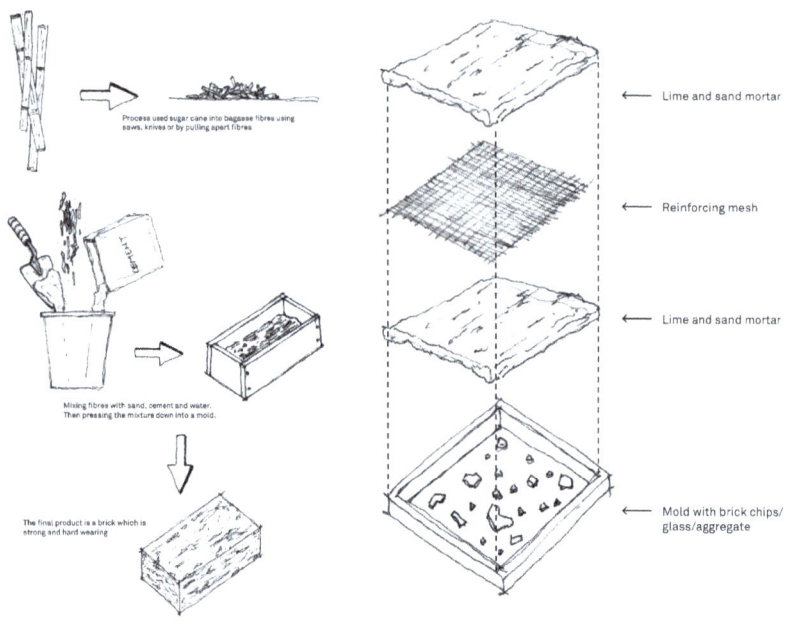

Far left: The initial idea was to use the waste bagasse fibres in a similar way to Hempcrete to form a flooring brick. The aim was to create a breathable floor finish which is also good at providing thermal mass to the building. It would be interesting to see if the bagasse fibres have similar insulating properties to hemp; which could help to reduce the amount of insulation we use in floors.

Left: Terrazzo experiment making a small square mould, using brick chips, glass and aggregate to form the pattern, held together with a lime and sand mortar with a reinforcing mesh layer in between. Lime floors have been used since the Roman times. These floor are extremely hard-wearing, breathable and water resistant.

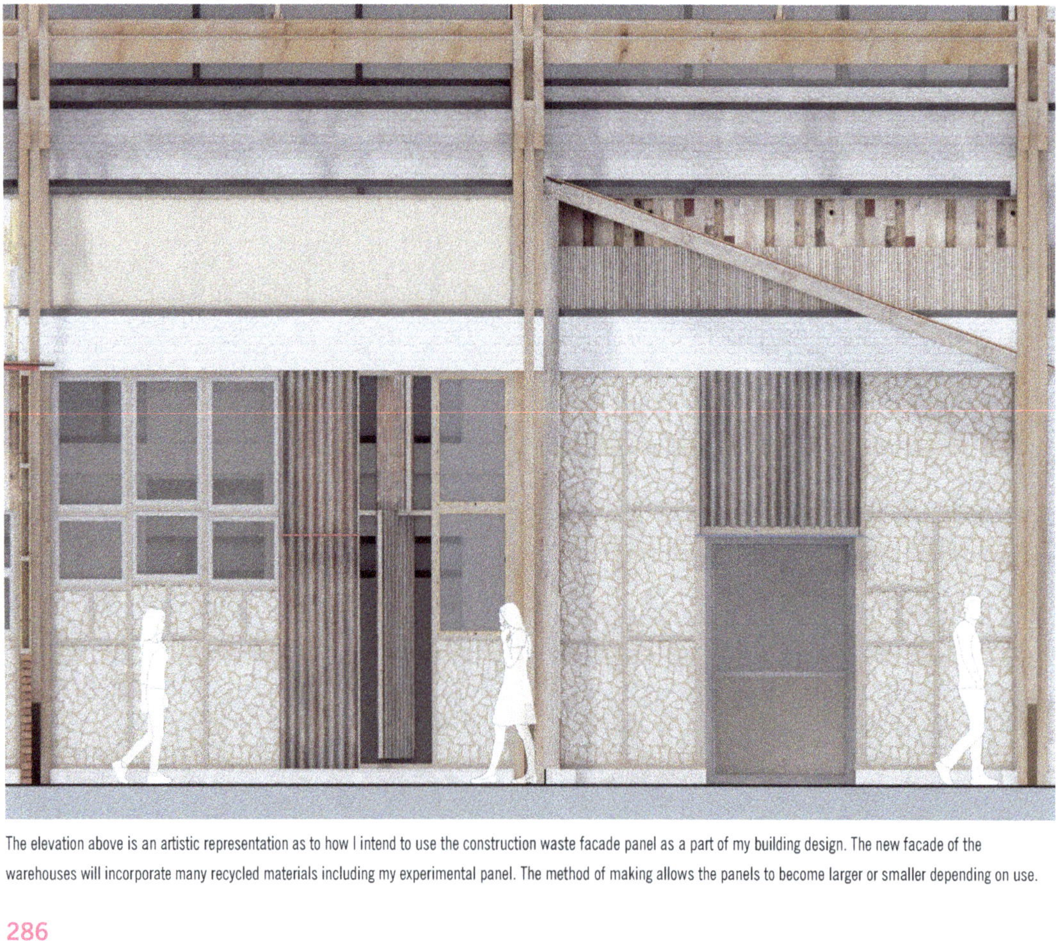

The elevation above is an artistic representation as to how I intend to use the construction waste facade panel as a part of my building design. The new facade of the warehouses will incorporate many recycled materials including my experimental panel. The method of making allows the panels to become larger or smaller depending on use.

WASTE+NATIVE MATERIALS MAKING

HARDEEPAK SINGH PANESAR

The Bagasse Brick - First Year

The 'PLSTR-core' Panel - Second year

Applied making is central to DS20's approach, bridging theory and practice through hands-on experimentation. By working directly with materials at a 1:1 scale, students gain embodied knowledge that informs both the live projects and our individual proposals. This method encourages investigation into sourcing, environmental impact, and local relevance - connecting design decisions to material histories, ecologies, and craft. Making helps test ideas in real time, grounding abstract concepts in tangible outcomes. It also fosters collaboration and skill-sharing, building a stronger relationship between designer, material, and context. In DS20, making is not an output - it's a critical part of the design process.

Second Year: The 'PLSTR-core' Panel.

While studying different improvised behaviours in the early stages of design development for the AdHoc Agora, I looked at how I could 'improvise' with waste plasterboard, timber and concrete (all common waste materials) creatively and integrate the end result into my building design. The process began by breaking down used plasterboard to extract the gypsum core, which I mixed with lime and a small amount of cement to form a more breathable and sustainable mortar. Using salvaged timber, I constructed a frame and filled it with shaped pieces of waste concrete, binding them together with the gypsum mix.

Lime alternatives are more breathable than cement but harder to work with. Lime is also more sustainable then cement as it has a lower carbon footprint during production and absorbs CO_2 during its curing process.

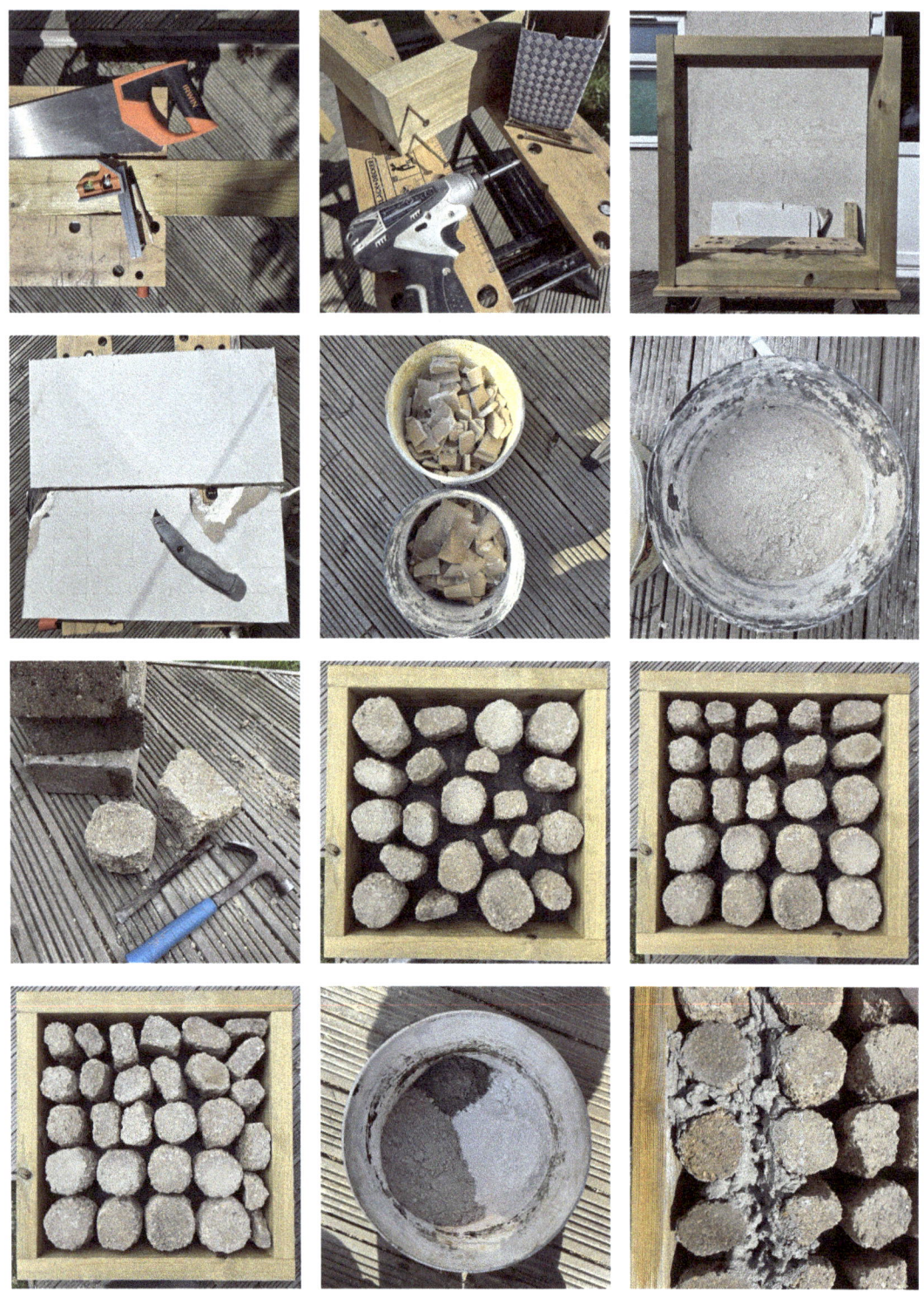

Images documenting the making process. From making the frame, to extracting the gypsum core, testing different arrangements and pouring the mixing between the concrete.

First Year: The Bagasse Brick.

My site during my first year of masters was located close to the Tate&Lyle sugar factory. I chose to use waste sugar cane (Bagasse) and recycle it to make a product which could be used within my proposed scheme. Taking inspiration from hempcrete, I decided to create a floor-finish brick, which could be used in order to add extra thermal mass to the building. The images below document the making process. Bagasse chips were mixed with lime and sand to form the main body of the brick. An 18mm layer of terrazzo was made to be used as the finishing layer; this was made using crushed brick, lime and sand. The brick would be laid on to a lean mix of sand and cement. As the brick is not fired, the embodied carbon of the brick is extremely low which is beneficial to the environment. The final brick measures 215x102.5x65mm.

Using bagasse chips as the substrate

Mixing with lime, sand and hemp fibres

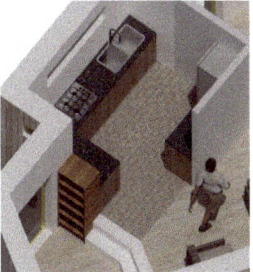
Brick in use as a finishing layer

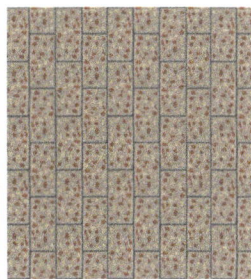
Brick texture

Pouring into the mould and tamping down

Adding brick chips to form the 'terrazzo'

Sanding brick to 2500 grit

Finishing the brick with linseed oil

Bagasse brick floor build up:
1. 65mm Bagasse brick
2. 25mm Sand and cement lean mix
3. Vapour control layer
4. 100mm Acoustic insulation
5. 220mm CLT slab
6. 25mm Battens (Service zone)
7. 12.5mm Fire rated plasterboard
8. 12.5mm Fire rated plasterboard
9. 3mm Plaster and paint finish

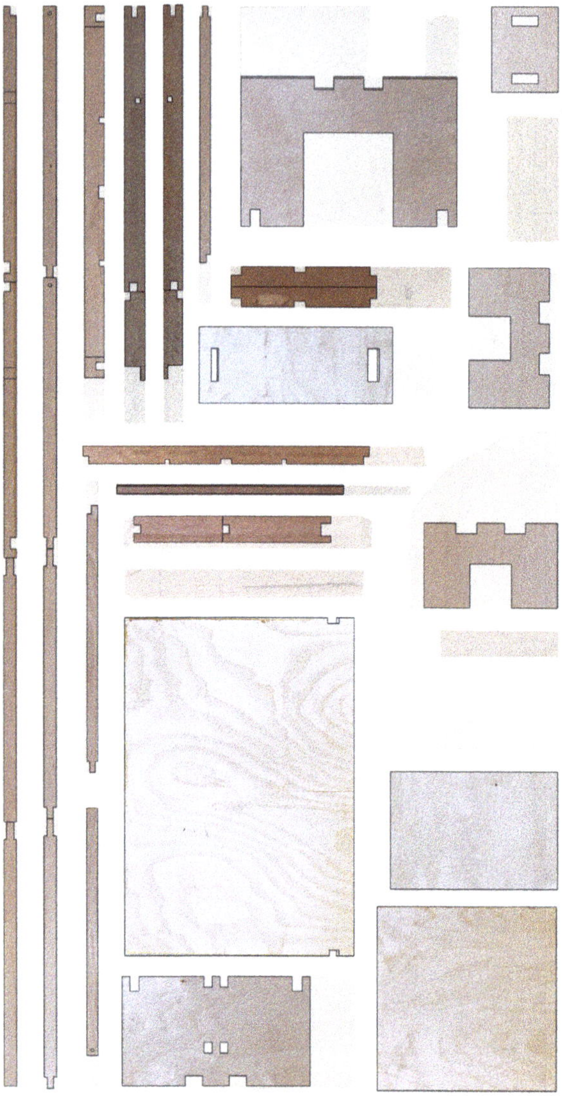

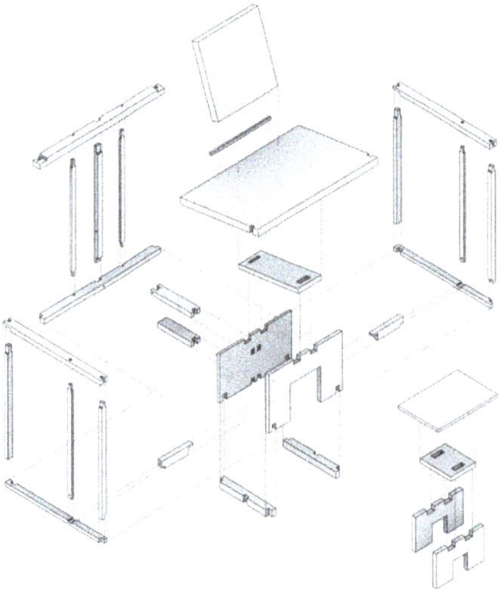

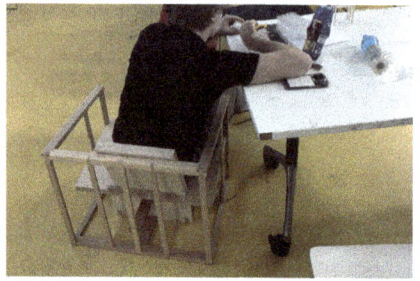

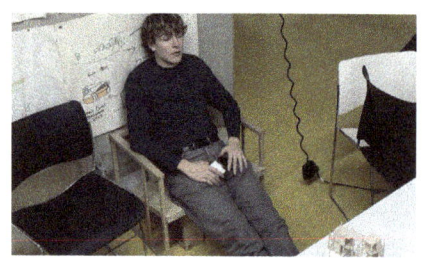

Top left: Designing the chair around the selected scrap. I marked and cut the elements from the pieces I'd collected, the chair was designed to utilise the scrap I found in the most efficient and considered way. Top right: Students enjoying the chair - from top left: Making, Presenting, Snoozing and Working. Left: Exploded axonometric view of the chair designed on Rhino to explore how the joints would be fitted together; Right: Hand cut joints designed for the chair.

I MADE IT MYSELF

DETACHING FROM CONSUMERISM BY HAND CRAFTING SCRAP

KITTY EMERY RAINBIRD

The final chair made from found scarps

I set myself the challenge of building a chair that embodied the principles of re-use and crafting. I began by collecting scrap timber from our FabLab, cataloguing the pieces, and modelling them in 3D to test how they might come together in a way that was both efficient, respectful of the material with aesthetic ambition. I produced a number of design iterations, moving between sketches, models, and digital studies before arriving at a solution that highlighted the joinery while still providing stability, even with the thin timbers available. Working with the constraints of irregular sizes pushed me to design with more care, ensuring that nothing was wasted.

The process of making was as important as the outcome: By refusing to rely on metal fixings, I limited myself to traditional joinery techniques, which not only offered structural integrity but also reinforced the principle of craft. It became a deliberate exercise in slowing down, in engaging directly with material and process. Once complete, the chair lived in our studio. I found real satisfaction in seeing others make use of it, sometimes while working, sometimes simply taking a break.

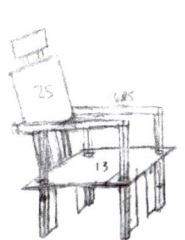 

MOVING FORWARD
LIVE PROJECTS AS EMBEDDED PRACTICE

Floating Forum Live Project at Cody Dock

CULTIVATING APPRECIATIVE JOY

Live Projects, for me, are also about celebrating the joy of design, architecture and construction, also with the public and the act of creating new possibilities. Finding joy in the creative process, in collaboration, in shared achievements. Taking pleasure in students' growth, in community flourishing that can make a difference in the built environment. They embody the possibility of contributing meaningfully to our shared environments, offering space for optimism and the hope that small-scale co-developed initiatives can lead to larger systemic change, a glimmer of hope.

Joy is also an act of resistance. It affirms a world view in which humans are inherently generous, capable of care for one another and for the broader human and non-human world. It's about celebrating and supporting community, fostering empathy and environmental stewardship. In a time when dominant systems often seem to promote unhealthy, aggressive, imbalanced and destructive competition, alienation and unsustainable values, such joy becomes a political and ethical stance - one we arguably need more than ever.

LIVE EXPERIMENTS

Live Projects function as live experiments. They test what is feasible within specific settings, often diverging from conventional relationships – such as the defined roles between client–contractor–architect–consultant - they offer the opportunity to explore alternative ways of working more closely and collaboratively.

Acting as project initiator, agent, and advocate can be empowering - promoting and undertaking one's own initiatives is something the architectural profession could champion more actively. This would expand the architect's role beyond simply responding to briefs with spatial and aesthetic ideas (where the profession is typically more involved, particularly in large-scale developments), toward being part of the brief development itself. Engaging in planning, urban design, and policy-making allows for a more holistic, systemic, and long-term contribution to shaping cities and societies - one that is more embedded, contextual, and situated. Architecture is, as Till also reminds us, "a dependent discipline, reliant on the flux of external forces and contingencies" (Till 2009, 25). Live Projects try to take these external forces on and question them - they are a form of holistic practice that works within the shifting ground of real-world complexity.

Live Projects create opportunities to step outside the constraints of conventional practice and imagine alternative futures. Academic freedom, if utilised (rather than staying within the safe and often referred to 'ivory tower' boundaries) offers the potential to provide a valuable seedbed in which longer engagement with process, rather than a focus on outcomes, can flourish. This contrasts with the often product and short-term driven orientated pressures of professional practice, shaped by economic constraints.

Live Projects give space for that learning and practice. As Donald Schön describes it, practitioners develop a kind of "knowing-in-action" (Schön 1983, 49), where learning happens through the doing itself. They offer a valuable way to bridge the siloed separation between theory and practice. In the words of Johann Wolfgang von Goethe, all theory is grey - Live Projects avoid the pitfalls of purely theoretical speculation by requiring action and tangible engagement.

GOING FORWARD

Live Projects introduce complex ecology of actors: students, tutors, local stakeholders, policy-makers, fabricators, specialist consultants and funding bodies. Within this already complex mix, one oscillates from exploring briefs, facilitating and cultivating relationships and managing solving problems. What emerges is not a singular methodology, but a plural field of approaches that are situated, collaborative and iterative, something difficult to achieve in a studio based brief. As the contributions in this book have shown, Live Projects are activities that are evolving components of architectural education and spatial practice. They offer a means of rethinking pedagogy, and authentic learning, re-situating the architect in society. They bridge the gap between academic inquiry, public engagement and practice, activating questions of agency, empowerment, methods, process, ethics, and accountability in real time. Live Projects can serve as a valuable source of research, provided that critical reflection occurs and tacit or implicit learnings are uncovered and analysed to generate new, transferable knowledge - often resulting in forms of insight that fall outside conventional academic methodologies, due to their reflection-in-action, situated, and sometimes retrospective modes of analysis.

Moving forward, a more sustainable platform is needed to continue experimenting and pushing innovation - in cross-collaboration, design processes, and construction. A key challenge is creating structures of continuity that allow Live Projects to evolve beyond one-off events into longer-term practices. This means recognising their potential and providing the resources and mentorship needed for growth. It also requires institutional support and a rethinking of educational value - one that acknowledges the social, material, and labour contributions of these projects. It calls for broader recognition of interdisciplinary alliances and a more expansive understanding of knowledge as central to both learning and practice.

For references, please see the end of the book.

The Growing Space Live Project at Cody Dock

AFTERWORD

PERSONAL JOURNEY

I never imagined I would write a book. I've always considered myself a visual thinker - more comfortable with images, drawings, and spatial ideas than with written words. Writing didn't come naturally to me. But through the process of writing a few articles and now this book, I've come to understand just how essential verbal communication is in the field of architecture. Even though much of our thinking remains non-verbal - spatial, visual, and intuitive - the ability to clearly articulate ideas in language is a skill that holds increasing importance.

During my BA studies at the University of Applied Arts in Vienna, my Masterclass tutor, Professor Wolf D. Prix, once told us: "Words are cheap." At the time, I took this at face value - believing that words could never carry the same weight as spatial exprience and architecture. Wolf led a uniquely "live" studio, where the boundary between academia and practice didn't exist. We visited construction sites, engaged with real-world briefs from his office, Coop Himmelb(l)au, and some of us - including myself - worked in parallel across both the university studio and the practice. That dual engagement grounded my understanding of architecture in the realities of design and construction.

So when I arrived in London on Erasmus and DAAD scholarships to pursue a Diploma and Master's, it was something of a cultural shift. Suddenly, I was immersed in an architectural discourse that operated independently of the built environment - more concerned with theory, speculation, and critique. This was the first time I experienced the tension between academia and practice - a divide that, at least in my own experience, feels far less pronounced within continental Europe.

This book, and the process of creating it, occupies the space between those two worlds: between making and thinking, action and reflection. I still believe that drawings, models and built work often communicate things that words cannot. But I also understand that writing serves a vital role. It refines thought. It's a space to reflect. It opens up conversation. It allows ideas and processes to move beyond the confines of a project or a place.

So perhaps, yes - words may be "cheap," but they are also powerful. Learning how to use them has been part of this Live Practice, too.

MEASURING THE IMMEASURABLE

Live Projects offer a unique space to explore the balance between what can be measured and what can be experienced. They are not just about delivering outcomes, but about engaging with process - a continual dialogue between the drawing board, the construction site, and the lived experience of the finished work.

For students, this becomes a bridge: between education and practice, between intention and reception, between the measurable and the immeasurable. While metrics like performance, cost, and efficiency are important, they don't capture the full value of design. Spatial generosity, material richness, emotional impact, and social connection all matter - even if they resist quantification.

Learning to articulate these qualitative dimensions is part of the project too. Words, reflections, and feedback become tools to give shape to the intangible. Through Live Projects, students not only learn to design - they learn to tell the story of what design does.

As Louis Kahn said: "A great building must begin with the immeasurable, must go through measurable means when it is being designed, and in the end must be unmeasured." Live Projects let us live that journey.

PROJECTS AS VEHICLES FOR INNOVATION

Live Projects hold great potential as tools for innovation. By bringing together individuals from diverse disciplines, backgrounds, and perspectives around a shared purpose, they can create fertile ground for experimentation and creative problem-solving. These projects allow ideas to be tested in real-world conditions, rather than remaining as speculative concepts confined to studio or theory. In many ways, innovation is not in short supply - the real challenge lies in application. New ideas often stall at the implementation stage - caught in a tangle of regulation, procurement challenges, perceived risk, or insurance constraints. Live Projects can help bridge this gap. Because they are time-bound and often operate at a smaller scale, they offer a contained space in which to test new approaches with reduced risk. They create a form of "safe failure - a place where lessons can be learned and successful outcomes can build a track record that encourages further adoption. These projects can demonstrate feasibility in tangible ways. They turn abstract ambition into built reality, providing evidence that innovation not only works but can deliver value. As such, Live Projects are not just academic exercises or community engagement tools; they have the potential as a strategic mechanisms for advancing the discipline - by proving, not just proposing, new ways forward.

REFERENCES

LIVE PROJECTS FROM SOCIAL SCIENCE PERSPECTIVES

ARLENE OAK

Anderson, J. (2017). Devising an inclusive and flexible taxonomy of international live projects. ARENA Journal of Architectural Research, 2(1), 3. https://doi.org/10.5334/ajar.5

Anderson, J. (2019). Live projects: Collaborative learning in and with authentic spaces. (pp. 161-173). Bilham, TH,

Claire; Hartog, Mary; Doolan, Martina A.(ed.) Reframing Space for Learning: Excellence and Innovation in University Teaching: Trentham Books, UCL IOE Press.
Bennett, J. (2010). Vibrant matter: A political ecology of things. Duke University Press.

Boysen, B. (2018). The embarrassment of being human: A critique of new materialism and object-oriented ontology. Orbis Litterarum, 73(3), 225–242. https://doi.org/10.1111/oli.12174

Brown, J. B., & Russell, P. (2022). When design-build met the live project – or – what is a live-build project anyway? In B. Pak & A. De Smet (Eds.), Experiential learning in architectural education (pp. 9–24).

Routledge. https://doi-org.login.ezproxy.library.ualberta.ca/10.4324/9781003267683
Cuff, D. (1991). Architecture: The story of practice. MIT Press.

Donald, I. (2022). Environmental and architectural psychology: The basics. Routledge. https://doi.org/10.4324/9780429274541

Doucet, I. (2016). Architecture wrestling the social: The "live" project as a site of contestation. Candide Journal for Architectural Knowledge, 10, 13–40, Article H1. https://candidejournal.net/article/architecture-wrestling-the-social-the-live-project-as-site-of-contestation/

Fenwick, T. J., Edwards, R., & Sawchuk, P. H. (2011). Emerging approaches to educational research: Tracing the socio-material. Routledge. https://doi.org/10.4324/9780203817582

Harriss, H., & Widder, L. (Eds.). (2014). Architecture live projects: Pedagogy into practice. Routledge. https://doi.org/10.4324/9781315780764

Ingold, T. (2021). Imagining for real: Essays on creation, attention and correspondence. Routledge. https://doi-org.login.ezproxy.library.ualberta.ca/10.4324/9781003171713
Ingold, T. (2020). Correspondences. Polity Press.

Ingold, T. (2013). Making: Anthropology, archaeology, art and architecture. Routledge. https://doi-org.login.ezproxy.library.ualberta.ca/10.4324/9780203559055

Jones, P. (2011). The sociology of architecture: Constructing identities. Liverpool University Press. https://doi.org/10.2307/j.ctt5vjjpk

Krasny, E. (2019). Architecture and care. In A. Fitz, E. Krasny (Eds.), Critical care: Architecture and urbanism for a broken planet. MIT Press. https://doi.org/10.7551/mitpress/12273.001.0001

Latour, B. (2017). Visualization and cognition: Drawing things together. Philosophical Literary Journal Logos, 27(2), 95–156. https://doi.org/10.22394/0869-5377-2017-2-95-151
Latour, B., & Yaneva, A. (2008). «Give me a gun and I will make all buildings move»: An ANT's view of architecture. Architectural Design Theory, 1, 103–111. https://doi.org/10.17454/ARDETH01.08

Lave, J. & Wenger, E. (1991). Situated learning: Legitimate peripheral participation. Cambridge University Press.
Marchand, T. H. J. (2010). Making knowledge: Explorations of the indissoluble relation between mind, body and environment. Journal of the Royal Anthropological Institute, 16(s1), S1–S21. https://doi-org.login.ezproxy.library.ualberta.ca/10.1111/j.1467-9655.2010.01607.x
Marchand, T. H. J. (2009). The masons of Djenné. Indiana University Press.

Marchand, T. H. J. (2007). Crafting knowledge: The role of 'parsing and production' in the communication of skill. In M. Harris (Ed.), Ways of knowing (pp. 181–202). Berghahn. https://doi-org.login.ezproxy.library.ualberta.ca/10.3167/9781845453640

Maynard, D. W., & Heritage, J. (2005). Conversation analysis, doctor-patient interaction and medical communication. Medical Education, 39(4), 428–435. https://doi-org.login.ezproxy.library.ualberta.ca/10.1111/j.1365-2929.2005.02111.x

Mazalán, P., Vinárčiková, J., & Hronsky, M. C. (2022). Architectural education in the context of social sciences. Architecture Papers of the Faculty of Architecture and Design STU, 27(2), 35–40. https://doi.org/10.2478/alfa-2022-0011

Mondada, L., & Miranda da Cruz, F. (2024). Requesting a colleague's independent opinion at work. Research on Language and Social Interaction, 57(4), 372–398. https://doi-org.login.ezproxy.library.ualberta.ca/10.1080/08351813.2024.2410130

Nicholas, C., & Oak, A. (2020). Make and break details: The architecture of design-build education. Design Studies, 66, 35–53. https://doi.org/10.1016/j.destud.2019.12.003

Niemi, J., & Hirvonen, L. (2019). Money talks: Customer-initiated price negotiation in business-to-business sales interaction. Discourse & Communication, 13(1), 95–118. https://doi-org.login.ezproxy.library.ualberta.ca/10.1177/1750481318801629

Oak, A. (2019). Interdisciplinary engagement through design/build education. In T. Cavanagh, A. Oak, & S. Verderber (Eds.), Thinking while doing: Explorations in educational design build (pp. 161–175). Birkhauser. https://doi.org/10.1515/9783035613476

Oak, A. (2013). 'As you said to me I said to them': Reported speech and the multi-vocal nature of collaborative design practice. Design Studies, 34(1), 34–56. https://doi.org/10.1016/j.destud.2012.08.002

Oak, A. (2011). What can talk tell us about design?: Analyzing conversation to understand practice. Design Studies, 32(3), 211–234. https://doi.org/10.1016/j.destud.2010.11.003

Lloyd (Eds.), About designing: Analyzing design meetings. CRC Press. https://doi-org.login.ezproxy.library.ualberta.ca/10.1201/9780429182433

Puig de la Bellacasa, M. (2017). Matters of care: Speculative ethics in more than human worlds. University of Minnesota Press. https://www.jstor.org/stable/10.5749/j.ctt1mmfspt

Schenck, J., & Cruickshank, J. (2015). Evolving Kolb: Experiential education in the age of neuroscience. Journal of Experiential Education, 38(1), 73–95. https://doi.org/10.1177/1053825914547153

Schwarz, B. B., Tsemach, U., Israeli, M., Nir, E. (2025). Actor-network theory as a new direction in research on educational dialogues. Instructional Science, 53, 173–201. https://doi-org.login.ezproxy.library.ualberta.ca/10.1007/s11251-024-09669-5

Sharif, A. A. (2020). Transfer ethnography: The recording of a heritage building. Archnet-IJAR: International Journal of Architecture Research, 14(2), 298–302. https://doi-org.login.ezproxy.library.ualberta.ca/10.1108/ARCH-02-2019-0039

Taylor, P. (2021). Developing a framework for describing, planning and evaluating empowerment in architectural making projects. [PhD thesis, University of Reading]. CentAUR: Central Archive at the University of Reading. https://doi.org/10.48683/1926.00108018

Woodward, S. (2020). Material methods: Researching and thinking with things. SAGE Publications Ltd. https://doi.org/10.4135/9781529799699

Yaneva, A. (2022). Latour for architects. Routledge. https://doi.org/10.4324/9780429328510

Yaneva, A. (2017). Five ways to make architecture political: An introduction to the politics of design practice. Bloomsbury Publishing Plc.

REFERENCES

CO-CREATING JUST STREETS

ENRICA PAPA, SABINA CIOBATA, MARIA KRAMER

Bertolini, L. (2020). From "streets for traffic" to "streets for people": Can street experiments transform urban mobility? Transport Reviews, 40(6), 734–753.

Cairns, S., Atkins, S., & Goodwin, P. (2002). Disappearing traffic? The story so far. Proceedings of the Institution of Civil Engineers – Municipal Engineer, 151(1), 13–22.

DfT & DCLG. (2007). Manual for Streets. London: Department for Transport and Department for Communities and Local Government.

Fokdal, J. Bina, O., Chiles, P., Ojamäe, L. & Paadam, K. (eds.) (2021). Enabling the City. Interdisciplinary and Transdisciplinary Encounters in Research and Practice. New York: Routledge.

Fricker, M. (2007). Epistemic Injustice: Power and the Ethics of Knowing. Oxford: Oxford University Press.

Gehl, J., & Gemzøe, L. (2003). New City Spaces. Copenhagen: The Danish Architectural Press.

Hamilton-Baillie, B. (2008). Shared space: Reconciling people, places and traffic. Built Environment, 34(2), 161–181.

Hass-Klau, C. (1993). Impact of pedestrianisation and traffic calming on retailing: A review of the evidence from Germany and the UK. Transport Policy, 1(1), 21–31.

Jacobs, J. (1993). The Death and Life of Great American Cities. New York: Modern Library Edition.

Jones, P., Boujenko, N., & Marshall, S. (2007). Link and Place: A Guide to Street Planning and Design. London: Landor Publishing.

Lees, L. (1998). Urban renaissance and the street: Spaces of control and contestation. In N. Fyfe (Ed.), Images of the Street: Planning, Identity and Control in Public Space. London: Routledge. pp. 236–253.

Lund, D. H. (2018). Co-creation in Urban Governance: From Inclusion to Innovation, Scandinavian Journal of Public Administration, 22(2), pp. 3-17

Martens, K. (2016). Transport Justice: Designing Fair Transportation Systems. New York: Routledge.

Natarajan, L., & Short, M. (Eds.) (2023). Engaged Urban Pedagogy: Participatory Practices in Planning and Place-Making. UCL Press.

Norton, P. D. (2008). Fighting Traffic: The Dawn of the Motor Age in the American City. Cambridge, MA: MIT Press.

Pereira, R. H. M., Schwanen, T., & Banister, D. (2016). Distributive justice and equity in transportation. Transport Reviews, 37(2), 170–191.

Pharoah, T. & Russel, R. E. (1991). Traffic calming policy and performance. The Netherlands, Denmark and Germany: Policy and Applications in Great Britain. Town Planning Review, 62(1).

PUBLICA (2025). Harley Street BID Masterplan. A Long Term Vision for the Public Realm of the Harley Street Area, London. Available at: chrome-extension://efaidnbmnnnibpcajpcglclefindmkaj/https://harleystreetbid.com/wp-content/uploads/2025/07/250630_0306_Harley-Street-Masterplan-report_digital_.pdf

Sheller, M. (2018). Mobility Justice: The Politics of Movement in an Age of Extremes. London: Verso.

Soja, E. W. (2010). Seeking Spatial Justice. Minneapolis: University of Minnesota Press.

Tolley, R. (1990). The Greening of Urban Transport: Planning for Walking and Cycling in Western Cities. London: Belhaven Press.

Vitale Brovarone, E., Staricco, L. & Verlinghieri, E. (2023). Whose is this street? Actors and conflicts in the governance of pedestrianisation processes. Journal of Transport Geography.

Westminster City Council (2021) Westminster City Plan 2019–2040. Adopted April 2021. London. Available at: chrome-extension://efaidnbmnnnibpcajpcglclefindmkaj/https://

THE LEA VALLEY - KINSHIP AND STAKEHOLDERS

CORINNA DEAN

Boelens, R., Escobar, A., Bakker, K., Hommes, L., Swyngedouw, E., Hogenboom, B., Huijbens, E., ... & Wantzen, K. M. (2022). Riverhood: political ecologies of socionature commoning and translocal struggles for water justice. The Journal of Peasant Studies, 50(3), 1125–1156.

Evans, Graeme (2018) Hydrocitizenship: Concepts and Insights from the Lee Valley, UK; in Rivers and Society: Landscapes, Governance and Livelihoods; Edited by Malcolm Cooper, Abhik Chakraborty, Shamik Chakraborty

Gandy, Matthew (2004), Rethinking urban metabolism: Water, space and the modern city, CITY, VOL. 8, NO. 3, December 2004
Gandy, Matthew. The Fabric of Space: Water, Modernity, and the Urban Imagination, MIT Press, 2014. ProQuest Ebook Central, http://ebookcentral.proquest.com/lib/westminster/detail.action?docID=3339897.
Snook, D.L., Whitehead, P.G., (2004). Water Quality and Ecology of the River Lee, Mass Balance and a Review of Temporal and Spatial Data, vol 8 Issue 4 636-650.

Tsing, A. L., Mathews, A. S., & Bubandt, N. (2019). Patchy anthropocene: Landscape structure, multispecies history, and the retooling of anthropology. Current Anthropology, 60(S20), S186–S197.

LIVE PROJECTS AS EMBEDDED PRACTICE

MARIA KRAMER

Till, J. (2009) Architecture Depends. Cambridge, MA: MIT Press.Sara, Rachel (2006) – Live Project Good Practice: A Guide for the Implementation of Live Projects.

Bell, B. and Wakeford, K. (eds) (2008) Expanding Architecture: Design as Activism. New York: Metropolis Books.

Schön, D. A. (1983) The Reflective Practitioner: How Professionals Think in Action. New York: Basic Books.

Ahmed, S. (2010) The Promise of Happiness. Durham: Duke University Press.

Brown, Valerie A., John A. Harris, and Jacqueline Y. Russell (2010) – Tackling Wicked Problems: Through the Transdisciplinary Imagination.

Segal, Rafi (ed.) (2020) – Designing for the Common Good: Theories and Practices of Architecture and Urbanism.

Live Projects - Live Practices
DS3.2+DS20

Maria Kramer

A University of Westminster, School of Architecture + Cities
Publication
Designed by Mark Boyce

All texts ©2025 the authors

This work is licensed under a CC BY-NC 4.0 license
ISBN 978-1-8383870-9-9

Books in the Studio as Book series are available to
purchase via OpenStudioWestminster here:
http://www.openstudiowestminster.org/studio-as-book/
or from online book stores.

The editors have attempted to acknowledge all sources of
images used and apologise for any errors or omissions.

School of Architecture + Cities
University of Westminster
35 Marylebone Road
London
NW1 5LS

www.ingramcontent.com/pod-product-compliance
Lightning Source LLC
Chambersburg PA
CBHW040931240426

43672CB00022B/2997